W9-DGH-742

ESSAYS ON THE ENGLISH LANGUAGE
MEDIEVAL AND MODERN

Essays on the English Language Medieval and Modern

Randolph Quirk
Quain Professor of English Language and Literature
in the University of London

INDIANA UNIVERSITY PRESS

Bloomington & London

Preface

It is a salutary, if at times harrowing, experience to go back in detail over material that one has written during a period of twenty years. If there is the repeated blush of humiliation at the painful reminders of brashness, and of past certainties difficult to reconcile with present doubts, these moments are offset by the occasional glow of pleasure at having done some things better than one surely now could – and at having done some things at all. Perhaps, one feels, the requests to reprint this or that paper have not, after all, been motivated purely by the kindness of friends or the piety of students.

In selecting the present group of papers in response to such requests, I have sought to concentrate attention upon two of the main areas within English studies to which I have devoted myself over the years: on the one hand, medieval English language and literature; and on the other, the Survey of English Usage in our own day. In both areas, whatever merit the papers have is to no small extent due to the great teachers in whose classes I was privileged to sit and whose work, I like to think, informs my own: R. W. Chambers and A. H. Smith, distinguished predecessors in the Quain Chair, as well as Daniel Jones and J. R. Firth, also in London; Bernard Bloch, Hans Kurath, C. C. Fries, and Kenneth L. Pike at Yale and Michigan. With their help and through their mediation, I have felt conscious of participating in some of the outstanding controversies in English philology and descriptive linguistics that have enlivened English studies since the nineteen thirties.

Six of the seventeen papers here presented were written in collaboration, and I am grateful to the friends and colleagues concerned for their willingness to allow our joint work to re-appear and for their willingness also to join me in editing it for the occasion. With these, as with the bulk of the papers, editing has involved little more than providing cross-references, standardizing conventions of presentation, improving on the formulation at certain points, and the correction of errors.

There has been no question of attempting any revision of the papers such as would take full and proper account of the work that has been done in the fields concerned since these contributions appeared in their original form.

It is a pleasure to acknowledge the kind co-operation of the editors and publishers who have so readily given permission to reprint, and a special pleasure to record my debt to Peggy Drinkwater of Longmans, Green for assuming with her customary skill and generosity the main burden of preparing the material for press.

R.Q.

University College London,
June, 1968.

Acknowledgments

For permission to reproduce the papers in this collection, we are grateful to the following:

Methuen & Co. Ltd for 'Poetic Language and Old English Metre' published in *Early English and Norse Studies* (A. H. Smith Festschrift) edited by Arthur Brown and Peter Foote, and for 'Research Problems and the Teaching of English', published in *English Teaching Abroad and the British Universities* edited by H. G. Wayment.

The Editorial Board of *The Journal of English and Germanic Philology* for 'Langland's Use of *kind wit* and *inwit*' (vol. 52, 1953) and 'Vis Imaginativa' (vol. 53, 1954).

Modern Humanities Research Association and the Editor of *The Modern Language Review* for 'On the Problem of Morphological Suture in Old English' (vol. 45, 1950).

Linguistic Society of America for the three papers published in *Language*: 'Descriptive Statement and Serial Relationship' (vol. 41, 1965); 'Some Recent Interpretations of Old English Digraph Spellings' (vol. 29, 1953) and 'The Old English Digraphs: A Reply' (vol. 31, 1955), the latter two written with Sherman M. Kuhn, whose permission also is gratefully acknowledged.

The Council of the Philological Society for 'The Survey of English Usage' published in *Transactions of the Philological Society 1960*.

The Editor of *English Studies* for 'Relative Clauses in Educated Spoken English' (vol. 38, 1957) and 'Complex Prepositions and Related Sequences' (vol. 45 supplement, 1964, the R. W. Zandvoort Festschrift). Oxford University Press and the Editor of *English Language Teaching* for 'From Descriptive to Prescriptive: An Example' (vol. 12, 1958).

The Nature Method Language Institute, Denmark, for 'Co-existing

Negative Preterite Forms of *dare*' published in *Language and Society* (A. M. Jensen Festschrift).

Mouton & Co. n.v. for 'Studies in the Correspondence of Prosodic to Grammatical Features in English' published in the *Proceedings of the IXth International Congress of Linguists* (1964).

Longmans, Green & Co. Ltd for 'On Scales of Contrast in Connected English Speech' published in *In Memory of J. R. Firth* edited by C. E. Bazell, J. C. Catford, M. A. K. Halliday, and R. H. Robins.

Jackson, Son & Co. (Booksellers) Ltd and the Editors of *Archivum Linguisticum* for 'Substitutions and Syntactical Research' (vol. 10, 1958).

The Editor of the *Proceedings of the University of Newcastle-upon-Tyne Philosophical Society* for 'Acceptability in Language' (vol. 1, 1966).

Contents

	Preface	v–vi
1	Poetic language and Old English metre	1–19
2	Langland's use of *kind wit* and *inwit*	20–26
3	Vis imaginativa	27–29
4	On the problem of inflexional juncture in Old English	30–37
5	Some recent interpretations of Old English digraph spellings (*with Sherman M. Kuhn*)	38–54
6	The Old English digraphs: a reply (*with Sherman M. Kuhn*)	55–69
7	The survey of English usage	70–87
8	Research problems and the teaching of English	88–93
9	Relative clauses in educated spoken English	94–108
10	From descriptive to prescriptive: an example	109–113
11	Co-existing negative preterite forms of *dare* (*with A. P. Duckworth*)	114–119
12	Studies in the correspondence of prosodic to grammatical features in English (*with J. Svartvik, A. P. Duckworth, J. P. L. Rusiecki, A. J. T. Colin*)	120–135
13	On scales of contrast in connected English speech (*with D. Crystal*)	136–147
14	Complex prepositions and related sequences (*with J. Mulholland*)	148–160
15	Substitutions and syntactical research	161–166
16	Descriptive statement and serial relationship	167–183
17	Acceptability in language	184–201

One

Poetic language and Old English metre†

1

Already in the nineteenth century, a good deal of interest was shown in
the function of fixed expressions – 'die epischen Formeln', as Banning
called them – in *Beowulf* and other early poems in the Germanic languages. More recently, several scholars have undertaken detailed com-
parative analyses to show the extent to which traditional formulas and
themes alike constitute the basis of such poetry.[1] Thus, the *Metodes
meahte* of Cædmon's Hymn is closely paralleled in a good many poems;[2]
the widespread use is itself an indication that there is no question of
specific borrowing, still less of plagiarism, but rather suggests that a
premium is set on the traditionally determined expression, and, as
Milman Parry said in discussing another literature, one poet is 'better
than another not because he has by himself found a more striking way of
expressing his own thought but because he has been better able to make
use of the tradition'.[3] Although there are obvious dangers and limitations in such an approach,[4] it is undoubtedly valuable for sharpening our
perspective as we try to evaluate our early poetry.

† This paper was written for the A. H. Smith Festschrift, *Early English and
Norse Studies* (London, 1963), where it appeared on pp. 150 ff.
[1] See especially Francis P. Magoun, Jr, in *Speculum* 28 (1953), 446 ff., and 30
(1955), 49 ff.
[2] To Professor Magoun's list (*Speculum* 30.62), one might add 'meotud
meahtum swið', *The Gifts of Men* 4 (Exeter Book, f. 78a).
[3] 'Studies in the Epic Technique of Oral Verse-making II: The Homeric
Language as the Language of an Oral Poetry', *Harvard Studies in Classical
Philology* 43 (1932), 13.
[4] Not least in helping to perpetuate the idea of *Beowulf* and other Old English
poems as the product of an early, primitive and ex tempore minstrelsy. The time
has come, perhaps, for a thorough reconsideration of the evidence for a very
early composition of *Beowulf*. Cf. Paper 4 below.

The formula is a habitual collocation, metrically defined, and is thus a stylization of something which is fundamental to linguistic expression, namely the expectation that a sequence of words will show lexical congruity, together with (and as a condition of) lexical and grammatical complementarity. It may be said of 'wide' and 'way', for example, that in Old English they set up a reciprocal expectancy of each other, which may operate strictly within the 'half-line' structure (as in 'wegas ofer widland', *Andreas* 198), but equally across half-lines (as in 'Wærun wegas ðine · on widne sæ', Paris Psalter 76.16), and also of course in prose: 'þæt geat ys swyðe wid, and se weg ys swyðe rum', Matt. 7.13.[5] An example with a thematically more powerful connexion (and in consequence one still more widely exploited) is the pair *mod* and *mægen*, perhaps most familiarly contrasted in Byrhtwold's words, 'mod sceal þe mare, · þe ure mægen lytlað' (*Maldon* 313). Hroðgar tells Beowulf, 'Þu eart mægenes strang · ond on mode frod' (l. 1844), which links with the treatment of 'sapientia et fortitudo' that R. E. Kaske has seen as being central to the theme of *Beowulf*, and in particular to the relationship of the hero with Hroðgar.[6] The collocation occurs frequently elsewhere: for instance, in *Gifts of Men* 98, *Elene* 408, the Paris Psalter 144.5, 150.2, and in prose, Bede's Eccl. Hist. Bk I Ch. 16 (p. 484, ll. 14–15 in the EETS edition).

It goes without saying, of course, that in discussing alliterative collocations in Old English, one must always remember that metrical demands may determine the connexion between words in a particular case; it is in fact easy to demonstrate that the connexion between words is frequently determined primarily by metrical demands. On the other hand, it is still more important to note that, given the natural phenomenon of collocation together with the existence in Old English (and kindred languages) of alliteration as a metrical device, the two work together so that alliteration becomes a regular mode of endorsing the linguistic connexion – whether complementary or contrastive – between collocated words. 'Hawk' and 'hand' are brought together in prose and verse from Old English times (as in 'heafoc on honda', *Fortunes of Men* 86) to our own times and the comic verse recited by Stanley Holloway:

[5] On the formulas found in OE diplomatic and epistolary prose, such as 'swa full 7 swa forð swa', 'binnan porte (∼byrig) 7 buton', 'on wudu 7 on felde', 'heora saca weorðe 7 heora socne', see F. E. Harmer, *Anglo-Saxon Writs* (1952), 61, 85 ff.
[6] See *Studies in Philology* 55 (1958), 423 ff. My quotations from *Beowulf* follow the text of C. L. Wrenn, from other OE poetry that of the Krapp and Dobbie, *Anglo-Saxon Poetic Records*.

and it may perhaps (through popular etymology) be the basis of Hamlet's 'I know a hawk from a handsaw'.

Since alliteration in Old English verse serves not only to connect stressed forms within the half-line but also to connect two half-lines to form the next higher metrical unit, the poet is necessarily involved not only in the simple collocation of pairs like those already illustrated but also in extended collocations. Thus, for example,

> Wid is þes westen,   wræcsetla fela
>
> (*Guthlac* 296)

extends the association of *wid* and *westen* (found for instance in Paris Ps. 74.6, Heptat. Deut. 32.10); *wid* and *wræc-* (as in *Christ and Satan* 119 f.); *westen-* and *wræc-* (as in Ælfric, Cath. Hom. I.560.22). The device of 'variation' is important in this process, since by its nature variation encourages extended collocation and at the same time allows the collocation to proceed beyond the two alliteratively bound units (the half-line and the full line); thus in

> ... mid hondum con   hearpan gretan;
> hafaþ him his gliwes giefe,   þe him God sealde
>
> (*Maxims I* 170 f.)

hand is collocated with *hearp* (as in *Genesis* 1079), *hearp* with *gretan* (as in *Beowulf* 2107 f. – also in an extended collocation), *hearp* with *gleo* or *gliw* (as in *Beowulf* 2262 f.); and all these connexions are manifested together in *Gifts of Men* 49 f. One might add that *giefu* and *God* are also closely collocated elsewhere (as in *Beowulf* 1271, 2182). The lines immediately following those quoted above from the Exeter Book *Maxims* provide a further example of the phenomenon:

> Earm biþ se þe sceal   ana lifgan,
> wineleas wunian   hafaþ him wyrd geteod   (172 f.)

where we have the connexion between *earm* and *an-* (as in *Beowulf* 2368), and between *earm*, *an-*, and *wineleas* (as in *Resignation* 89 ff.).

2

It may therefore be fairly claimed that an expectation of the congruous and complementary, expressed through recurrent collocations, is built into the poetic system of Old English, and it may be supposed that this is close to the starting point in estimating the original audience's pleasurable experience, as it is close to our starting point in criticism of the poetry today. There is evidently a prime satisfaction in the propriety of like belonging with like, of traditional correspondences being observed. 'Ellen sceal on eorle' as surely as 'wulf sceal on bearwe' or as 'gim sceal on hringe · standan steap and geap', we gather from the Cotton Tiberius gnomic verses: each must be where each belongs. So it will happen (through the corresponding association of *eorl* and *æþeling*, witnessed for instance in the *Rune Poem* 55, 84) that the right heroic tone can be established at the opening of *Beowulf* by the assurance that the Danish *æþelingas ellen fremedon*; indeed *wæs seo þeod tilu*, as we are told later (1250): the behaviour of their princes fits the heroic ideal, enshrined in the metrical and lexical system. The idea that the setting up of lexical expectations is basic in the composition and enjoyment of the early poetry would seem to be supported[7] by the description of Hroðgar's *scop*, 'se ðe eal-fela eald-gesegena worn gemunde, word oþer fand soðe gebunden' (896 ff.), the latter part recalling the quest for wisdom and expression in *Hávamál*:

> Þá nam ek frævaz
> ok fróðr vera
> ok vaxa ok vel hafaz;
> orð mér af orði
> orz leitaði,
> verk mér af verki
> verks leitaði.
>
> (st. 141)[8]

If however one were to reduce Old English poetry to metrically endorsed habitual collocations, lexically and syntactically complementary, this would be merely to agree with Milman Parry's view quoted earlier that the best poet was the one who knew and adhered most completely to the conventional diction. And this – to put it at its highest – would be a misleading conclusion, failing to account for much of our experience of the poetry. There are several ways in which the sophisticated poet, well learned in the conventions, could 'shade and knit anew the patch of words', as Dylan Thomas puts it. One of the most widely used devices is to allow the conventional lexical connexions and the conventional grammatical connexions (normally in unison, as in 'Sum mid hondum mæg · hearpan gretan' *Gifts of Men* 49) some degree of independence, with an

[7] As has been suggested: see R. W. Chambers, *Beowulf* (1914), note to ll. 870–1.

[8] Ed. Jón Helgason, *Eddadigte* I (1951).

area of overlap. The phenomenon is easily illustrated from post-Renaissance poetry also; in Shakespeare's thirty-third sonnet, we have

> Full many a glorious morning have I seen
> Flatter the mountain-tops with sovereign eye

where the lexical congruity of *flatter* and *sovereign* effects one valuable connexion (since there is some similarity with the courtly situation in which sovereigns are flattered), but where the grammatical connexion is necessarily independent of this, since here it is the majestic sun itself that performs the flattery. Again, in Shelley's 'The World's Wanderers',

> Tell me, moon, thou pale and gray
> Pilgrim of heaven's homeless way

homeless works in a grammatical connexion ('space provides no homes') and in an independent lexical connexion (with *pilgrim*). One might further illustrate the point from the complementary but independent lexical and grammatical relations of *human* and *softly* in these lines by W. H. Auden:

> Lay your sleeping head, my love,
> Human on my faithless arm

and

> Let the winds of dawn that blow
> Softly round your dreaming head.[9]

It can be shown that in a good deal of Old English poetry, too, words 'interanimate' each other, to use Donne's admirable expression. The name *Grendel*, for instance, is alliteratively linked in more than half its two score occurrences with words congruently indicative of fierceness, especially *guð* and *gryre*: and it is surely unnecessary to point out that there is no question of the poet's being obliged to make such selections by reason of a scarcity of words which will alliterate.

---

[9] The power of a collocation may, however, result from purely contextual developments and need not depend on previous experience of a particular lexical connexion. In *Richard II*, for example, when it has become painfully clear how feeble a substitute for kingship is the *name* of kingship, the king – who is almost alone in failing to see the gulf between the two – cries:

> Is not the king's name twenty thousand names?
> Arm, arm, my name! A puny subject strikes
> At thy great glory.   (III.ii.85 ff.)

The lexical relationship between 'my name' and 'puny' effectively deflates the preceding line.

Frequently, the lexical connexion is in unison with the grammatical one; for instance: 'he hraðe wolde Grendle forgyldan guð-ræsa fela' (*Beowulf* 1576 f.; and similarly 483, 591, and elsewhere). But we find notable instances in which the lexical connexion is maintained without a grammatical one, an effect which can be achieved not only because the particular type of lexical connexion is already established in the poem, but also because the whole metrical tradition has, as we have seen, established an expectation of lexical connexion. There is a good example in Unferð's flyting:

Ðonne wene ic to þe   wyrsan geþingea,
ðeah þu heaðo-ræsa   gehwær dohte,
grimre guðe,   gif þu Grendles dearst
niht-longne fyrst   nean bidan. (525 ff.)

The grammatical connexion of *grimre guðe* here is with Beowulf's skill in the past, but its equally potent lexical connexion is with Grendel and his present threat. Similar relationships appear in lines 819, 1538, and elsewhere.

When Beowulf's ten cowardly comrades rejoin Wiglaf after the fatal combat, it is said of them, 'hy scamiende · scyldas bæran' (2850). The lexical and metrical connexion between *scamiende* and *scyldas* points the irony of their external equipment and their internal inadequacy, which is made explicit in the context, especially by Wiglaf's words in ll. 2865–6. The syntactic connexions state that, feeling shame, the men approached with their shields; the metrically endorsed lexical connexion states that their shame actually lay in their shields, their own well-protected condition.[10]

The establishment of a lexical connexion 'by secretly evoking powerful associations', as C. S. Lewis put it,[11] is well demonstrated in the relationship of *death* and *doom*. The lexical and grammatical connexions are concurrent in *Beowulf* 1387 ff.:

wyrce se þe mote
domes ær deaþe;   þæt bið driht-guman
unlifgendum   æfter selest

---

[10] The double relationship finds a parallel in the 'prosodic counterpoint' that J. W. Lever sees in Sidney and other poets, the one depending upon syntax, the other (which may reinforce it or be in contrast) depending upon rhyme-scheme; see *The Elizabethan Love Sonnet* (1956), for example, p. 62. One should also refer, of course, to the complexity of effects that W. Empson is able to see generated by polysemy and the concurrent operation of lexical and grammatical connexions: *Seven Types of Ambiguity* (second edn, 1947), 30 ff., 49 ff., for example.

[11] *Studies in Words* (1960), 218.

as they are also in *Hávamál*:

> ek veit einn,
> at aldri deyr:
> dómr of dauðan hvern.
>
> (st. 77)[12]

In the Tiberius gnomic verses, the lexical connexion is independent:

> and ealle þa gastas   þe for gode hweorfað
> æfter deaðdæge,   domes bidað
> on fæder fæðme
>
> (*Maxims II* 59 ff.)

with which we may compare *Beowulf* 885 'æfter deað-dæge · dom unlytel'; the connexion is also independent of grammar later in the poem, l. 1490 f.:

> ic me mid Hruntinge
> dom gewyrce,   oþðe mec deað nimeð

and in the Exeter Book maxims:

> holen sceal inæled,   yrfe gedæled
> deades monnes.   Dom biþ selast.
>
> (*Maxims I* 79 f.)

With differing degrees of grammatical independence, there is an identical lexical connexion between the root 'lie' and *líc* in

> þær his lichoma,   leger-bedde fæst,
> swefeþ æfter symle
>
> (*Beowulf* 1007 f.)

and

> þæt he for mund-gripe   minum scolde
> licgean lif-bysig,   butan his lic swice.
>
> (*ibid.* 965 f.)

The well-established connexion between *brucan* and *beag*, the very type and symbol of reward, is exemplified concurrently with a grammatical connexion in *Beowulf* 894 ('he beah-hordes · brucan moste'), but occurs independently with no less effectiveness, as when lexical collocation proclaims that bright treasure may now be enjoyed again in Heorot:

> Heorot is gefælsod,
> beah-sele beorhta;   bruc, þenden þu mote,
> manigra medo . . .   (1176 ff.)

12 Ed. Helgason, *op. cit.*

We have the same independent relationship a little later:

> ... ic gum-cystum   godne funde
> beaga bryttan,   breac þonne moste.
>
> (1486 f.)

It would take more space than is available here to explore this phenomenon as it manifests itself in a poem as thematically rich as *Beowulf*, but
mention might be made of a passage in the Finn episode where it occurs
with particular density and effectiveness, especially perhaps in lines
1103, 1113, 1121, 1122, 1123.

3

Most of the examples we have considered so far have been of metrical
two-stress units being complementary to each other. But strong as is the
expectation of this, it is important to note that there is comparable
power in the expectation of parity, of equivalence, of grammatical
apposition – the relationship which has as its primary vehicle the metrical
convention known as 'variation'. This is so common as to need little
illustration. One well-known type is seen in 'Beowulf maðelode, · bearn
Ecgþeowes' or 'Eala Ioseph min, · Iacobes bearn' (*Christ* 164). When
Hroðgar says to Beowulf, 'gemyne mærþo, · mægen-ellen cyð' (659),
the lexical congruity of *mærþo* and *mægen-ellen* (well attested in hymns
and psalms, for instance), together with the grammatical parallelism of
the two metrical units (imperative plus object), would prompt an
audience used to the patterns of Old English poetry to see a variation-
equation here: bearing glory in mind is one aspect of showing mighty
valour. So too when we are told (of Byrhtnoð's avengers),

> Þa hi forð eodon,   feores hi ne rohton
>
> (*Maldon* 260)

it is the expectations determined by the metrical conventions as much
as by the context that make us aware that going forward *meant* not
caring about their own lives. The plight of the pagan Danes in *Beowulf*
is expressed by this means: their *hyht* is collocated – significantly – with
hell:

> Swylc wæs þeaw hyra,
> hæþenra hyht;   helle gemundon
> in mod-sefan,   Metod hie ne cuþon ...
>
> (178 ff.)

By contrast, it is said of the hero:

> Huru Geata leod   georne truwode
> modgan mægnes,   Metodes hyldo
>
> (669 f.)

and the metrical dependences thus directly attribute Beowulf's might to the Lord's favour. In the same way, the description of Grendel's *glof*, 'gegyrwed deofles cræftum ond dracan fellum' (2087 f.), is not to be read as sylleptic. One further illustration may be offered to show how close this idea of an equation between metrical units in variation is to the idea discussed earlier of congruity between such units when they are complementary:

> Ful oft gebeotedon   beore druncne
> ofer ealo-wæge   oret-mecgas . . .
>
> (*Beowulf* 480 f.)

In these transverse sets (*beot–beor*; *ealo–oret*), we have a witness to the dependence of challenge upon beer that would be difficult to parallel.

Now that we have seen to some extent how immensely powerful are the tendencies towards a relationship of at least lexical congruity between metrical units, and have observed some of the ways in which Old English poets exploited these tendencies to sharpen communication, we may turn to what would seem to be the most attractive potentiality for exploitation provided by the system of conventions. For the very reason that there was a high expectation of congruity at specific points in metrical structure, the impact of the incongruous at such points could be the greater.[13]

After *sæl* in the sense of 'happiness' has been used three times in *Beowulf* in a congruent context (the occurrence in line 643 collocates with *sige-folca sweg* as a variation), we have Hroðgar's reply to Beowulf's polite inquiry on the morning after the attack by Grendel's mother:

> Ne frin þu æfter sælum;   sorh is geniwod
> Denigea leodum.   Dead is Æschere . . .
>
> (1322 f.)

Later on in the same poem, it is said of Unferð that he did not dare 'drihtscipe dreogan; · þær he dome forleas' (1470). The turned tide of Beowulf's fortunes as he embarks on the dragon fight is symbolized by the contrast between *goldwine* (which invites exultant collocations) and

---

[13] See the discussion of 'warranted' and 'frustrated expectations' by Roman Jakobson, 'Linguistics and Poetics', in *Style in Language*, ed. T. A. Sebeok (1960), 350–77.

geomor sefa, with which it is metrically linked (2419). In a similar way, the incongruity of youth and sadness, external gaiety and inward grief, is sharpened in the *Wife's Lament*:

> A scyle geong man   wesan geomormod,
> heard heortan geþoht,   swylce habban sceal
> bliþe gebæro,   eac þon breostceare ...
>
> (42 ff.)

In *Beowulf*, line 281, *bealu* is contrasted with a redeeming *bot*, and the line which follows provides a good example of what could be done with lexical and metrical patterning:

> þa cear-wylmas   colran wurðaþ ...

The collocation of *care* with *cool* would in itself be a congruous commonplace (compare l. 2396 or – an illustration with greater morphological and semantic complexity – *Seafarer* 14). But here (as in l. 2066, equally effectively and in a far more pregnant passage) the semantic relationship is enriched by the presence of *wylm*, the lexical relations of which elsewhere are often the antithesis of cold:[14] compare *Genesis* 2586, *Juliana* 583, *Christ* 831, 965, *Phoenix* 283, *Daniel* 463, and *Beowulf* 2546. The collocation thus subtly implies the possibility of both a contrast and a paradox, parallel on the one hand to the change from *bealu* to *bot* (281) and on the other to the connexion between conjugal love and slaughterous enmity (2065).[15]

Metrical and lexical links which are incongruous may have a sharply poignant effect, as when Hildeburh is forced to commit her son to the funeral pyre ('hire selfre sunu · sweoloðe befæstan' 1115),[16] or when Hroðgar knows that his noble thane Æschere is lifeless, 'aldor-þegn · unlyfigendne, / þone deorestan · deadne' (1308 f.). There is a whole series of such incongruities in the description of the mourning father (*Beowulf* 2444 ff.), such as the link of *sunu* with *sarig sang* (2447) and with *sorh* (2455), of *hearp* with *hæleð in hoðman* (2458).

Again, incongruous links may be sinister, as when it is said of Heorot, at the triumphant moment of completion, that 'heah ond horn-geap, ·

---

[14] In *Elene* 1257, the same compound *cearwylm* is in construction with the verb *cnyssan*, and the image in this instance relates emotion rather to a storm at sea.

[15] See p. 16 below.

[16] There is a poignant irony with similar exponence in *Hildebrandslied*: 'nû scal mih suâsat chind · suertu hauwan'; it is implicit earlier too: 'muotîn ... untar heriun tuêm,/sunufatarungo; · iro saro rihtun,/garutun se iro gûðhamun'. Cf. also *Beowulf* 1261 f.: 'Cain wearð to ecg-banan angan breþer', perhaps used to emphasize – by the parallel – Unferð's baseness.

heaðo-wylma bad' (82).[17] Or they may point an ironic antithesis. In
Beowulf 1709, *hæleðum to helpe* (predicted of the hero) is collocated with
Heremod, the symbol of evil kingship, and the passage which follows
develops this antithesis between the good and evil types of king, with
several pairs of alliterating units defying congruous complementarity:

> ne geweox he him to willan,   ac to wæl-fealle
> ond to deað-cwalum   Deniga leodum.
>
> Breat bolgen-mod   beod-geneatas,
> eaxl-gesteallan,   oþþæt he ana hwearf,
> mære þeoden,   mon-dreamum from,
> ðeah þe hine mihtig God   mægenes wynnum,
> eafeþum stepte,   ofer ealle men
> forð gefremede.   Hwæþere him on ferhþe greow
> breost-hord blod-reow;   nallas beagas geaf
> Denum æfter dome.   Dream-leas gebad ...
>
> (1711 ff.)

The ironical presentation of antitheses, 'not *this* (as might be expected)
but *that*', is clearly of great appeal as a rhetorical device, and it is
something for which the features of poetic style that we have been considering have an extraordinary potential, exploited in many poems. For
instance:

> Warað hine wræclast,   nales wunden gold,
> ferðloca freorig,   nalæs foldan blæd.
>
> (*Wanderer* 32 f.)

> Abraham sealde
> wig to wedde,   nalles wunden gold,
> for his suhtrigan,   sloh and fylde
> feond on fitte.   (*Genesis* 2069 ff.)

> Þæt þam banan ne wearð
> hleahtre behworfen,   ah in helle ceafl
> sið asette   (*Andreas* 1702 ff.)

> Hwilum ylfete song
> dyde ic me to gomene,   ganetes hleoþor
> ond huilpan sweg   fore hleahtor wera,
> mæw singende   fore medodrince.
>
> (*Seafarer* 19 ff.)

[17] See p. 15 below.

> (Welund) hæfde him to gesiþþe   sorge ond longaþ,
>   wintercealde . . . wræce   (*Deor* 3 f.)

While the ironies here are achieved through the juxtaposition of incompatibles like 'laughter' and 'hell' at points in the metrical structure where lexical relationship is expected, one may also find a comparable effect achieved by retaining complementary and normal collocations rendered contextually ironical. In the flood which is brought about by Andreas's prayer, his revelling and feasting tormenters find rather different *byrlas* serving up a great deal of unwelcome 'drink':

>   Fæge swulton,
>   geonge on geofene   guðræs fornam
>   þurh sealtne weg.   Þæt wæs sorgbyrþen,
>   biter beorþegu.   Byrlas ne gældon,
>   ombehtþegnas.   Þær wæs ælcum genog
>   fram dæges orde   drync sona gearu.
>
>   (*Andreas* 1530 ff.)

The ironical tones can be dissipated into the almost wholly commonplace in descriptions of retribution, for which this rhetorical device (as we have already seen) is very commonly used; words for 'payment' or 'repayment' all too readily connote 'punishment':

>   Gyldað nu mid gyrne,   þæt heo goda ussa
>   meaht forhogde,   ond mec swiþast
>   geminsade,   þæt ic to meldan wearð.
>   Lætað hy laþra   leana hleotan
>   þurh wæpnes spor   (*Juliana* 619 ff.)
>
>   Þæs hi longe sculon
>   ferðwerige onfon   in fyrbaðe,
>   wælmum biwrecene,   wraþlic ondlean
>   (*Christ* 829 ff.)
>
>   sealde him wites clom,
>   atole to æhte   (*Christ and Satan* 451 f.)[18]

At times, however, the conjunction of words, metre, and situation have a very powerful effect, as in Byrhtnoð's reply to the Vikings' demand for tribute:

>   Gehyrst þu, sælida,   hwæt þis folc segeð?
>   Hi willað eow to gafole   garas syllan,

---

[18] Compare such expressions as 'for recompense he will receive great torment' in the OS *Heliand*, ll. 4585, 5424, 5563, etc.

> ættrynne ord   and ealde swurd,
> þa heregeatu   þe eow æt hilde ne deah.
>
> (*Maldon* 45 ff.)[19]

And similarly, Hadubrand's rejection of the gifts offered by the man whom he cannot believe to be his father:

> Mit gêru scal man   geba infâhan,
> ort widar orte.   (*Hildebrandslied*)

In the Edda, likewise:

> Kvǫddo síðan   Sigmundar bur
> auðs ok hringa   Hundings synir,
> þvíat þeir átto   iǫfri at gialda
> fiárnám mikit   ok fǫður dauða.
>
> Létat buðlungr   bótir uppi,
> né niðia in heldr   nefgiǫld fá;
> ván kvað hann mundo   veðrs ens mikla
> grára geira   ok gremi Oðins.
>
> (*Helgakviða Hundingsbana I*, st. 11 and 12)[20]

---

[19] I am grateful to Professor I. L. Foster for discussing and expounding (in correspondence) a notable Welsh parallel. The poem *Armes Prydein* in the Book of Taliesin (ed. J. G. Evans, 1915) has 'tribute' and 'pay' used ironically several times in prophesying the lot of King Athelstan's stewards. For example, *anaeleu dretheu, dy · chynullant* (1. 72) – 'grief (will be) the tributes that they gather'.

[20] Ed. Jón Helgason, *Eddadigte* III (1952). The device is used with comic effect in *Þrymskviða*, st. 29,32:

> Inn kom in arma   iǫtna systir,
> hin er brúðfiár   biðia þorði:
> 'Láttu þér af hǫndom   hringa rauða,
> ef þú ǫðlaz vill   ástir mínar,
> ástir minar,   alla hylli' . . .
>
> Drap hann ina ǫldno   iǫtna systur,
> hin er brúðfiár   of beðit hafði;
> hón skell um hlaut   fyr skillinga,
> en hǫgg hamars   fyr hringa fiǫlð.

(Ed. Helgason, *Eddadigte* II, 1952). It has a similar comic effect in the prose Edda too, as we find in the account of how Thor dealt with the smith from Jotunheim:
'Galt hann þá smíðarkaupit, ok eigi sól ok tungl [as had been agreed], heldr synjaði hann honum at byggva í Jötunheimum ok laust þat it fyrsta hǫgg, er haussinn brotnaði í smán mola, ok sendi hann niðr undir Niflheim' (*SnE* 47, normalized).

When, in the *Nibelungenlied*, the sight of Hagen's gold armring attracts the avaricious Danube ferryman, we are told:

> dô wold' er verdienen   daz Hagenen golt sô rôt:
> des leit er von dem degene   den swertgrimmigen tôt.
>
> (st. 1554)

Among the many other occasions on which we find expressions of similar irony in medieval literature, one might mention the fourteenth-century German poem on the Battle of Sempach where the Swiss defensive resolution before the battle is expressed in terms of penance. A priest can certainly be found to hear confession:

> er kan wol büsse geben:
> mit scharpfen hallenbarten
> so gibt man inen den segen.
> Das ist ein scharpfe büsse . . .[21]

4

It is with irony of this kind that the extreme bitterness is expressed towards the close of *Beowulf*; the dead hero is surrounded by incongruous wealth:

> þa sceall brond fretan,
> æled þeccean,   nalles eorl wegan
> maððum to gemyndum,   ne mægð scyne
> habban on healse   hring-weorðunge,
> ac sceal geomor-mod,   golde bereafod,
> oft, nalles æne,   elland tredan,
> nu se here-wisa   hleahtor alegde,
> gamen ond gleo-dream.   Forðon sceall gar wesan
> monig morgen-ceald   mundum bewunden,
> hæfen on handa,   nalles hearpan sweg
> wigend weccean,   ac se wonna hrefn
> fus ofer fægum   fela reordian,

[21] Ludwig Tobler, *Schweizerische Volkslieder* II (1884), 10 f. We may compare our use of 'short shrift'. In Sir Walter Scott's version of the poem, we have:

> The Switzer priest has ta'en the field,
>   He deals a penance drear.
> Right heavily upon your head
>   He'll lay his hand of steel;
> And with his trusty partisan
>   Your absolution deal.

earne secgan,   hu him æt æte speow,
þenden he wið wulf   wæl reafode.

(3014 ff.)

This passage, however, is more than merely an additional example of a recurrent theme, contrasting comfortable possibility with bitter fact through what can now be seen as a characteristic departure from the basic metrical and lexical conditions: we see here the use of incongruous collocations to form a critical undercurrent of a kind which notably enriches *Beowulf* from time to time and which is prominent among the features making it a great poem. Mention has already been made of the predicted fate of Heorot (82): this is immediately followed by a direct link between *ecg-hete* and *aþum-swerian* (84);[22] somewhat later, we see the sinister character of Unferð – particularly in relation to his past faithlessness towards kin (587) – and his sinister proximity to Hroðgar (500). In Fitte XV, we have an important passage as follows:

Ne gefrægen ic þa mægþe   maran weorode
ymb hyra sinc-gyfan   sel gebæran.
Bugon þa to bence   blæd-agande,
fylle gefægon;   fægere geþægon
medo-ful manig   magas þara,
swið-hicgende,   on sele þam hean,
Hroðgar ond Hroþulf.   Heorot innan wæs
freondum afylled;   nalles facen-stafas
Þeod-Scyldingas   þenden fremedon.

(1011 ff.)

The passage begins by portraying *comitatus* solidarity and reflecting this in the stable, traditional and congruous heroic collocations: kinsmen united over mead, brave-minded in a brave hall; the metrical arrangement should also suggest the unity of Hroðgar and Hroþulf within Heorot (1017), but this has been made equivocal (84) and irony is explicit in 1018 with the link between *freondum* and *facen-stafas* – a link which however is metrical without being syntactic.[23] The sinister suggestions become more explicit a hundred and fifty lines later when what Jakobson calls a 'warranted' link (metrically and lexically) between 'suhtergefæderan' and 'sib' is broken by the foreboding *gyt*.[24] The

---

[22] See the excellent note on this passage in C. L. Wrenn's edition.
[23] As J. W. Lever says (*op. cit.* 6), the 'progressive logic of syntax' can be 'overborne by the emotional suggestions of rhyme'.
[24] See n. 13, p. 9, above.

metre gives a further hint of Unferð's place in the ultimate tragedy:

> þær þa godan twegen
> sæton suhtergefæderan;   þa gyt wæs hiera sib ætgædere,
> æghwylc oðrum trywe.   Swylce þær Unferþ þyle
> æt fotum sæt frean Scyldinga;   gehwylc hiora his ferhþe treowde,
> þæt he hæfde mod micel,   þeah þe he his magum nære
> ar-fæst æt ecga gelacum.   (1163 ff.)

By the time we come to Wealhþeow's speech beginning at line 1216, we are no longer disposed to take 'warranted' links at their face value; as for instance:

> Her is æghwylc eorl   oþrum getrywe . . .
> (1228)

The internal disharmonies of a subsequent *comitatus* scene are even more forcibly emphasized by lexical disharmonies pointed by the metre. After the description of the Queen's and Freawaru's relations with the court of Heorot (2016 ff., a passage characterized by congruence of vocabulary, syntax, and metre), mention is made of the marriage to Ingeld, and at once an undercurrent becomes noticeable, running independently of and at first in opposition to the syntax, with the lexical-metrical links of *wif* and *wæl-fæhð* (2028), *bon-gar* and *bryd* (2031). The tragedy moves to its climax with the goading of a young Heatho-bard by the 'eald æsc-wiga' (2042) who says of the Danish courtier that he 'morðres gylpeð · ond þone maðþum byreð' (2055). The metre here achieves the inciter's end by seeming (in terms of variation) to give equal authority to the *fact* (wearing the sword) and the *inference* (exulting in the earlier slaughter of Heathobards). The rhetorical equation – 'morð-res gylpeð' *in that* 'maðþum byreð' – is given further point by the alliterative link and syntactic parallelism of *murder* and *sword*. So too, the absence of direct responsibility on the part of those who now suffer is emphasized in the metrical and grammatical parallelism of 'se fæmnan þegn · fore fæder dædum' (2059); and the bitterness of Ingeld's situation is summed up in the collocation (independent of grammar) of *wæl-niðas* and *wif-lufan* (2065).

With the dragon fight, and beginning in Fitte XXXII, we find all the devices of metre, word-relationship, and grammar so far discussed being used to mark what is surely the most important thematic undercurrent in the poem: an undermining of the heroic values attached to gold. The treatment of the lone survivor emphasizes the dubious and transient value of treasure by such metrically endorsed collocations as *deore maðmas* and *deað* (2236), *lytel fæc* and *long-gestreona* (2240), and syntactic connexions like *hæðen gold* (2276). The fitte ends with the metrical link of *sinc* and *sar*, confirming a connexion between the hero's death and a distorted valuation of treasure, and anticipating the same collocation in 2746, where it applies to the dragon, whose death (also brought about by the gold) is explicitly compared with Beowulf's in 2844. From the thirty-second fitte onwards, whatever the difficulties we have with the narrative account of the treasure's history,[25] *hord* is a suspect word (it is collocated with 'hate' in 2319), and *hord-weard* is identified with the dragon (2293, 2302, 2554). The damning collocations of treasure continue: *wrætta ond wira* is linked metrically to *weard unhiore* (the dragon) in 2413, *gold* to *guð* (2414, 2536), to *geomor* (2419, 3018), to *grim* (3012), to *bær* (3105), and to *greot* (3167); *feoh* to *fyren* (2441); *beah-hord* to *bealu* (2826). There is a metrical but not syntactic relation of *searu* with *sinc* at the very point where we have the explicit condemnation of treasure as such:

> ... earm-beaga fela
> searwum gesæled.   Sinc eaðe mæg,
> gold on grunde,   gum-cynnes gehwone
> oferhigian ...   (2763 ff.)

The devaluation is completed when we have the supreme irony of the lines describing the disposal of the gold for which Beowulf died:

> Hi on beorg dydon   beg ond siglu,
> eall swylce hyrsta,   swylce on horde ær
> nið-hedige men   genumen hæfdon;
> forleton eorla gestreon   eorðan healdan,
> gold on greote,   þær hit nu gen lifað
> eldum swa unnyt,   swa hit æror wæs.
>   (3163 ff.)

And that it *is* the supreme irony, the poet's elaborately equivocal use of familiar formulas has made perfectly clear. Over the last seven hundred lines of the poem, the dragon fight is repeatedly referred to as a pitifully unequal bargain of Beowulf's life in exchange for gold, terms like *ceap*

---

[25] See, for example, K. Sisam in *Review of English Studies* 9 (1958), 129 ff.; C. L. Wrenn, edition, notes to ll. 3051 ff., 3074 ff.; G. V. Smithers in *English and Germanic Studies* 4 (1951–2), 75 ff.

both enhancing the irony and probing the morality of wordly purchase
and wealth:

> Weard unhiore,
> gearo guð-freca   gold-maðmas heold,
> eald under eorðan;   næs þæt yðe ceap
> to gegangenne   gumena ænigum.
>
> (2413 ff.)

Beowulf finds himself recalling another 'feoh-leas gefeoht' (2441),
which in turn leads to his parable of the mourning father who is brought
in grief to see the worthlessness of material treasures (2455 ff., especially
2461 f.). Beowulf mentions life in terms of bargaining, 'ealdre gebohte,
heardan ceape' (2481 f.), and after the fight he uses the same expression
to describe the price he has paid:

> Nu ic on maðma hord   mine bebohte
> frode feorh-lege . . .   (2799 f.)

So too, a little later, we are told that

> Biowulfe wearð
> dryht-maðma dæl   deaðe forgolden
>
> (2842 f.)

and the immensity of the treasure that his death has secured, the 'hord
. . . grimme gegongen' (3084 f.), only emphasizes its ultimate, compara-
tive worthlessness:

> þær is maðma hord,
> gold unrime,   grimme geceapod;
> ond nu æt siðestan   sylfes feore
> beagas gebohte: þa sceall brond fretan,
> æled þeccean,   nalles eorl wegan
> maððum to gemyndum . . .   (3011 ff.)[26]

In view of this, it is worth recalling that, at the point where Beowulf
was represented as seeking out the dragon's hoard, the poet has told us –
in one of his most telling ironic uses of familiar collocations – that *wyrd*
would be seeking out the treasure-hoard of the hero's soul and that the
only dividing up that day would be of life from body:

> wyrd ungemete neah,
> se ðone gomelan   gretan sceolde,
> secean sawle hord,   sundur gedælan
> lif wið lice . . .   (2420 ff.)

[26] Accepting the usual editorial readings in ll. 3012, 3014.

It should therefore be emphasized that, while formulaic utterances and habitual collocations are the necessary starting point in the study of the early alliterative poetry, they are *only* the starting point. The very fact that he could depend on his audience having a firm expectation of certain dependences and determined sequences involving metre, vocabulary, and grammar gave the poet his opportunity to stretch linguistic expression beyond the ordinary potentialities of prose, and to achieve a disturbing and richly suggestive poetry.

Two

Langland's use of *kind wit* and *inwit*†

One has only to glance at the *NED* article on *wit* to realise its vast range of meaning in ME. In this respect, Langland's usage corresponds very much to that of his contemporaries. To name some outstanding functions, we find the word applied, for example, to any mental or sensual faculty. It is used of the 'outer' senses (thus, B xiv.54), just as Gower uses it of 'the gates, Thurgh whiche ... Comth alle thing' (*Confessio Amantis* i.296); it is used of a special skill or art, as in B xix. 118 where we read that Christ's turning water into wine was 'bi no witte · but thorw worde one', just as the translator of Guy de Chauliac's *Grande Cirurgie* (New York Academy of Medicine MS, fol. 4b) discourses of 'þe witte of extracciou of arwes'. It is grouped broadly with *wisdom* as in 'wytte and wisdome · the welle of alle craftes' (B. xv. 30), a popular coupling in ME, to be compared for example with 'þe welle of wytte and of wysdome' in *Ayenbite of Inwyt* (EETS.OS 23.251). And it is used of acumen ranging from the basest cunning (as in C vii.259; compare *Alexander B* 534[1]) to the wisdom which is the formulator of philosophic thought (for example, B ix *passim*, xix.78; compare *Speculum Gy de Warewyke*, EETS.ES 75. l. 227: 'God ʒaf him wit as his owen, God and yuel for to knowen'[2]). In short, there appears to be no use of the word in *Piers Plowman* that was not completely commonplace in Langland's time.

† Reprinted from *The Journal of English and Germanic Philology* 52 (1953), 182 ff. I am greatly indebted to Professor Hans Kurath, University of Michigan, for allowing me full and prolonged use of the *Middle English Dictionary* material and library in the preparation of this and the next paper in the present volume.
    [1] *The Gests of King Alexander of Macedon*, ed. F. P. Magoun, Jr (Cambridge, Mass., 1929).
    [2] Cf.: 'þe zoþe wyt þet þe holy gost tekþ to godes uryendes is ine knauynge wyþoute wyþnimynge þet ech þing is worþ' *Ayenbite* 82.

The position is rather different with the related but narrowed concepts, *kind wit* and *inwit*.

Kind wit is not different from *wit*, in the sense that *wanhope* is different from *hope*; indeed, it *is* 'wit', but 'wit' looked at from a particular point of view and (with Langland) in only one of its senses. The term *kind wit* can always be replaced by *wit*, with only the risk of some loss in precision;[3] but though *wit* can similarly be replaced by *kind wit*, this is not always – nor even frequently – possible.

This general statement of the relation between *kind wit* and *wit* holds for all ME usage, but the exact terms of the relationship show some variation from writer to writer. In some authors, Wiclif for example, *kind(ly)* defines *wit* as one of the five bodily senses.[4] This is rare, however, and it is more usual to find *wit* in this group signifying 'ratio', the reasoning faculty which supremely marks off the powers of man from those of beasts, the qualifying *kind* being introduced to distinguish this in its turn from absolute or divine reason. Thus Trevisa speaks of men being turned into animals and retaining nevertheless 'kyndeliche witte and reasoun', this whole expression translating Higden's *mens rationalis* (*op. cit.* II.425). Similarly Mandeville speaks of birds as having 'no kyndely wytt ne resoun' (EETS.OS 153.39). This is obviously quite different from the concept in *Piers Plowman*, where it is made clear that animals had at least some degree of 'kind wit'; thus in C xv.164 we learn of Nature's giving, not only to Adam and Eve, but to 'other bestes alle A cantel of kynde witt · here kynde to saue', just as Chanticleer 'knew by kind' when it was time to crow (*Canterbury Tales* B 4386). Presumably, therefore, Langland's *kind wit* corresponds to Pecock's 'natural logik', which is also common to beasts and unlearned men (*Folewer* 37 f., EETS.OS 164), rather than to his concept of 'kindeli witt' which in *Repressor* I.132 (ed. C. Babington, London, 1860) Pecock equates with 'reason' or rather 'natural reason', the limiting 'natural' (like 'kindeli') being used, as he points out in *Folewer* 72 f., to draw attention to the fact that it is not a *miraculous* attribute of men. Compare likewise his distinction between the law of faith and the 'law of natural resoun in moral gouernauncis' (*Reule of Crysten Religioun*, 322, EETS.OS 171). Similarly, it seems to be Trevisa's *kindly wit* not Langland's *kind wit* that is meant by 'kindly reason' (='humana racio') in *The Three Kings of*

---

[3] Thus *wit* clearly stands for *kind wit* in B vii.52.

[4] E.g. 'kyndely wittes', *Select English Works* (ed. T. Arnold, Oxford, 1871) III. 405. On the equation of *kind* and *kindly* in this connexion, see Trevisa's translation of Higden (Rolls Series 41) III.217, where the manuscripts are divided between *kyndly* and *kynde* (*wytt*).

Cologne, p. 50 (EETS.OS 85), and by 'natural reason' in *The Assembly of Gods*, l. 1622 (ed. O. L. Triggs, Chicago, 1895).[5]

By contrast, Langland uses *kind* not to emphasize as 'human', 'mortal' the *wit* thus designated but to draw attention to the fact that it is natural and inborn in creatures. This is brought out clearly in B xii. 225 where we are told that neither 'Clergie ne kynde witte' – neither wisdom by learning nor wisdom by nature – has ever known the secrets of God,[6] and the gulf between *kind wit* and *reason* has been emphasized a hundred lines earlier in the statement that 'letterure' leads 'lewed men to resoun', whereas 'a kynde-witted man ... for al his kynde witte' cannot be saved unless 'clerkes hym teche'. Further, *kind wit* is intimately connected with the bodily senses; it comes 'of alkynnes siʒtes, Of bryddes and of bestes · of tastes of treuthe, and of deceytes' (B xii.130), whereas reason is capable of comprehending all things imaginable and sensible without recourse to the imagination or the senses, as any reader of Boethius knew perfectly well (Bk. v, Pr. 4).

On the other hand, *kind wit* is far superior to the lowly faculty called *common wit* by writers on anatomy and philosophy.[7] Itself the gift of Kind, God the Creator, Kind Wit is the companion and teacher of Conscience (A iii.281, B iii.282, xix.357), and in B i.140 Holy Church announces that it is 'kind knowing' (elsewhere clearly identified with 'kind wit': cf. B xii.130–37) that

> kenneth in thine herte
> For to louye thi lorde · leuer than thi-selue;
> No dedly synne to do · dey thouʒ thow sholdest.

Moreover, to 'Scripture the wise' Kind Wit is both cousin and confessor, and one can reach him by travelling with *omnia probate* to 'the burgh *quod-bonum-est-tenete*' where Kind Wit lives (A xii.38–52).

Thus although it is not easy to find a close parallel to Langland's

---

[5] That Langland's *kind wit* can be distinct from the *scientia* aspect of *wit* (contrast D. W. Robertson, Jr, B. F. Huppé, *Piers Plowman and Scriptural Tradition*, Princeton, N.J. (1951), 27, 103, 152, 223) is supported not only by the development of the allegory, particularly in Passus x–xii of A, but by the attribution of *kind wit* to animals. In his translation of Bartholomæus Anglicus, Trevisa says that, though 'unreasonable', beasts have 'wonder redynesse of witte' (Lat. *prudentia*) 'but in hem is no science propurliche to speken of science but in hem liknesse of science is yfounde for þey haueþ redynesse of witte' (Lat. *solertia*) 'in bredȳg and of rerynge of hire brood' (British Museum Add. MS 27944, fol. 259a).

[6] Cf. 'Kynde-wittede men han · a cleregie by hem-selue' C xv. 72.

[7] Corresponding to the Latin *sensus communis*; cf. the ME translation of Chauliac, *MS cit.*, fol. 11a, and Trevisa's Bartholomæus, *MS cit.*, fol. 21a, 77a.

kind wit elsewhere in ME, either in form or meaning, we are no doubt near it in Trevisa's Higden when we are told that primitive men 'by besynesse of kynde witte . . . beþouʒt hem of buldynge' and proceeded to erect cabins and the like.[8] We are reminded that 'Kynde wit and the comune · contreuede alle craftes' (C i.144) and that Kind Wit taught Conscience to defend Holy Church and 'comaunded · al Crystene peple, For to deluen a dyche · depe a-boute Vnite' (B xix.357 ff.).

From the foregoing, it seems that the refinement of terminology in Langland – *kind wit ∼ wit* – is to be interpreted as follows. The two terms are an attempt to represent the unity of and at the same time the distinction between the *vis cogitativa* (which corresponds to the *vis aestimativa* in animals) and the *ratio particularis*; they conveniently express these two aspects of the same faculty: *quod bonum est tenete* and *wit wolle the wisse*.[9]

There is general agreement among most ME writers that *inwit* is a faculty or collection of faculties relatively far removed from the bodily senses and can therefore be naturally contrasted with 'outwit(s)', as in Wiclif, *Select English Works* II.311. On one occasion Langland too seems to think of *inwit* in this general sense: 'With inwit and with outwitt · ymagenen and studye' (B xiii.289); according to *The Lay Folks' Catechism* (EETS.OS 118.19) this collection of the 'five inwits' comprises 'will, reason, mind, imagination and thought'. Nevertheless, just as some writers used *kind wit* of the outer senses, so we find occasionally *inwit* used likewise; Trevisa[10] talks of 'þe inwitte of smellynge' a line or so after he has used *inwit* also to translate *intellectus*.

The distinction between the soul and the highest mental faculty, intellect, was never established to the complete satisfaction of all the scholastic philosophers, and we see this reflected in the difficulty ME writers experienced in expressing the concept *animus*. One finds something akin to the unprecise coupling of 'wit and wisdom' in the grouping 'inwit and soul', as for example in Rolle's Psalter.[11] Trevisa often renders Higden's *animus* by *inwit* where the anonymous Harleian

---

[8] *Op. cit.* II.227; the Latin has *naturali solertia* which the anonymous translator in the Harleian MS renders 'natural reason'. Cf. also 'natural understanding' in Usk (*Testament of Love* 78.42), 'kindly understanding' in Chaucer (*Book of the Duchess* 761), 'natural wit' in *Ayenbite* 18, 'kindly wit' in *Cloud of Unknowing* 30.

[9] Cf. Thomas Aquinas, *Summa Theologica* I, Quest. 78, Art. 1 ff. See also C. A. Hart, *The Thomistic Concept of Mental Faculty* (Washington, D. C., 1930) Ch. V, and L. Schütz, *Thomas-Lexikon* (Paderborn, 1895) s.vv. *ratio, cogitativus*.

[10] Bartholomæus, *MS cit.*, fol. 312a.

[11] *Western Reserve University Bulletins* xxi.52–3.

manuscript has *soule* instead,[12] and where in his 1382 version of the Bible Wiclif translates *animus* as *inwit*, he almost always substitutes *soul* in 1388.[13] Thus we can find *inwit* recorded in practically all the senses of the Latin *animus*, not only 'soul' and 'intellect' but 'spirit, heart, disposition, feeling': 'Inwitte of god is makere of alle þinges' Trevisa's Higden III.65, where the Harleian manuscript reads *wille* for *inwitte*; 'I counceile ȝou for to be of good ynwitt *or herte*' (1388: *of good coumfort* (Lat. *bono animo*) Wiclif, *Deeds of the Apostles* 27.32.

For the most part, however, *inwit* signifies – more or less vaguely – the human faculty of comprehension. Trevisa talks of man's 'vndirstondinge & inwit' where Bartholomæus uses simply *intellectus* (*MS cit.*, fol. 12a; so too fol. 14a), and of 'þe siȝt of here īwitt' where Bartholomæus has *mentis aciem* (fol. 16a). Pecock demonstrates that the multiples of finites are still finite, however much this may 'astonye ... oure inwitt and ymaginacioun' (*Reule of Crysten Religioun* 50). In the prose Vegetius, an emperor is addressed who holds all the laws and statutes in his 'hiȝe in-witt and wisdom'.[14] In a similar way, Walton's rendering of Boethius groups *inwit* and *reason* (EETS.OS 170.158), apparently an expansion of Chaucer's *reason*. The word is also found in expressions meaning little more than 'to my mind':

> He sais Scotland is in his hand for now & ay,
> At myn inwitte it is not ȝit alle at our fay.[15]

This usage is found in Langland occasionally: 'hit semeth, to myn inwitt' (C x.117), 'me thynketh, by myn inwyt' (B xvii.278).

Now 'conscience', in the modern sense, is a relatively rare meaning of *animus*, and it is correspondingly a relatively rare meaning of *inwit*. In Furnivall's edition of Brunne's *Chronicle* II (London, 1887, 575), we learn that a good while had passed before the English had finished settling their newly-won land – 'As mannes in-wyt may þat well knowe'. Furnivall glosses *in-wyt* as 'conscience', but a less likely operation of conscience would be hard to imagine. At the same time, both from the point of view of its etymology as well as by an easy semantic development of its most frequent use, it is not unreasonable to expect that *inwit* could on occasion have the meaning 'conscience'. It is possible to find

---

[12] E.g. III.223 (Rolls Series 41).
[13] E.g. Genesis 26:35, Deuteronomy 21:14, Judges 16:20, 1 Kings (=1 Samuel) 1:10, 2 Maccabees 9:7.
[14] MS Douce 291, fol. 26b; two other manuscripts read *witte*.
[15] *Peter Langtoft's Chronicle* II (ed. T. Hearne, London, 1810), 282; cf. also 1.155.

examples where the meaning hovers between 'intellect', 'awareness of things' and 'conscience':

> How shul þey þan help þe at þy nede,
> Whan þou hem drawyst to þy falshede;
> And þyn inwyt, þyn ownë skyle,
> Aȝen þe seyþ and euermore wylle.[16]

If all the examples were as equivocal as this, we should not be able to say with certainty that *inwit* ever bore the meaning 'conscience', but, although this sense was certainly rarer than has been supposed, a few examples establish it beyond doubt. One of the fifteen accusers of the wicked, according to *The Pricke of Conscience* (ed. R. Morris, Berlin, 1863, l. 5428) will be 'Conscience þat es called Ynwitt'. Indeed, this sense was apparently current quite early in ME: 'þeos riwle is chearite of schir heorte 7 cleane inwit 7 treowe bileaue' (*Ancrene Riwle*, Corpus MS, fol. 1a); 'ure ahne cōscience þat is ure ínwit forculiende hire seoluen wið þe fur of sunne' (*ibid.* fol. 83a). And it seems clear that this is the main meaning throughout the *Ayenbite of Inwyt*.

In considering Langland's usage in the light of what has been said, it is necessary to note some points arising from the presentation so far: that *inwit* is the 'classic' translation of *animus*, that in general use it referred to man's intellectual powers, and that the more narrowly the word is applied to the scholastic concept of *intellectus*, the nearer its meaning becomes to 'conscience' and hence the harder it is to distinguish therefrom.

Inductively, one might assume from the fact that there is a figure in *Piers Plowman* called 'Conscience' (functioning as we understand 'conscience' today) that the figure and concept 'Inwit' in the poem is unlikely to have the same signification. Nor does it. Apart from sporadic 'popular' uses of the term, Langland's usage is precise and technical to a degree hard to parallel in ME; *inwit* is 'intellect', the *agens* aspect of *intellectus* in Thomist terms, and since the intellect is concerned with the apprehension of truth, it is therefore concerned with the distinction between true and false, good and evil; hence its functions can come near to, and be confused with, those of conscience. All this is admirably demonstrated in the synoptic allegory describing the relation of *inwit* to *anima*. Kind has built a castle called Caro in which he has settled his sweetheart, the lady Anima, and her servants Dowel, Dobet, and Dobest. For the love of Anima, a 'wise knight', Sir Inwit, is made

---

[16] *Handlyng Synne* (EETS.OS 119), l. 645. Cf. *Piers Plowman* C vii.421.

constable of the castle and protects them all from his point of vantage in the head, along with his five sons, the good actions. The awe inspired by the dignity of Inwit's office is thus considerable:

> Inwit is the help · that *Anima* desyreth;
> After the grace of god · the gretteste is Inwit.   (A x.47–48)

He is 'godes owen good · hus grace and hus tresoure' (C xi.175). Some, such as madmen, lack this grace and others find they lose it easily; so much the more, then, should we treasure it; so much the more 'wo worth hym · that Inwitt mys-speyneth' and 'leeseth · thorw lykerouse drynke'.

Langland is not one of the ME writers who use 'inwit' for 'conscience'; he maintains a consistent and scholastically accurate distinction between the two concepts, and if to us today the distinction at times seems blurred, it is our unfamiliarity with medieval thought that blurs it. This is not to say that he makes 'conscience' a separate faculty from 'inwit'; conscience is rather one aspect of inwit's activity; it is inwit's awareness of right and wrong brought to bear upon one's actions; it is inwit in action.[17]

It was not the purpose of this paper to attempt a complete interpretation of Langland's concepts *kind wit* and *inwit* in terms of medieval philosophy, but rather to compare Langland's use of the terms with the usage of other ME writers. It is important however to note in conclusion that while, as we have seen, his usage differed considerably from that of most writers, the difference lay in his need to find terms with which he could express in a consistent allegorical framework complex concepts of scholastic philosophy which would yet be intelligible to an English public. The familiar cognate expressions he chose admirably demonstrated the close relation between the concepts thus designated, and at the same time the elements bore meanings in general usage which must have made the specialized senses he intended readily comprehensible to his contemporaries.

[17] Cf. *Summa Theologica* I, Quest. 79, Art. 13.

Three

Vis imaginativa†

In his enlightening article 'Imaginatif in Piers Plowman', H. S. V. Jones[1] did not see fit to make it clear that Langland's use of the term is extremely rare in Middle English, and by this same token omitted therefore to explain the long-lasting failure to understand the concept. There were two main technical uses of the term in Middle English, and the commoner sense – reproductive imagination – is not that found in Langland. While a study of the Victorines, as Jones showed, can help to interpret Langland's usage, it does not explain its rarity nor how the split conception arose. This goes back, it seems, to the binary character of Aristotle's analysis: φαντασία is either calculative and deliberative or sensitive.[2] Most philosophers tended to concentrate on the latter function,[3] and Thomas Aquinas is little different from his predecessors or successors when he says 'est . . . phantasia sive imaginatio quasi thesaurus

---

† Reprinted from *The Journal of English and Germanic Philology* 53 (1954), 81 ff.

[1] *JEGP* 13, 583–88.

[2] *De Anima* III.11.

[3] It was the difficulty of reconciling the two apparently mutually exclusive deliberative and sensory aspects of the faculty which made 'fewe philesofris accorde in her writyng' on localizing it, as Pecock says (*Folewer*, EETS.OS 164.32). The difficulty is reflected in the modifications to the concept of three brain ventricles; while some Arab writers try to solve it by putting imagination in both front (sensory) and middle (logistic) cells, as Algazel of Baghdad, other early anatomists and psychologists made a distinction between *phantasia* and (*vis*) *imaginativa* (notably Avicenna and Albertus Magnus), others again postulated four instead of three ventricles: thus, for example, Constantine. The readiness with which Albertus set up sub-cells within the three ventricles, while enabling him to apportion the facets of *imaginativa* satisfactorily, led others to transfer the deliberative aspect of Aristotle's φαντασία to a 'cogitative' faculty allied with *ratio* and sharing the latter's middle ventricle: thus for instance Guy de Chauliac. For a general account of this subject, see W. Sudhoff, 'Die Lehre von den Hirnventrikeln', *Archiv für Geschichte der Medizin* 7, 149–205.

quidam formarum per sensum acceptarum'[4]; the same concept is seen in Roger Bacon: 'imaginatio ... est arca ac repositorium sensus communis'.[5] Imagination as a sort of memory[6] for sensory data, 'a tresorie to þe ... comune witt' (*Folewer* 26) is the doctrine taught by Pecock, who distinguishes a *fantasy* which is the productive imagination, albeit its products are such trivialities as an object 'maad of a lions heed, of a gootis bodi, and of a dragons tail'.[7]

Aristotle's deliberative function, which appears as what we may call 'creative reflection' in Langland's *Imaginatif*, was not transmitted (except incidentally[8]) through the main stream of medieval psychological learning. Since it has been demonstrated[9] that the Victorine allegory of contemplation is useful to us in interpreting Langland's *Imaginatif*, it is of interest to note the way in which Richard and Hugo analysed and determined the functions of *imaginatio*. Both distinguished between an *imaginatio bestialis* (~*reparatrix*) and what Hugo called an *affectio imaginaria* and Richard *imaginatio formatrix seu moderatrix*; as Hugo puts it, this higher aspect of imagination acts as a medium between the purely corporal and the purely spiritual, while Richard goes further in saying that, in so far as it creatively synthesizes the totality of images, the *imaginatio moderatrix* is actually a part of the reasoning process, even when it acts contrary to reason.[10] Dante, too, saw imagination as having

---

[4] *Summa Theologiae* I, Quaestio 78.

[5] *Opus Majus* v.ii.

[6] Memory 'þerby þe soule biholdiþ þe liknes of bodiliche þinges þat beþ absent' Trevisa's *Bartholomæus*, Brit. Mus. Add. MS 27944, f. 20b. The distinction between this memory and *memoria* in the cell *Puppis* is made clear by Aquinas, *Expositio in Librum Aristotelis de Memoria et Reminiscentia* 3.

[7] *Folewer* 26; cf. *Donet* (EETS.OS 156), 10.

[8] Aquinas, for example, allows that *phantasms* formed in man's mind by God's aid express divine truths more effectively than those received through the senses (*Summa Theologiae* I, Quaestio 12) and Bartholomæus (*De Proprietatibus Rerum* II.ix) implies that *imaginativa* provides men imperfectly with the vision of God which the cherubim have as a divine gift.

[9] Jones, *op. cit.* 584 ff.

[10] See the recent study of Victorine psychology in E. de Bruyne, *Études D'Esthétique Médiévale* II (Bruges, 1946), 218 ff. Richard's succinct statement 'sine imaginatione, ratio nihil sciret, sine sensualitate, affectio nil saperet' is not as significant in itself as Jones would have us believe, since *all* anatomists and philosophers were agreed that reason drew on imagination for its raw materials; Lanfranc,'*Chirurgia Magna* II.i, is typical in pointing out that reason's cell presented a broad receptive front towards the cell containing *imaginativa* in order to be supplied the more readily with images; compare Bartholomæus v.iii. We are told in *The Cloud of Unknowing* (EETS.OS 218.117) that imagination 'is as it were seruaunt' to reason. The dependence of reason upon imagination is further illustrated by Lydgate's lines (*Troy Book* I.123 f.): 'So febled was his celle

a higher function than being merely a 'repositorium sensus communis'; the *alta fantasia* of *Paradiso* xxxiii.142 shows that Dante, in the words of E. G. Gardner, 'admits knowledge of spiritual things, not merely by abstraction from sensible experience, but through the working of the higher imagination'.[11] A ready source of this notion for any medieval writer lay to hand of course in the words of Boethius, 'Imaginatio ... conlustrat non sensibili sed imaginaria ratione iudicandi'.[12]

Nevertheless, beside Langland, the only Middle English writer to attribute to *imaginatif* a deliberative function seems to be Lydgate:

> Seoþe and considerþe in youre ymaginatyf
> For Adams synne howe Cryst was crucefyed[13]

Still more clearly, in saying that he cannot undertake to describe what happened when Jason and Medea were in bed, because he is a dull man in everything and especially in matters beyond his personal knowledge, the poet observes:

> For-dullid is myn ymagynatif,
> To deme in practik or in speculatif.[14]

---

retentif And fordirked his ymaginatif, That lost were bothe memorie and resoun'.

[11] 'Imagination and Memory in the Psychology of Dante', *A Miscellany of Studies in Romance Languages and Literatures* (Cambridge, 1932), 279.

[12] *Philosophiae Consolationis* v, pr. 4.

[13] *A Procession of Corpus Christi*, EETS.ES 107.36.

[14] *Troy Book* 1.3577. There is nothing corresponding to these lines in the Latin of Guido delle Colonne.

Four

On the problem of inflexional juncture in Old English†

In Old English, contracted and athematic verbs differ in their infinitive and present tense forms from other verbs in having no consonant between the stem vowel and the inflexional ending. These forms have been regarded almost universally as monosyllabic, with stem and inflexion forming together a monophthong or diphthong: for example, *fōn – fōð, tēon – tēoð, slēan – slēað, ʒān – ʒāð, dōn – dōð, bēon – bēoð.* Thus, in speaking of the strong *verba contracta* of class I, Wright says, 'In the pres. the *ēo* from older *īo* regularly fell together with the *ēo* from Germanic *eu* . . .'.[1] Similarly, while making some exceptions, Girvan makes it clear that the contracted verbs followed the general patterns of Old English phonology in that the loss of medial *h* caused contraction between stem and ending so that 'De tweeklanken *ěa, ěo, ǐo, ǐe* absorbeeren elke volgende vocaal, waarbij dan de korte diphthongen lang worden'.[2] In the same vein, we read elsewhere, 'Ae. *ō* + Vokal bleibt *ō*',[3] as examples of which we have *fōn, hōn.* On the other hand, 'Urspr. *ū* + Vokal bleibt unkontrahiert',[4] as in *būan.*

It may well be that this widespread contraction of stem vowel and verbal ending to form a monosyllable took place as the grammarians say. Certainly the form of Old English which is most represented in literary remains – the West Saxon 'Gemeinsprache' – provides ample material inviting this conclusion; and against any objection that the

† A slightly revised version of a paper first published in *The Modern Language Review* 45 (1950), 1 ff.
[1] *Old English Grammar,* §492.
[2] *Angelsaksisch Handboek,* §110.
[3] Sievers-Brunner, *Altenglische Grammatik,* §131.
[4] *Ibid.* §132.

spelling conventions in this material have been interpreted too mechanically, we may claim corroboration in the parallel syncopation of inflexional vowels in the second and third persons singular of the present indicative which appear in such forms as *bintst*, *bint*. Nevertheless, spellings occur in a large number of texts which suggest that contraction has either not taken place or has been followed by analogical re-formation. Such spellings are generally noted by grammarians as exceptions to the contraction rules already mentioned: 'Nordh. kommen auch unkontrahierte (zweisilbige, mit analogisch zu anderen Verben angetretener Endung) Formen vor, wie Inf. *dōa*, *fōa*, *hōa*, Präs. Ind. Pl. *dōaŏ*, *dōeŏ*....'.[5] In the Lindisfarne Gospels we find the present participle of *sēon* as *seende*, *seȝende*, the second person singular present indicative as *siis*, *siistu*, the third as *siiŏ*, *siis*, the singular present subjunctive as *sii* ('die Formen mit *ii* sind vielleicht zweisilbige mit analogisch angetretener oder nicht kontrahierter Endung'),[6] the plural as *see*, *seæ*, *seȝe*. Analogical re-formation is mentioned by Girvan as a Northumbrian feature,[7] and we are told that 'R.¹, Li. hebben den analogischen infin. *wrígan* voor *wríon* Li. ook een 3ᵉⁿ sg. ind. *wrígaŏ*'.[8] But these phenomena are not confined to Northumbria: clear traces of the absence of contraction, although to a lesser extent, are to be found in Mercian and Kentish monuments. Thus the Vespasian Psalter has *doan* 'facere' (142.10), and a Kentish charter of 837 (Cotton Aug. II.42) has the infinitive form *ȝedoan*.

Outside the West Saxon area, then, there is no part of the country which we can definitely say was without at least a sporadic tendency either to preserve uncontracted forms after the loss (where applicable) of medial *h* or to re-form the verbal paradigm after contraction had taken place. When we ask why this tendency displayed such a virility over whole areas which may have had little or no linguistic influence on each other, we find the answer near at hand. The majority of Old English verbs had stems ending in a consonant, and thus the most influential morphological pattern would be that followed by this type of verb. That is to say, the most frequently used marks of correlation between the first person singular present indicative, the first person plural and the infinitive are *-e* (*u*, *o*), *-aŏ*, *-an*. Thus we have *binde*, *helpe*, *fare*; *bindaŏ*, *helpaŏ*, *faraŏ*; *bindan*, *helpan*, *faran*. In the case of contracted and athematic verbs, the corresponding forms are usually

[5] *Ibid.* §131 Anm.
[6] *Ibid.* §374 Anm. 5.
[7] *Op. cit.* §109 Aanm.
[8] *Ibid.* §370 Aanm. 2.

spelt as follows: *seo, slea, do*; *seoð, sleað, doð*; *seon, slean, don*. According to the contraction rules, the marks of correlation between the parts here must be reckoned as being *nil, -ð, -n* – a very different pattern from that followed in the uncontracted verbs. The variant spellings, however, which occur in a large number of non-West Saxon texts[9] suggest marks of correlation on the uncontracted pattern: vowel, vowel + *ð*, vowel + *n*.

The latter state of affairs can hardly be regarded as unexpected. Throughout the history of English, morphological forms have tended to follow the patterns of the majority, and these analogical processes were already very much alive in Old English. Moreover, inflexional juncture is a living phenomenon which can be observed in Modern English keeping vowels apart as disyllables which might otherwise contract into diphthongs or monophthongs. The present participle of the verb 'to saw' is the disyllable [sɔːiŋ]; we do not contract the two vowels into the diphthong [ɔi] which we have in words like *loin, point*, and which most nearly resembles the vowel-group heard in *sawing*. There seems no reason, therefore, why we should not presume inflexional juncture in such verbal forms of Old English as *siið, doan*, where the scribes seem to be deliberately expressing disyllables, whether they occur in Northumbrian, Mercian, or Kentish records. Since some of these forms are palpably late, they cannot all be related to the loss of medial *h* or to the other contraction phenomena, and for this reason it seems fitting to concentrate for once on the question of uncontracted forms as a morphological problem.

So far we have glanced only at non-West Saxon forms where occasionally the dimorphemic structures can be picked out from the spelling. In the West Saxon dialect such spellings are of the greatest rarity, but that does not mean that the dimorphemic type is entirely absent. Before turning, however, to the difficult question of interpreting the apparently monosyllabic spellings of West Saxon, it may be observed that open juncture is not easy to express in spelling however 'phonetic' one's orthographic principles. Moreover, where the elements of a junctural sequence resemble a diphthong existing in the language, it is particularly difficult to express the distinction in writing. This may be illustrated by the words *sure* and *bluer* in Modern English, which might be written in phonetic script [ʃuə], [bluə], using the same vowel symbols in each case. Yet the latter word has morphological juncture while the former has not, and this may be proved by reflecting that while the former may

---

[9] For further examples like *food, foæð*, see Johannes Hedberg, *The Syncope of the Old English Present Endings* (Lund, 1945), 47–55.

have the phonetic realization [ʃɔː], *bluer* can have no corresponding variant.[10]

The Old English poetic measure affords us a means (though not always an entirely satisfactory means) of determining whether or not a contracted form normally monosyllabic is disyllabic, regardless of the spelling in which it has come down to us. Thus the half-line 'man ȝeþeon', *Beowulf*, l. 25, only fits into one of the chief verse patterns when we assume that -*þeon* is disyllabic. Similarly, 'and on deað slean' (first stress on *deað*), *Genesis*, l. 1267, 'ond on seoð' (from *sēon*), *Christ*, l. 1245, 'þæs þa bearn doð' (from *dōn*), *Riddle* 41.7 (*Old English Riddles*, ed. Wyatt, 1912), all contain disyllabic verbs.[11] Such poetic material has not always, however, been related by scholars to the disyllabic spellings occurring in prose. Instead, a disyllabic *seoð* has been used to prove that the poem in which it occurs was composed before the medial *h* disappeared from **sehan* (or rather from **seohan*, with the breaking that is assumed in such circumstances), or so soon afterwards that the inevitable syncope had not taken place. In this way, the prose disyllables came chiefly to be mentioned as criteria of dialect, the poetic disyllables chiefly as criteria of date, in neither case with very satisfactory or fruitful results.

There has, however, been a salutary reaction against using absence of contraction in poetry as a dating criterion.[12] Professor Norman's remarks on the subject in his edition of *Waldere*[13] are worth quoting in full:

> The form *fleon* [he says] is frequently regarded as supplying evidence of early date since a line such as *oððe on weal fleon* (first stress on *weal*) is said to be irregular unless we assume still the existence of intervocalic *h* (cf. Gothic *þliuhan*). Since this intervocalic *h* seems to have disappeared at the latest by the first half of the eighth century, we should thus obtain a linguistic *terminus ad quem* for our original poem. No satisfactory evidence has ever been brought forward to enable us to determine when the *eo* in such words as *fleon* (arising from *ēo + a*) ceased to be *e + o* and became a true diphthong. Even if we assume that the *eo* in *fleon* became a diphthong at an early date

---

[10] Cf. B. Trnka, *A Phonological Analysis of Present-day Standard English* (Prague, 1935), 13.

[11] See Sievers' article, 'Zur Rhythmik des Germanischen Alliterationsverses', *Beiträge* 10, esp. 268 f., 475–8.

[12] An early critic of such misuse of linguistic data was Schücking in his article 'Wann entstand der Beowulf?', *Beiträge* 42, esp. 356–9.

[13] (London, 1933), 6–7.

we do not know whether, to what extent and for how long such a word could be continued to be treated as disyllabic in poetic tradition.

Similarly, Girvan denies the validity of contraction as a test of date. Undoubtedly there was contraction at the time at which *Beowulf* was composed. 'On the other hand, uncontracted forms occur in poetry which is demonstrably late, and analogical addition of the normal endings in verb, noun and adjective is easy and frequent in prose as well as verse.'[14]

In a late Old English prose manuscript which I have studied in this connexion, there is a certain amount of evidence which clearly seems to support the argument of these scholars. The manuscript is the Cambridge Fragment of the Old English Heptateuch[15] written in a form of late Old English, the unconventional spellings of which enable the student to make certain deductions concerning the phonology.[16] Briefly, we may say that the OE *ĕa* is preserved as a diphthong, to express which the scribe frequently uses the symbols *ia, ya, iea* and the like, a reaction against the use of *ea* which clearly implies a first element more raised than the sound associated with the symbol *e*. On the other hand, the *eo* spelling for OE *ĕo* is almost universally retained, but the fact that *eo* is also used occasionally for *o* after *w* and for unstressed *e*, while *ĕo* is a few times spelt *y, u, o*, strongly suggests that OE *ĕo* is a front-round monophthong in the dialect of this manuscript.

The only material of the manuscript which seriously challenges these conclusions is a handful of present tense verbal forms. In the first place, the spellings for the breaking of WGmc. *ă*, where they are not the traditional *ea*, are variously *ia, iea, ie, yea, ye*. Thus we have *ʒesieah* (pret. sing. of *-sēon, Gen.* xix.1), while the only other non-*ea* spelling of original *ă* before *h* flatly contradicts the evidence of this form: *þwæað* (imperat. pl., xix.2). In the view of most grammarians, the vowel of *þwēan* is derived from an earlier short diphthong by breaking, subsequently lengthened with the loss of *h* and contraction. If this view is justified, we have the peculiar situation of most diphthongs by breaking in this manuscript showing a more palatal first element than that implied by the conventional spelling, while one such diphthong (and that a lengthened one, with its implication therefore of increased

---

[14] *Beowulf and the Seventh Century* (London, 1935), 17.

[15] The first forty-four pages of Cambridge University Library MS Ii.1.33.

[16] See S. J. Crawford, *TPS 1917–20*, 41–7, and *The Old English Version of the Heptateuch*, EETS.OS 160 (London, 1922). Some account of the fragment is also provided by F. H. Chase, *Archiv* 100, 241–66.

tenseness) is spelt with a symbol implying a lower vowel than that used in the conventional spelling. The evidence for the assumption of breaking in *verba contracta* (apart from obvious cases like the imperative singular) is by no means satisfactory, of course; Sievers, in the third edition of his *Angelsächsische Grammatik* (§84 Anm.2), expresses more doubt on this issue than in the previous editions. But whether the *ea* in *þwēan* has arisen from a broken vowel or from the contraction of two simple vowels, the spelling *þwæað* in this manuscript strongly suggests that the 'diphthong' is not classed phonemically with either the conditioned or etymological *ea* diphthong. It is more likely that the digraph symbol represents a disyllable, with the long vowel *æ* (lengthened by loss of *h*) separated acoustically from the inflexional vowel by morphological juncture, so that there is no glide in the phonological sense.

Secondly, certain forms from the **bheu* root of the verb 'to be' suggest that the vowel has not developed parallel to the conditioned or etymological *eo* diphthong. Apart from the conventional (and usual) spelling *eo*, the 'long' diphthong *ēo* from all sources appears in various forms: 'she' appears as *hu* (Preface, 1. 46, and *Gen.* xxi.15), -*þēod*- as -*þud*- (xii.10), 'fell' (pret. sing.) as *fúl* (xvii.3), *lēof* as *lyf* (xxiii.6), *lēode* (dative) as *lyde* (xxiv.8). At the same time, *ēo* occurs once as *yo* in *lyof* for *lēof* (xxiii.11), but this is the only use of an unconventional digraph spelling for long or short *eo* outside the paradigm of the verb 'to be'.

On the other hand, the present tense forms of 'to be' which are usually spelt *eo* occur several times with a different digraph spelling; thus we have *byoð* (imperat.pl., ix.7), *bioð* (3 p.pl.pres.indic., xviii.29), *byoð* (3 p. pl. pres. indic., xxii.18), *byo* (3 p. sg. pres. subj., xxiii.11). Moreover, although *y* and *i* forms also occur, there are no *u* spellings. It seems reasonable to conclude that the vowel in these verbal forms cannot be equated with that of such words as *þēod*. It is equally reasonable to conclude that if the vowel of the verbal forms had been consistently diphthongal, it would then indeed have developed exactly as in *þēod*. The digraph spellings like *byoð* imply rather a disyllabic pronunciation than a diphthongal one, and this again is to be attributed to inflexional juncture.

Thus, *bēoð* is spelt in three ways in the manuscript. The spelling *beoð* is impossible to assess phonetically because it is the conventional one: at the date at which this Heptateuch manuscript is judged to have been written, this spelling had been in regular use for several centuries.

The variant digraph forms like *byoð* seem, as we have seen, to imply disyllables, and finally we have the *bið*, *byð* type (for example, xviii.24), which imply not only monosyllables but monophthongs. It appears then that relevant parts of the verb 'to be' in the late Old English and early Middle English periods could be pronounced as disyllables or could have the vowel of the ending elided so that the whole formed a monosyllable. But, as is well known, when the *Beowulf* poet composed his poem, he must have had verbs like *dōn – dōð*, *sēon – sēoð* in two similarly coexisting permissible forms, disyllabic and monosyllabic. Unless this merely means that 'uncontracted' forms cannot be used as evidence of early date, the conclusion seems unavoidable that morphological juncture was an active if spasmodic force operating throughout this period of the language just as it operates in our own.

If this is so, certain general conclusions may also be drawn. In the first place, we should beware of regarding 'uncontracted' forms of verbs as evidence of date, and likewise of connecting this phenomenon necessarily with loss of medial *h*. Moreover, before we can accept such forms even as general evidence of dialect, we must satisfy ourselves that the spellings of *fōn*, *sēon*, *dōn* and the like which occur with remarkable regularity in the West Saxon 'Gemeinsprache' are to be regarded as universally monosyllabic. This would seem a difficult point to settle, but what evidence there is seems to suggest that disyllabic forms undoubtedly occurred beside the monosyllabic ones. Finally, for these reasons, the history and development of the sounds spelt *ea* and *eo* in verbs like *slēan* and *sēon* should not be used as evidence of the history and development of the etymological or conditioned diphthongs: in a given dialect at a given time, they may well have been at least as distinct from each other as the vowel sounds in *bluer* and *sure* are today, with the one class resisting for morphological reasons the trend of development being followed by the other.

Even when we accept the thesis that such open juncture existed in Old English, however, we are still very far from being able to estimate its extent. As we have observed from some Modern English examples, the line between juncture and no juncture can often be an extremely fine one. Moreover, the distinction is by no means stable, and the dimorphemic structure of a word may not be preserved indefinitely: nor need contraction itself, once achieved, be a permanent feature, since so long as the particular morphological element is living in the language, a contracted monosyllable may be re-formed and made dimorphemic again. In Shakespeare's time, a disyllabic *doeth* seems to have been common in non-auxiliary usage. In the pronunciation of many English people there is today a distinction between 'the hen is a good *layer*', 'brick-*layers*' and '*layers* of dirt', between 'four tennis *players*' and 'twenty *Players*, please'. So in Old English, we know that certain forms are without contraction, while in many cases we can definitely say that we have contraction; unfortunately, however, the majority of forms may be either contracted or not without our being able to say which. In these cases we should be wise to avoid tacit assumption of contraction and to bear both possibilities in mind.

Five

Some recent interpretations of Old English digraph spellings†

Three attempts have been made in recent years to apply the techniques of modern descriptive linguistics to the Old English spellings produced by breaking, palatal diphthongization, *i*-umlaut, and velar-umlaut. Desirable as such attempts are, the authors of the present article find the results still far from satisfactory.

In 1939, Marjorie Daunt proposed a reinterpretation of the OE digraph spellings *ea, eo, io, ie*, claiming that, with a few exceptions, the only real diphthongs of OE were the *ēa, ēo, īo,* and *īe*, derived from West Germanic *au, eu,* and *iu*, and that the conditioned forms of OE (as in *healt, heorte, liomu, ierre*) must be regarded as monophthongal allophones of the *æ, e,* and *i* phonemes.[1] A similar reinterpretation has been incorporated by Fernand Mossé in the phonological section of his recent OE grammar.[2] The newest effort in this direction is that of R. P. Stockwell and C. W. Barritt, who limit themselves to maintaining that *æ* and *ea* are merely graphic variants representing one short vocalic nucleus.[3] We shall try here to ascertain the position which these scholars take, noting some of the implications of their views, and then re-examine the bases of their arguments.[4]

† This article, written in collaboration with Sherman M. Kuhn, is an expansion of a paper read in the Linguistic Forum of the University of Michigan Summer Session, 23 July 1952. It is reprinted here from *Language* 29 (1953), 143 ff.

[1] 'Old English Sound Changes Reconsidered in Relation to Scribal Tradition and Practice', *TPS 1939*, 108–37.

[2] *Manuel de l'anglais du Moyen-Âge, I. Vieil-anglais* (Bibliothèque de philologie germanique, Vol. 8; Paris, 1945).

[3] *Some Old English Graphemic-Phonemic Correspondences – ae, ea,* and *a* (*Studies in Linguistics*: Occasional papers, No. 4; Washington, 1951).

[4] These scholars are not, of course, the first to question the diphthongal

All four scholars make it abundantly clear that they find the commonly accepted diphthongal interpretation objectionable, but it is not easy to determine precisely what interpretation they have to offer as a substitute. In the first place, Miss Daunt and Mossé are not clear as to what sounds the digraph spellings represent.

Miss Daunt, at times, argues that the spellings *ea, eo, io* in conditioned positions represented the simple vowels, which she interprets [æ], [e], [i], with a diacritical symbol qualifying the neighbouring consonant (121–2, 128); thus OE *weorpan* is said to have [e] plus a retroflex *r*, West Saxon *feaht* [æ] plus a velar fricative, and Anglian *liomu* [i] plus some sort of velarized *m*. At other times, however, she seems to regard such digraphs as representations of diphthongal sounds, 'conditioned diphthongs', in which a short vowel 'acquires a slightly diphthongal sound in combination with the off- or on-glide of a preceding or following consonant' (109). She admits that in words like *feoh* (oblique *feo*) the *eo* represents a real diphthong when the *h* is lost (132). She favours interpreting the spelling *ie*, not as a conditioned diphthong, but as [i] (131).

Mossé's indecision is even more obvious. In Old English, he says, *ea, eo, ie* may represent either diphthongs or simple vowels (30), depending on whether they refer to long or to short nuclei. In speaking of the short nuclei, he states that 'le premier élément vocalique après une consonne palatale et le second devant une consonne vélaire sont des signes diacritiques destinés à indiquer la prononciation palatale, vélaire ou arrondie de la consonne' (31). At the same time, he holds that long or lengthened vowels under these same conditions (as in *gēar, scēap, nēah, mēares*) became diphthongs, phonemically identical with the *ēa* resulting from WGmc. *au* (32, 42). In another place, we find the breaking of short vowels defined as 'la naissance d'une voyelle furtive ou "glide" qui a été notée *a* après *æ* . . . *o* après *e* et *i*' (41). Similarly, although we had been led to believe that there was no such sound change as palatal diphthongization, we are informed (43) that this too is a glide phenomenon, the digraphs of which are explicitly contrasted with those in *geoc, giong, geōmor*. In the latter group 'les graphies ğe-, ği- ne sont pas

---

interpretation of OE digraph spellings. Many grammarians assume that in words like *geoc*, the *e* is diacritical; and as early as 1868, W. Scherer suggested that *ea* and *eo* in breaking and velar-umlaut positions indicated no more than that the following consonants were pronounced in a certain way. See *Zur Geschichte der Deutschen Sprache* (Berlin, 1868), 141.

autre chose que la notation du son [j]', and the sound of the vowel is said to be unaffected.

Stockwell and Barritt take a more definite stand in this matter. They explain the short *ea* by contrasting it with long *ēa* from WGmc. *au*. The latter they describe as '/æ/ plus phonemic off-glide /h/' or phonetically [æə], the off-glide being a part of the syllabic nucleus. The short *ea*, in breaking and velar-umlaut positions, they describe as a 'back allophone' of /æ/ (spelled *e*) plus an off-glide [ə] which they regard, not as a part of the vocalic nucleus, but as part of the following consonant (13). The short *ea* after palatal consonants is also explained as partly vowel, partly consonant, the *e* denoting the palatal value of the consonant, the *a* representing a 'front allophone' of /æ/ (14). We may point out that the use of *e* for a back sound, *a* for a more raised and fronted sound, is not in keeping with the usual practices of Anglo-Saxon scribes. Although the short *ie* (as in WS *giefan*) is outside the scope of their study, this digraph is said to be a representation of the /i/ phoneme, rather than diacritic plus unchanged vowel (26). Thus palatal diphthongization of *e* is treated as both a phonetic and a phonemic change, while palatal diphthongization of *æ* is assumed to be no sound change at all. The analysis by Stockwell and Barritt, upon closer inspection, turns out to be wholly a matter of segmentation: *hēah* they would divide h-ea-h;[5] *neaht*, n-e-ah-t; *geat*, ge-a-t; and *giefan*, g-ie-f-a-n.

None of these four faces the problem of the consonantal allophones and allographs which must be postulated if this system of segmentation is correct. Instead of short diphthongs *ea*, *eo*, *io*, and *ie*, we should have a large number of consonant allophones, individually represented by graphs. A description of the consonants of the early West Saxon of King Alfred's time would call for all of the graphs now recognized, plus such additional symbols as *ah* in *meaht*, *al* in *healt*, *ar* in *earm*, *ce* in *ceaster*, *ge* in *geat*, *of* in *heofon*, *oh* in *feoht*, *ol* in *seolfor*, *op* in *cleopode*, *or* in *eorl*, *os* in *sweoster*, *sce* in *sceal*. These are by no means all of the new 'consonants' which would be needed; anyone familiar with the Alfredian texts will recall numerous others of less frequent occurrence.

The Anglian texts would require an even greater array of graphic symbols. One illustration will suffice. To represent the consonants in the Vespasian Psalter (British Museum MS Cotton Vespasian A.1), one

---

[5] They do not attempt an explanation of *nēah*, in which we have an earlier *ǣ* in breaking position, or of *gēar*, in which *ǣ* apparently underwent palatal diphthongization.

would have to set up the following allographs[6] and interpret them phonetically:

ac in *hreacan*	*oc* in *spreocan*	*c* in *bec* and *ic*			
ad *feadur*	*od* *gebeodu*	*d* *bed*			
af *heafuces*	*of* *eofur*	*f* *cælf* and *hefig*			
ag *weagas*	*og* *weogum*	*g* *oferhogan* and *megen*			
		h *haldan* and *ðuerh*			
		i *iuguðe*			
	ol *feolu*	*l* *hwalas* and *cild*			
am *freamsum*	*om* *liomu*	*m* *rum*			
an *deanum*	*on* *hionan*	*n* *ðanan*			
ap *leappan*	*op* *cleopung*	*p* *stepum*			
ar *hearpe*	*or* *heorut*	*r* *hwer*			
as *feasum*	*os* *geostran*	*s* *blis* and *ðusend*			
asc *eascan*		*sc* *fiscas*			
at *leata*	*ot* *uðweotan*	*t* *weter*			
að *hreaða*	*oð* *cweoðu*	*ð* *muð* and *oðer*			
		þ *þæt* and *muþe*			
		u *ðuerh*			
		w *sawul*			
		x *oxan*			

A description of Old English in general would have to include not only the graphs mentioned thus far, but many more which occur in other dialects and texts. It is remarkable that Mossé makes no mention of such graphs, or of the allophones which they would presumably stand for, in his handling of the OE consonants. The other scholars avoid the problem by reason of the limitations placed upon the scope of their studies; nevertheless, we believe that a scholar dealing with a limited problem is responsible for the broader implications of any solution he may propose.

On one point the three treatments are internally consistent and in agreement with one another: the graphic distinction between *æ* and *ea* does not reflect a phonemic distinction. Mossé, without offering any clear argument, seems to have been convinced by the fact that *ea* is usually a predictable positional variant of *æ*. In addition, Miss Daunt points to the supposed identity of OE *æ* and *ea* in Middle English. Stockwell and Barritt claim that *ea* and *æ* cannot represent separate phonemes because there are, they say, no minimal pairs so distinguished. These arguments will be dealt with later.

[6] This list is the irreducible minimum; several other symbols might be needed, depending upon the mode of analysis.

The manner in which these scholars treat the whole series of OE sound changes calls for some comment.

Mossé is least aware of the consequences of his statements regarding conditioned diphthongs. He merely repeats the traditional views concerning the relative chronology of breaking, palatal diphthongization, *i*-umlaut, and other changes. He even discusses the first two as vocalic changes, ignoring them in his treatment of the consonants. In short, he presents the traditional sound changes in the traditional order without any attempt to reconcile them with his new theory.

Stockwell and Barritt make an effort to transpose the results of earlier scholarship into their own system. Their principal modification consists in reversing the order of certain changes:[7] (1) velar-umlaut is dated earlier (instead of later) than *i*-umlaut; (2) palatal diphthongization is dated later (instead of earlier) than *i*-umlaut. The first revision ignores strong evidence which has long been familiar to historical linguists. The earliest OE texts show *i*-umlaut virtually, probably altogether, complete; on the other hand, they show fluctuations in spelling which indicate that the influences causing velar-umlaut were still active in the language. In the Corpus Glossary (eighth-century Mercian), we find *sibun-* (later Mercian *seofen*), *heben-* (later *heofen*), *gelo* (later *geolu*), *quedol* (later -*cweodul-*); in the proper names of the Moore MS of Bede's *Ecclesiastical History* (eighth-century Northumbrian), we find *herut-* (later Nthb. *heorut*, *hearta*, etc.), *hefen-* (later *heofun*, *heafnas*, etc.). These are but a few typical illustrations; many others could be cited. Moreover, there are several OE words in which a front vowel from *i*-umlaut has undergone velar-umlaut; to cite one example, *ondsweorian* in the Vespasian Psalter corresponds regularly to WS *ondswerian* (< *-swarjan*). In this instance, the sequence *i*-umlaut – velar-umlaut was made possible when the verb shifted from the 7th strong class to the 2nd weak class. Further examples may be found in the handbooks.[8]

The second of their revisions, they admit, is unnecessary if *ea* and *ie* are regarded as diphthongs. Their reorganization of the chronology is necessitated by their own interpretation of *ea* as /æ/ and *ie* as /i/, the latter being assumed without evidence (26). Unless they place *i*-umlaut

---

[7] We approve their shifting the second fronting of WGmc. *a* (Luick's 'zweite Aufhellung') to a period after *i*-umlaut. See further R. Girvan, *Angelsaksisch Handboek* (Haarlem, 1931), 79, 81, 83; and S. Kuhn, 'The Dialect of the Corpus Glossary', *PMLA* 54, (1939), 13–16.

[8] E.g. K. Luick, *Historische Grammatik der Englischen Sprache* (Leipzig, 1921) 210; K. Brunner, *Altenglische Grammatik nach der Angelsächsischen Grammatik von Eduard Sievers* (Halle, 1951), 90.

before palatal diphthongization, they are in the awkward position of having to suppose that /æ/ was changed directly to /i/ by *i*-umlaut (whereas elsewhere in Old English, /æ/ was umlauted to /e/): **gæst-* /æ/, by pal. diph. > **geast-* still /æ/, by *i*-uml. > *giest* /i/. They therefore place *i*-umlaut before palatal diphthongization: **gæst-*, by *i*-uml. > **gest-*, by pal. diph. > *giest*. In this rather arbitrary procedure, they ignore the well-known test word for the relative dating of palatal diphthongization and *i*-umlaut. Latin *cāseus* was borrowed early by the English and underwent both changes, resulting in a late WS *cȳse*. The development here must have been *ā* > *ǣ* (fronting) > *ēa* (pal. diph.) > *īe* (*i*-uml.) > *ȳ* (late WS). If *i*-umlaut had preceded palatal diphthongization, in accordance with the chronology of Stockwell and Barritt, the development would have been *ā* > *ǣ* (fronting) – *ǣ* (*i*-umlaut had no effect upon *ǣ*) > *ēa* (pal. diph.), resulting in a form **cēase*.

Miss Daunt goes further than the others, in that she entirely discards breaking, palatal diphthongization, and velar-umlaut as sound changes (134). These, she says, 'should be omitted from any account of the sounds of Old English' (122). As a substitute for the traditional series of sound changes, she offers 'progressive palatalization' (134), a general process covering practically all the OE changes in vowels and consonants except nasalization, rounding, and 'loss of sounds and contraction' (136). This substitution of an amorphous theory of development for a set of accurately described sound changes which can be proved or disproved by means of objective evidence seems to us a retreat from that scientific conception of historical linguistics which has produced such revolutionary discoveries since the end of the eighteenth century. It certainly knocks the props from under many of the criteria for differentiating Old and Middle English dialects.

Unless we have misunderstood Miss Daunt's views regarding the effect of an *i* or *j* on a preceding consonant (109, 129), she has confused two phenomena: the automatic, partial palatalization of a consonant in the neighbourhood of *i/j* (as in German *ich* versus *ach*), and the considerably greater palatalization, limited to a specific and datable period, which we know as *i*-umlaut. If, as she seems to suggest, the palatalizing influence was so strong, so immediate, and so progressive that a preceding consonant could not remain velar enough 'to have a distinctly velar on-glide', we must suppose that *i*-umlaut began as soon as any *i* or *j* came to follow an Indo-European stressed vowel.[9]

[9] Yet there is no such universal effect of *i/j* upon preceding consonants, as we may see from modern English *fielding* beside *field*, in both of which many speakers pronounce a velar *l* with a velar or centring on-glide.

From an examination of the theories themselves, we turn now to the bases on which they are founded.[10]

Both Miss Daunt and Mossé find arguments to justify their interpretations of the OE digraph spellings by referring to well-known views on consonant colour in Old Irish. Mossé treats the matter briefly: 'Il ne faut pas oublier que ce sont des Irlandais qui ont appris aux Anglais à noter par écrit les sons de leur langue. Or en irlandais on se servait également de voyelles diacritiques pour indiquer l'articulation des consonnes voisines' (31). Six years earlier a fuller version of this view had been expressed by Miss Daunt: 'In the first instance, the Irish teachers, listening as foreigners to a strange tongue and trying to write it down, would hear shades of pronunciation which the English speakers would not have heard in themselves, and the Anglo-Saxons would probably try to follow their example and establish an orthographic method and tradition, for native English writing, on their lines' (115).

It would seem that these scholars have started from the accepted fact that the Irish taught the English to write Latin and have gone on to assume that the Irish also taught the English to write English. This assumption, while not inherently improbable, is difficult to verify. It is easy to prove that the Irish were frequent visitors to Anglo-Saxon England, and most of the visitors seem to have been clerics; but there is no early Old English manuscript in the vernacular which can be traced to an Irish scribe. The first half of the seventh century is the period during which the Irish met the Anglo-Saxons as foreigners and pre-

---

[10] One point they make is of such a nature that an attempt at direct refutation would lead to no very conclusive or worthwhile results. It assumes that linguists are in possession of universal truths regarding languages in general, and that it is possible to say what can and what cannot exist in language. According to Miss Daunt, 'in existing languages there is, so far as my knowledge and information go, no example of "long" and "short" diphthongs, differentiated only by quantity, being phonemic, and it seems very unlikely that Old English had what is now non-existent' (110). Stockwell and Barritt, after discussing the vocalic nuclei represented by *nama*, *nām*, *nearu*, and *nēar*, say: 'We think it is an accurate statement that no languages have been found that utilize more than three of these four theoretically possible distinctions, or of any other four that might be set up, i.e. three types of syllabic nuclei seem to be a generalizable maximum. On the *a priori* grounds that OE was a real language and ought to act like one, the set of four distinctions is objectionable' (5). We wish merely to offer the following objections. (1) Present linguistic knowledge is probably insufficient for such generalizations. There are literally hundreds of living languages which have not yet been analysed. (2) This sort of statement seems to deny the possibility that a language may have a unique feature. (3) *A priori* reasoning loses its validity when it comes into conflict with objective data. The statements of Miss Daunt and of Stockwell and Barritt regarding Old English must ultimately stand or fall upon the evidence of the manuscripts.

sumably gave them the art of writing. By the close of that century, the English were copying Latin manuscripts with a skill indicative of long practice in the art. But the earliest manuscripts wholly in English can be dated no earlier than the ninth century, and even the Anglo-Latin glossaries are no earlier than the eighth. The Irish, also, wrote principally Latin before the eighth century; the earlier Old Irish records consist of a few brief glosses and other fragments.[11] For evidence of Irish influence, one must look to the resemblances between the scribal practices of the two peoples.

Miss Daunt lists six features of OIr. orthography which are paralleled to some extent in Old English. The first five do not concern conditioned diphthongization, and are, as Miss Daunt says, of 'minor importance'. The sixth is the indication of consonant colour in Old Irish manuscripts, a feature which produced forms like *tuaith*, *diglae*, *fiur* (the boldface letters representing the so-called diacritics). From this practice, thinks Miss Daunt, the Anglo-Saxons developed the habit of writing digraph spellings in the neighbourhood of certain consonants. Quite apart from any question of similarity between the Old Irish and the Old English phenomena, it should be noted that the English manuscripts nearest in time and place of origin to the fountainhead of Irish influence show the least development of digraph spellings. Thus spellings like *heben* are common in the proper names of the Moore MS of Bede, spellings like *sparuua* are frequent in the Epinal Glossary, and spellings like *half* are universal in the Corpus Glossary. The spellings which Miss Daunt seeks to attribute to Irish influence, e.g. *heofon*, *spearwa*, *healf*, *fiellan*, do not become regular forms until the ninth century, the last two in West Saxon, the dialect furthest removed from the great centres of Irish influence. But let us examine the Old Irish spellings more closely.

The most common of the 'diacritics' in Old Irish was apparently *i*, as in *maith*, *teist*, *slóig*.[12] The influence of this orthographic feature might therefore be expected to appear most strongly in Old English; yet OE forms that might be considered analogous (such as *dæig*) are rare and usually late. The second most common diacritic in OIr. was *u*, as in *daum*, *neurt*, *fiur*.[13] Analogous *u*-forms are extremely rare in Old

[11] On the dates and character of early English and Irish manuscripts, see E. A. Lowe, *Codices Latini Antiquiores*, Pt. 2 (Oxford, 1935); E. M. Thompson, *An Introduction to Greek and Latin Palaeography* (Oxford, 1912), 371–402; W. Stokes and J. Strachan, *Thesaurus Palaeohibernicus* (Cambridge, 1901–3), 1. xiii–xxvi and 2. ix–xl.

[12] R. Thurneysen, *A Grammar of Old Irish* (rev. ed., trans. by D. A. Binchy and O. Bergin; Dublin, 1946), 56.

[13] *Ibid.* 57.

English; in fact, most texts have none at all. Thirdly there are the Irish
a-forms, which belong to Middle Irish and in Old Irish are still very
rare.[14] Thus spellings like *deacht*, for which it is easy to find OE parallels, were scarcely used by the Irish until after they had appeared in Old
English.

Furthermore, the OE digraphs differ fundamentally from such OIr.
spellings as *ai* and *iu* in the manner of determining the glide element. In
Old Irish, *e* or *a* or *i* can be followed by a *u*-spelling, and *a* or *e* or *o* or *u*
can be followed by an *i*-spelling, according to the particular phonetic
quality of the following consonant. In OE *ea*, *eo*, etc., the use of *a* or *o* is
not determined by the following consonant; instead, *a* appears if the
original vowel was *æ*, *o* appears if the original vowel was *e* or *i*. In other
words, in Old Irish the choice of the second element in the digraph
spelling is determined by the nature of the consonant and not by the
original vowel; in Old English it is determined by the original vowel
and not by the nature of the consonant.

Finally, we may point out that scholars in the field of Irish are not
unanimous in regarding the OIr. spellings as pure diacritics. Thurneysen speaks repeatedly of *i* and *u* as 'glides' (55–7); the case of *i* is
elaborated as follows: 'the existence of an audible sound is suggested
by the remarkable consistency with which *i* is inserted, and still more
by the fact that a word like *immalle*, notwithstanding the palatalized *ll*,
is written without *i* (as contrasted with *aill* neut. "other", etc.); in
the unstressed pretonic interior syllable full development of the glide
could not take place' (56–7).

Another argument in support of the new views is drawn from a consideration of Middle English phonology. Miss Daunt and Stockwell and
Barritt appear to be under the impression that OE *æ* and *ea* developed
identically in Middle English, and that OE *e* and *eo* fell together in a
similar manner. 'A supporting reason in favour of regarding the writings
eo and *ea* as only variants of [e] and [æ], in certain conditions,' says Miss
Daunt, 'is that in the overwhelming majority of cases the forms to be
traced in Middle English show exactly the development to be expected
of [e] and [æ]' (128). Stockwell and Barritt fall into the same error: '*Æ*
and *ea* fall together in Middle English, resulting in /æ/ in Modern
English, when secondary developments do not intervene. When secondary influences operate, they operate to affect *ae* and *ea* in identical ways
when all other conditions are identical' (8).

This view derives from some of the old treatments of English

[14] *Loc. cit.*

phonology, in which Old English is represented by the WS dialect of Alfred's time and Middle English by the Southeast Midland of Chaucer's, the two being presented as though the later type of English were directly descended from the earlier. In point of fact, of course, the two dialects belonged to different regions as well as to different periods; Chaucer's *old* is a later form, not of Alfred's *eald*, but of an Anglian *ald*.

A closer examination of Middle English would have revealed to these scholars large bodies of evidence which refute their statements. While the simple short *æ* of Alfred's West Saxon appears as *a* in Southwestern Middle English, there is much place-name material of this area which shows that short *ea* did not develop in the same way.[15] This material has been systematically studied by Hjördis Bohman[16] and Henning Hallqvist,[17] who give many examples of forms which seem to indicate a diphthongal pronunciation; for example, *Estharabyar* < WS-*bearu* (Cornwall, 1324), *Trendelbiare* (Devon, 1314), *Wydebyer* (Devon, 1249), *la Hyele* < WS *healh* (Somerset, 1243), *la Hyales* (Devon, 1280), *Fiernham* < WS *fearn-* (Hants, fourteenth century), *Vialepitte* < WS *fealw-* (Devon, 1316), *Dyalediche* < WS *Dealla-* (Devon, 1281), *Piarrecumbe* < WS *pearroc-* (Devon, 1312). It may be worth while to point out in passing that, if OE *ea* represents a back allophone of /æ/ (as Stockwell and Barritt say), it is strange to find it replaced by ME *ia, ya, ie*; there are also many forms in which the reduced diphthong is spelled *i* or *y*, indicating that the vowel was high and front. To complete the anomaly, Stockwell and Barritt's front allophone of /æ/ is spelled *a* in Southwestern Middle English, as in *Blakepol* < WS *blæc-* (Devon, 1238).

It is generally recognized that the dialect of the early ME legends of the Katherine Group corresponds most nearly of all Middle English to the Mercian of the Vespasian Psalter. In the gloss to this Psalter, short *ea* represents a breaking diphthong before *r* plus consonant (as in *earm*) and a velar-umlaut diphthong (as in *geðeafung-*); short *æ* appears in several fairly well defined environments in a small number of words, for instance in such smoothed forms as *mæht*; elsewhere WGmc. *a* usually appears as *e*. MS Bodley 34 of the Katherine Group shows the following: (1) *ea* corresponding to the *ea* of the Vespasian Psalter, (2) *a* correspond-

---

[15] J. E. B. Gover, A. Mawer, and F. M. Stenton, *The Place-names of Devon* I (London, 1931–2) xxxiii. Because of the scarcity of ME literary texts from this area (especially texts which are linguistically reliable), it is necessary to depend largely upon place-names for evidence of local pronunciation.

[16] *Studies in the ME dialects of Devon and London* (Gothenburg, 1944).

[17] *Studies in Old English Fractured* ea (Lund, 1948).

ing generally to the *æ*, and (3) *e* corresponding to the *e*. In the legend of St Margaret, for example, we find:[18] (1) *earme, heardeste, hearm, feaderes* (gen. sg., VPs. *feadur*), *fearen, heatele, heatieð, þeauieð*; (2) *lahhe* (VPs. **hlæhhan*, cf. *hlæhað*), *mahte, mahten*; (3) *dei, efter, feder* (nom. sg., VPs *feder*), *hefden, schefte*. We do not wish to suggest that these spellings are distinguished with perfect consistency, although the regularity of the MS Bodley 34 seems extraordinary when one compares it with most manuscripts of the thirteenth century. Nor do we propose to interpret the *ea*-spellings of the Katherine Group as diphthongal. Our purpose is merely to show that there is ample evidence that ME scribes did not treat diphthongized and undiphthongized results of WGmc. *a* alike – evidently because they did not sound alike.[19]

As regards the ME developments of *e* and *eo*, there are abundant forms testifying to the fact that ME scribes did not treat them alike. While WS *e* remained in the spelling, the WS short *eo* assumed a number of forms: in addition to *e*, there were *eo, u, o*, sometimes *ue* and *oe*, these variants being usually interpreted as representing a front-round vowel.[20] Examples drawn from the place-names of Southwest England could be cited at great length, but a few will suffice: *Sturte* < WS *steort* (Dorset, 1327), *Sturtyl* (Dorset, 1250), *Sturte* (Surrey, 1332), *Sturrey* < WS *steorra* (Surrey, 1312), *Chorleton* < WS *ceorl-* (Dorset, 1345), *Churlewod* (Surrey, 1333), *Choerle-* (Devon, 1338), *Cheorle-* (Devon, 1337), *le Hort* < WS *heorot* (Dorset, 1327), *Hurt* (Dorset, 1280), *Hurtescroft* (Surrey, 1336), *Huertemere* (Surrey, circa 1270), *Hurtishole* (Devon, 1299), *Mukeswurde* < WS *meox, weorðig* (Devon, 1185), *Hurdewik* < WS *heorde-* (Devon, 1333).[21]

In the Mercian area, where in Old English the distinction between *e*

[18] Frances M. Mack, *Seinte Marharete* (EETS.OS 193; London, 1934). Further evidence of the same sort will be found in E. Einenkel, *The Life of Saint Katherine* (EETS.OS 80; London, 1884), and in S. T. R. O. d'Ardenne, *Seinte Iuliene* (Paris, 1936). Examples used here have been verified in Ragnar Furuskog, 'A Collation of the Katherine Group (MS Bodley 34)', *Studia Neophilologica* 19 (1946–7), 119–66.

[19] This discussion, limited to two OE dialects and their ME developments, makes no claim to completeness. An examination of other dialects would reveal further evidence; for example, breaking took place in Kentish as well as in West Saxon, and the Kentish diphthongs may have been preserved as late as the fourteenth century in such forms as *zyalde* 'sold', *hyealde* 'hold'. See R. Morris, *Ayenbite of Inwyt* (EETS.OS 23; London, 1866).

[20] See, for example, R. Jordan, *Handbuch der Mittelenglischen Grammatik* (Heidelberg, 1934), 86–8; Luick, *op. cit.* 333.

[21] Bohman, *op. cit.* and B. Sundby, *The Dialect and Provenance of the Middle English Poem* The Owl and the Nightingale (Lund, 1950).

and *eo* also obtained, we find a distinction likewise in Middle English. The short *e* remains so spelled, but short *eo* from breaking or velar-umlaut of WGmc. *e* or *i* appears in a variety of spellings (*eo, o, u,* etc.) pointing to a rounded vowel. Again we cite examples from the Bodley MS of the legend of St Margaret: (1) for breaking of WGmc. *e*: *beornind, dorkest, eorðliche, feor, heorte, steorren*; (2) for velar-umlaut of WGmc. *e*: *beoden* 'prayers', *beoreð, eoten, heouene* (Royal MS: *houene*), *seoueðe*; (3) for velar-umlaut of WGmc. *i*: *cleopieð, leome* 'limbs', *neomeð, neoðer, seonewwen* (or *seonewen*).

In view of such evidence, it is hardly possible to dismiss the OE distinctions *æ/ea, e/eo* on the ground that no such distinctions obtained in Middle English. Whatever one's phonetic interpretation of the forms, it is clear that there were ME distinctions parallel to those in Old English, which the scribes recognized and tried to record in their spellings.

A third argument for the monophthongal interpretation is based upon a consideration of the OE forms. Miss Daunt and Mossé confine themselves pretty much to the well-known examples given in the grammars; they offer nothing new in the way of evidence, however much their interpretations depart from those commonly accepted. Stockwell and Barritt present new material, but in a manner which will probably nullify its effect upon the majority of linguists.

Stockwell and Barritt describe their monograph (3) as a graphemic survey of Old English between A.D. 700 and 900. They give the impression of having examined, and phonemically interpreted, all of the *ae-, ea-,* and *a-*spellings in every OE text of the eighth and ninth centuries. They speak of certain forms as 'statistically predictable' (15), which would suggest to us that they have taken fair samplings directly from the manuscripts or from facsimiles or at least from reliable editions of the texts covered by the study. Yet we are nowhere given a list of the texts or portions of texts which have actually been used, and the two occasions on which they do specify a text show that they have gone outside their prescribed period. Data are cited (15–16) from the gloss to the Lindisfarne Gospels,[22] written in the tenth century, and a single form 'in Bede' is quoted (31), which turns out to be from the Cambridge University Library MS Kk. 3.18, of the eleventh century.

[22] British Museum MS Cotton Nero D.4. Incidentally, their suggestion that previous scholars were unaware of *ea*-spellings after *c, g, sc* in the Lindisfarne Gospels is unfair to the 'handbooks' which they appear to find deficient. The phenomena in question are dealt with in Brunner–Sievers 63–4; Luick 161; Girvan 68–9; K. Bülbring, *Altenglisches Elementarbuch* (Heidelberg, 1902), 62–3.

4

They also make statements about early OE phonology which lead one to suspect that their survey is based in part on late texts, WS copies of Anglian originals, and the like. For example, their 'statistically predictable' dialect spellings of six OE words (15) include four in which one can have little confidence. Thus *sceaft* is said to be the typical Anglian form, whereas we have been unable to find any *ea*-forms in Anglian texts of 700–900. Their Anglian *gæt* is extremely rare in the early texts; *ludgæt* in the Corpus Glossary, corresponding to *-gaet* in the Epinal and Erfurt Glossaries, seems to be the only example.[23] It is true that one would regard *cæster*, or *caestir*, as typical in an eighth-century Mercian or Northumbrian text, but the ninth-century Vespasian Psalter has only *e*-spellings, and there are no pure ninth-century Northumbrian texts. The form *cæfl* 'halter', said to be the typical WS form, does not appear (to the best of our knowledge) in any WS text of the period 700–900.[24]

Their mode of describing the practices of the early OE scribes is not likely to reassure historical linguists (including, of course, structural linguists who deal with historical problems). They ignore the fact that the grapheme *æ* appears in the manuscripts in three forms (*æ*, *ae*, and *ę*), and speak as though the only symbol to be contrasted with *ea* and *a* were *ae* (3). They also suggest that vowel length was indicated in the manuscripts by a macron. A macron-like sign was used by the scribes, it is true, but primarily as a substitute for *m*, occasionally to indicate an *n* or a contraction. If, for example, a scribe had written the word *la* (i.e. *lā* 'lo') with a macron over the *a*, his contemporaries would have read an entirely different word, *lam* (i.e. *lām*, 'loam').

While presenting old evidence or unreliable new evidence, all four scholars have overlooked many forms which tend to show that the conditioned diphthongs were phonetically distinct from the OE simple vowels. Among the clearest indications is the fact that the short *io* from WGmc. *i* in velar-umlaut position fell together with the short *eo* from WGmc. *e*. The spelling *eo* was commonly substituted for *io* in the ninth century; in later Old English the two diphthongs fell together completely and were regularly spelled *eo*; in Middle English they appear not

---

[23] The three glossaries mentioned appear in Corpus Christi College, Cambridge, MS 144; MS Épinal 17; and MS 42 of the Amplonian Library at Erfurt.

[24] In words of the type represented by *cæster*, *gæt*, and *sceaft*, eighth-century Anglian texts regularly have *æ* (also spelled *ae* and *ę*) or *e*; ninth-century Mercian has regularly *e*. The word entered in dictionaries as *cæfl* is attested (in early Mercian and late WS glossaries) in an instrumental form *cæfli* or *caefli*, apparently from **cafuli* and, if so, having secondary *i*-umlaut. An early WS nominative reconstructed from this might be **cæfl* or **ceafl* or **cafol*.

to have been distinguished.[25] Mossé mentions this falling together (46) but fails to see its bearing upon his theory. If the digraph spellings represented unchanged simple vowels, this phenomenon can be explained only as a falling together of simple [e] and [i]. One must then explain why [e] and [i] did not fall together in other positions too.

Both Miss Daunt and Mossé agree that short *ea* and *eo* upon lengthening behaved like *ēa* and *ēo* (< WGmc. *au* and *eu/iu*): *mearh* – *mēares*, *feoh* – *fēo*, etc.[26] Neither of them satisfactorily explains how lengthening of [æ] and [ɛ] could cause diphthongization in those contexts and not elsewhere.

There are late Old English manuscripts which contain evidence of another sort; again one example must suffice. The Cambridge University Library MS Ii.i.33, written soon after 1100, contains part of the Ælfrician translation of Genesis, in which the spelling tradition is less fixed than in some of the better known WS texts. Certain of the forms show consistent departures from the WS spelling tradition and give such indications of phonetic values as to preclude the possibility that *ea* and *eo* were either allographic variants of *æ* and *e* or minute allophonic variants of /æ/ and /e/.[27]

Broken and unbroken forms of WGmc. *a* are kept clearly apart. The scribe frequently reacted against the *ea*-spelling, not in order to use any symbol suggesting a monophthong, but rather to emphasize the diphthongal character of the sound and to indicate a more palatal first element than that suggested by *e*: *biarn*, *wiarð* (also *wierð*, *wiearð*, pret. of *weorðan*), *cyealf*, *getiald* (ppl. of *tellan*), *sialde* (also *syelde*, pret. of *sellan*), *sielt-*, etc. It may be noted that the scribe frequently replaced *ēa* (< WGmc. *au*) with a similar range of spellings: *biagas*, *dieadan*, *gelyafan*, *geliefen*, *lyeuum*, etc.

Broken and unbroken forms of WGmc. *e* were likewise kept apart. Occasionally the scribe spelled the broken forms with *u* or *o*: *furen* (for *feorran*), *orþan*. But departures from *eo* are relatively rare; on the contrary, we find the reverse phenomenon. The scribe sometimes used *eo* in place of stressed *o* (as in *geweorhte*, *weorde*) and in place of unstressed

[25] These statements apply to the WS and Mercian dialects; the distinction was retained longer in Northumbrian and Kentish. In Northumbrian, on the other hand, the scribes did not distinguish *ea* and *eo*, although they rather consistently preserved the distinction between *æ* and *e*.

[26] Daunt 132; Mossé 31–2, 41.

[27] The relevant portions of this manuscript are accessible in S. J. Crawford, *The Old English Version of the Heptateuch* (EETS.OS 160; London, 1922). Crawford studies the significant forms in an appendix to this edition, and in *TPS 1917–20*, 41–7; see also Paper 4 in the present volume.

vowels (as in *beotwux, beo* prep., *þeo* rel. pron.). From these facts we draw some important conclusions. First, it is clear that at the time the manuscript was written, *eo* in breaking positions represented a sound so far removed from [ɛ] that the symbol could be used for a vowel pronounced with lip-rounding or even for [ə]. Second, the *o* of *eo* was not part of any consonant nor a diacritic of any consonant, but was an integral part of the vocalic symbol *eo*, which could be transferred as a whole from its original predictable contexts.[28] Third, and most obviously, broken and unbroken forms of WGmc. *e* had diverged so far as to be recognized by the scribe as being 'differents'.

Having shown that there is strong evidence in Old English that *ea* and *eo* were phonetically distinct from *æ* and *e*, we are now ready to present some of the evidence which might be taken as indicating that they were phonemically distinct. Those forms cited immediately above, in which *eo* has been transferred from its original limited context to represent other sounds phonemically distinct from /e/, point to a phonemic distinction in the uses of *eo* and *e*.

Other forms could be cited at length from the Vespasian Psalter to show that *æ* and *ea*, *e* and *eo*, were no longer in strict complementary distribution as early as the first part of the ninth century. *Heofen* 'heaven', the usual form of the word, shows the *eo* remaining although the conditioning velar vowel of the final syllable has been weakened to a sound represented by *e*; similarly *seofen*. The plural *steaðelas* has *ea*, either retained from the time when the second syllable had a velar vowel or transferred by analogy from the singular *steaðul*. A similar *ea* which cannot be called conditioned appears in the preterite plural *hneapedun*, beside the singular *hneapade*. The conditioned *ea* in such present-tense forms as *-fearað* is found transferred by analogy to the participle *fearende*. In like manner, we find *beorende*, in which the *eo* is not conditioned, beside *beorað*, *cweoðende* beside *cweoðað*, and *cleopiende* beside preterite forms like *cleopade*. Any phonemic analysis which rejects the distinction between *ea* and *æ*, *eo* and *e*, must account in some way for these non-conditioned forms, as well as many others; the following are selected examples: *amearedes, eadesan, gedeafenað, gleadie, gongeweafre, hreaðedon, spearede; gemeodemad, geweolegað, hehseotle, heolstur, heoretas, ofergeotelas, spreocende*.

Although Stockwell and Barritt maintain that there are no minimal

---

[28] This can be observed sporadically in the codices of OE poetry; e.g. *freom* for *from* 'valiant' (Exodus 14), *weorn* for *worn* (Azarias 185), *weordum* for *wordum* (Phoenix 425).

pairs in Old English distinguished by *æ* and *ea*, we find a number of pairs which seem to have all the requirements of minimal distinctiveness. Naturally there cannot be many, since short *ea* regularly originated as an allophonic variant of /æ/; but the simplification of certain final consonant clusters, the loss of unstressed medial vowels, and late borrowings from Latin made it possible for minimal pairs to evolve.[29] Examples are *ærn* 'house':*earn* 'eagle'; *bærn* imperative 'burn':*bearn* 'child'; *fær* 'journey':*fear* 'bull'; *(wudu)mær* 'echo':*(ge)mear* 'wicked'; *pæll* 'pallium':*peall* 'defrutum'; *stæl* 'place':*steal* 'stall'; *wæl* 'slaughter': *weal* 'wall'; *wær* 'wary':*wear* 'a callous'; *wærna* 'wren':*wearna* gen. pl. 'of hindrances'.[30]

The technique of analogous pairs would uncover further evidence. To show that short diphthongs are distinguished from simple vowels in analogous environments, one could pair off such forms as these: *cwealmes*:*ælmes*, *ears*:*bærs*, *eall*:*pæll*, *hearm* or *bearn*:*hærn*, *pearfendlic*: *hærfest*, *heolfor*:*delfan*, *seolfor*:*selfum*, *heor*:*here*, *meord* or *weorc*:*mersc*, *feorm*:*fersc*. Minimal and analogous pairs of this kind are not necessarily found in any single manuscript or text, but all are from the same dialect, namely West Saxon, and show no features not found in the manuscripts of the Alfredian period.

In conclusion, we recognize the usefulness of descriptive techniques in the treatment of historical problems, but we believe that the new interpretations of the digraph spellings, as they have been thus far presented, are untenable. Before the new theories can make much head-

---

[29] There is a parallel case in the *i*-umlaut of WGmc. *u*, which in a specific context produced a predictable variant of *u*, written *y* and phonetically distinct from the then existing sounds in the OE phonological system. Although minimal pairs developed (e.g. *mund*:*mynd*), they are rare, and it is easier to demonstrate the phonemic identity of *y* by the use of analogous pairs, such as *tyrnan*:*murnan*. On this method of analysis, see B. Bloch, 'A Set of Postulates for Phonemic Analysis', *Lg.* 24 (1948), 30–2; *id.*, 'Studies in Colloquial Japanese, IV. Phonemics', *Lg.* 26 (1950), 86–125; K. L. Pike, *Phonemics* (Ann Arbor, 1947); *id.*, *Tone Languages* (Ann Arbor, 1948), 50–4. As Bloch points out (*Lg.* 26.96), 'Although minimally different pairs are not necessary to prove that a given phonemic difference is distinctive in a particular language, they illustrate such differences more strikingly than other examples'.

[30] Stockwell and Barritt attempt to explain away some of the pairs made possible by metathesis (31–2). Their first argument is a restatement of the contention that the ME development shows the sounds undifferentiated, a matter already dealt with in this article. Their other arguments are equally weak. They allow a single late spelling *earn* (for *ærn*) to carry as much weight as an abundance of early and irreproachable spellings with *æ*. They argue that *cærse* and *gærs* were so spelled because the scribes wished to distinguish the unpalatalized *c* and *g* from the palatalized varieties; yet the scribes made no such effort in scores of similar cases, such as *cēne* 'bold' and *genge* 'going'.

way, certain steps must be taken: (1) the new phonetic values to be assigned to the spellings *ea, eo, io, ie* must be clarified; (2) the consonant phonemes and allophones of Old English must be systematized and brought into harmony with the new vowel system; (3) the whole series of OE sound changes must be explained in terms of the new theories, without recourse to explanations which seem to contradict known facts or which render the changes unverifiable by means of objective evidence.

Even with such clarification and amplification, the theories will remain untenable so long as serious objections to their three major bases remain unanswered. First, the argument from Old Irish rests upon the unverified assumption that the Irish taught the Anglo-Saxons to write English, and upon vague resemblances between two sets of digraph spellings which were fundamentally different. Second, the argument that the OE short diphthongs and short vowels developed identically in Middle English is contradicted by the practice of a number of ME scribes who kept them apart in their spelling. Third, the arguments based upon OE scribal practices either fail to take into account or lightly dismiss a great deal of evidence bearing upon the phonetic and phonemic interpretation of the digraph spellings. For the present, we see no reason to depart from the established view – namely, that short diphthongs were produced in Old English by breaking, velar-umlaut, and palatal diphthongization, or by a combination of any one of these with *i*-umlaut. We have furnished some evidence to show that, within the historical period of Old English, short diphthongs were phonetically distinct from short vowels. We believe that a good case can be made for their having been phonemically distinct as well.

Six

The Old English digraphs: a reply†

The frank withdrawal of several claims and statements originally made by Stockwell and Barritt has answered some of our objections; but, for the most part, their rebuttal ('The Old English Short Digraphs: Some Considerations') has not only failed to convince us of the soundness of their general position, but has provided further evidence of its unsatisfactory nature and basis. We shall be as brief as possible, and for ease of reference, our comments are so arranged and labelled as to correspond with the numbered sections of the rebuttal.[1]

We begin with the revisions and emendations which Stockwell and Barritt propose to make in their first article.[2]

§2.12. In their interpretation of the phenomenon of 'slur', they go far beyond anything that we can find in Martin Joos's monograph.[3]

---

† This paper, written like the preceding one in collaboration with Sherman M. Kuhn, is a reply to an article by R. P. Stockwell and C. W. Barritt in *Language* 31 (1955), 372–89, which sought to rebut the essay that appears as Paper 5 in the present volume. Our reply appeared in the same volume of *Language* (pp. 390 ff.) as the rebuttal which it seeks in turn to refute.

[1] Since we wrote the paper which appeared in *Lg.* 29 (1953), 143–56, four further discussions of this subject have come to our attention: M. L. Samuels, 'The Study of Old English Phonology', *Transactions of the Philological Society 1952* (London, 1953), 15–47; M. Daunt, 'Some Notes on Old English Phonology', *ibid.* 48–54; K. Brunner, 'The Old English Vowel Phonemes', *English Studies* 34 (1953), 247–51; and C. E. Bazell, review in *Litera* 1 (1954), 75–7. Further reference will be made to these studies wherever they contribute to the present discussion, but in order not to obscure the points at issue between Stockwell and Barritt and ourselves, we shall confine such contributions to the footnotes.

[2] *Some Old English Graphemic-Phonemic Correspondences*—ae, ea, *and* a (*Studies in Linguistics:* Occasional Papers, No. 4; Washington, 1951). This study will be referred to hereafter by page, the rebuttal in *Language* 31 by section.

[3] *Language Monograph No. 23* (Baltimore, 1948), 104–9.

We suggest that slur alone cannot account for the combinative sound changes which gave rise to OE *ea, eo, io, ie*. Breaking, to take the simplest example, affected only certain vowels. Slur, according to Joos, affects all of the speech sounds. Breaking occurred only in certain environments, although the resulting sound might later be transferred analogically to a limited number of other environments. Slur takes place in any environment, the phoneme being modified by any sound that immediately precedes or follows it. In the words of Joos, 'The speaker has, in the articulatory and acoustic aspects, a whole vowel-phone system for the context [d – d], another system for the context [s – p], and so on. And in each context he articulates the appropriate allophone' (108). Breaking must have involved consciousness. If the Anglo-Saxons had been unconscious of the difference between simple vowels and the sounds represented by *ea, eo, io, ie*, they could not have distinguished them in spelling, e.g. *ærn:earn*. When, through phonetic change, they lost the distinction in sound (e.g. /i/ and /ie/ in one stage of West Saxon, cf. our fn. 4 below), they also lost the ability to make the orthographical distinction. Slur, on the other hand, is automatic and unconscious. Breaking could lead to phonemic change, as Stockwell and Barritt observe (§7). Slur (if we assume that the phenomenon is phonetic and not purely acoustic) produces a multitude of allophones, but Joos does not seem to regard these as phonemically significant. That the phenomenon of slur, as revealed by the spectrograph in languages today, was also present in Old English, seems to us very probable; but OE spellings like *dyde–sype*, *Dodda–soppian* indicate that it was, then as now, unconscious and non-phonemic.

§2.13. The substitution of *scæft* for *sceaft* in the 'Anglian column' merely replaces one misleading form with another equally misleading. Both here and in §9.6, Stockwell and Barritt show a surprising lack of caution in the treatment of OE dialects. *Scæft, sceft, sceaft, cæster, cester, ceaster, gæt, get, geat* – these are all Anglian forms, in that spellings like these turn up in manuscripts of known Anglian provenience. But the form to be expected depends upon which of the Anglian dialects, and what period of its development, one is dealing with. The error lies in selecting a single form and treating it as though it were typical for all varieties of Anglian.

As for *cæfli* (§9.6), this does not occur in any pure WS text. We cannot even be certain that it is a WS word, for the late glossaries often contain matter copied from older Anglian sources.

§2.14. The revised sequence of OE sound changes is more plausible than that originally proposed by Stockwell and Barritt (24–6), but *i*-umlaut is still dated earlier than palatal diphthongization. The defence of this order (§§8–8.2) will be dealt with later.[4]

[4] Stockwell and Barritt follow the traditional chronology in regarding *i*-umlaut as later than breaking. On this point we agree with them rather than with Samuels who argues that breaking was contemporaneous with *i*-umlaut and continued after *i*-umlaut was complete (33–46). Although we are in substantial agreement with Samuels in many of his views and conclusions, the evidence that he has so far presented in favour of the lateness of breaking seems to us inadequate. The non-WS material (21, 36–7) consists of fourteen spellings collected from eight different texts written in three (possibly four) dialects at various times from about the sixth to the ninth century. These sporadic monophthongal forms should not be allowed to outweigh the abundant evidence of breaking that we find in the earliest manuscripts, especially since the fourteen spellings (and some others like them, which Samuels did not include) have already been explained by other scholars. We should like to point out, moreover, that the proper names in Bede's *Ecclesiastical History*, from which Samuels takes four of his forms, also include spellings like *guruiorum* (=*gyrwa*), -*angli* (=*engle*), *strenaes halc* (=*strēones*-), *estranglorum* (=*ēastengla*), and that the two Kentish charters used contain the forms *hlothari* (=*hlōðhere*), *enfridi* (=*ēanfriðes*), and *bercuald* (=*beorht*-). If sporadic Latinisms and scribal errors can be used to prove that breaking had not occurred when these texts were written, they can also be used to prove that *i*-umlaut was not yet complete in the eighth century, or that WGmc. *au* and *eu* were monophthongal in early Old English, or that the cluster *htw* lost its *t* in early Kentish. How much to infer from occasional spellings is a matter for personal judgment, but Samuels goes further than we are prepared to follow.

The WS material used to illustrate WS phonology before the time of King Alfred (43–5) consists of eight forms, which appear to be non-WS or local dialect, taken from two documents of the ninth century. It seems to us unsafe to treat these texts as though they contained typical pre-Alfredian West Saxon, first, because of the evidences of dialect mixture and, second, because of the dates at which they were written. The one mentions the date of Alfred's accession, and the other cannot have been composed earlier than the year preceding his birth. Both texts are available in H. Sweet, *Oldest English Texts*, EETS.OS 83.179, 433–4 (1885).

For the Age of Alfred, Samuels cites *ie*-spellings (chiefly from Bodleian MS Hatton 20 of Alfred's translation of the *Pastoral Care*) such as *iernan* and *gewrietum*, to show that breaking occurred after the period of *i*-umlaut in the first type of word, and that something akin to velar-umlaut occurred in the second. But can forms like these be treated in isolation from other *ie*-spellings in the Hatton MS? It is difficult to assume a diphthong of any kind or of any origin in forms like the following: *briengan, hieder, nieðemeſð, siendon, sient, tieglan, ðieder, ðienga, ungeriesenlice, wieten* (opt.). These examples of *ie* for historical /i/ are paralleled in the same manuscript by forms with *ie* for /i:/; e.g. *adriefð, flietað, gegriepð, gestieganne, iedelnes, riece*. We should have liked to see Samuels take account of such forms as these in postulating his revised chronology. He might have explained why they and the examples which he himself cites should no longer be regarded as reverse spellings, i.e. as an indication that early WS *īe* and *ie* were well on their way to becoming monophthongal by the close of the ninth century.

It would, therefore, seem necessary to have further evidence and discussion before we proceed with Samuels to assume a new sound-change in the form of a

We proceed to the clarifications in §§2.41–44, thence to the heavier arguments which follow.

§2.41. The disagreement over the manuscript diacritic which Stockwell and Barritt wish to call a 'macron' may be more than a simple matter of 'transparent but nontraditional' terminology. It would appear that the authors regard the acute accents in OE manuscripts as identical in distribution and function with the macrons in OE grammars. If so, their original statement concerning '"short" vocalic nuclei ... over which a macron was not written in the manuscripts' (3) reflects a double misconception: first as to the shape of the manuscript diacritic in question, and second as to the linguistic inferences which can be drawn from its occurrence or non-occurrence over any specific form in a manuscript.[5]

§2.43. We can see nothing to be gained by arbitrarily defining 700–900 as 'The Old English period'. There are more good OE manuscripts from the tenth and eleventh centuries than from the eighth and ninth.

§§5.1–3. The vowel system here posited for Old English is too indefinite and fragmentary for effective evaluation. We notice, however, that the sound represented by OE *io* seems to have been overlooked,[6] and we wonder on what evidence the sound represented by *a* (as in WS *dagas, faran*) has been classified as a rounded vowel.[7] As far as Old

---

secondary *i*-umlaut (45) to account for the *ie* in WS *wielle, fiellan*. Caution seems all the more desirable when we note that forms like *tellan* and *hærfest* (adequately accounted for, along with *wielle* and *fiellan*, in the accepted chronology) are not satisfactorily explained by Samuels' hypothesis. Nor, by the same token and for the reasons previously stated, do we feel able to accept his arguments as regards the lateness of breaking in relation to *i*-umlaut.

[5] Usage varies from manuscript to manuscript: in the Vespasian Psalter (British Museum MS Cotton Vespasian A.1), long vowels and diphthongs are never distinguished by diacritics; in *Beowulf* and *Judith* (MS Cotton Vitellius A.15), there is on the average about one acute in every twenty lines of poetry, and all appear over long vowels or long diphthongs; in the Caedmonian poems (Bodleian MS Junius 11), somewhere between half and two-thirds of the lines contain one or more acutes, but these appear over short as well as long vowel elements. The use of the acute over diphthongs is rare in all of the manuscripts, so rare that it might be termed sporadic. For detailed information on the usage in the poetic manuscripts, one may consult the introductions to the various volumes of the *Anglo-Saxon Poetic Records* (New York and London, 1931–53). Information concerning other manuscripts must be sought in scattered sources, too numerous to be listed here.

[6] This diphthong is indispensable for the description of Northumbrian, Kentish, early Mercian, and early West Saxon.

[7] When lengthened before a consonant cluster (as in Merc. *āld*), the vowel became rounded in some dialects of Middle English. But this development is too late to be included in a description of Old English: cf. K. Luick, *Historische*

English is concerned, the use of /h/ and /w/ as phonemes of length (or glide vowels, or whatever they are in this modification of the Trager-Smith system) is certainly undesirable. Consonantal /w/ occurs initially, medially, and finally, before vowels, after vowels, and between vowels. The same is true of /h/, if we recognize the initial [h] and the final [x] of *hēah* as allophones, and the [xx] of *hliehhan* as a geminated /h/.[8] If Stockwell and Barritt retain the consonantal phonemes and use /h/ and /w/ also as phonemic constituents of vowel nuclei, the results may be economical of phonemes (or rather of symbols for phonemes), but not of the user's time, especially when he begins to phonemicize forms like *blōwan, cnēow, hēawan, lǣwede, nīewe, sāwan, lēoht, līehtan, nēah, pūhte, wōh,* and *wrāh*.[9] Apart from the fact that it distorts the linguistic facts by grouping under one phoneme sounds which are phonetically and historically unrelated, such a system would be cumbersome and confusing, and therefore undesirable.

§§7–7.6 In these sections, Stockwell and Barritt present an elaborate and ingenious attack upon our arguments in Paper 5 above, pp. 46–9. But they apparently agree with our contention that *æ* and *ea* (and also *e* and *eo*) did not develop identically in Middle English.

§7.11. They have overstated the argument in Paper 5 above, p. 47. We did not separate *æ* and *ea* in the first place, and we should hardly have done so on the basis of the ME evidence alone. The evidence which led nineteenth-century linguists to separate the two and to associate *ea* with *ēa* is too well known to be catalogued here. Probably they were most strongly influenced by the fact that OE scribes wrote the letters *ea* in both *hearpe* and *hēafod*, as well as in many similar words, rarely distinguishing the long sound from the short. The problem of separating *ea* from *ēa* was much greater than that of distinguishing *ea* from *æ*, or *ēa* from *ǣ*. But the knotty problems of yesterday, once solved, are apt to be

---

Grammatik der Englischen Sprache (Leipzig, 1921) 358–64; R. Jordan, *Handbuch der Mittelenglischen Sprache* (Heidelberg, 1934), 68–71; K. Brunner, *Die Englische Sprache* I (Halle, 1950), 224–5; F. Mossé, *Manuel de l'anglais du moyen âge, II. Moyen anglais* I (Paris, 1949), 41; and other standard secondary sources.

[8] For the generally accepted phonetic interpretation of OE *h* as [h] initially (except perhaps before /w/) and as [x] elsewhere, see K. Bülbring, *Altenglisches Elementarbuch* (Heidelberg, 1902), 188–9; J. Wright and E. M. Wright, *Old English Grammar* (Oxford, 1925), 169–72; H. C. Wyld, *A Short History of English* (New York, 1927), 61; etc.

[9] We also anticipate some confusion in the phonemicization of pairs like *bȳ, byge; hēa* (pl. of *hēah*), *hēaw* (imperative); *hygd, hȳd; sǣ, sēaw; sēo, sēow* (pt. of *sāwan*); *þē, þēo* (dat. sg. of *þēoh*); *wǣg, wēa; wē, weg*.

forgotten; and now there are several scholars who seek to disregard the evidence of the OE spelling practices, one of their chief arguments being the alleged sameness of the ME reflexes of *æ* and *ea*. We merely pointed out a portion of the evidence which indicates that the ME reflexes were not the same in certain dialects.

§7.12. Stockwell and Barritt now recognize that OE *æ* and *ea* did not develop identically in Middle English. They admit that the reflexes of OE *ea* in Southern ME place-names were often treated like the reflexes of OE *ēa*.[10] Having thus gained our point, we ought perhaps to be satisfied and to let the matter rest.

We feel, however, that faulty interpretation of the evidence in this section of the rebuttal should not go unchallenged. It is true that the ME spellings of the Southern place-names are by no means uniform. The lack of uniformity has been observed by many scholars and accounted for in several ways: the Southern dialect area was not uniform even in OE times,[11] Southern documents of the ME period were frequently copied by royal scribes whose dialect and scribal habits were Midland rather than Southern,[12] etc. The existence of a large body of diphthongal spellings (like *Fiernham*) may be used as evidence that a diphthongal pronunciation existed in Southern Middle English. It does not prove that this was the sole pronunciation, nor have we at any time made any such claim. Other spellings (like *Fernlegh*) may be evidence that some speakers, somewhere in the Southern area, monophthongized

---

[10] Even if they are correct in supposing that OE *ea* was lengthened in all such cases, it is nevertheless true that they separate the Southern ME reflexes of WS *ea* from the reflexes of *æ*. We do not accept some of the theories of lengthening advanced. Although we believe that we understand what Stockwell and Barritt mean by 'analogical' lengthening (§7.13), the process is still too vague and undefined to be acceptable as an explanation of any large body of linguistic facts. Lengthening 'by processes not now described in the traditional handbooks' (§7.12, fn. 4) is so general and all-inclusive as to be meaningless.

[11] At the present time this area is so lacking in uniformity that modern dialectologists recognize several distinct dialects in Southern England. All of the major dialect areas of modern England contain smaller sub-areas, speech islands, etc. In OE times the major areas may have been more homogeneous than at present, but the evidence suggests that they were by no means uniform.

[12] As an example of the way in which a scribe might respell place-names, we offer the following pairs of spellings from two different manuscript copies of a single document in Walter de Gray Birch, *Cartularium Saxonicum* 1 (London, 1885–93), 466–7: *Appincg lond*, *Apping Land*; *Fefresham*, *Febresham*; *Grafon aea*, *Grafonea*. Four spellings of *Worcester* occur in two copies of a single document (*ibid.* 2.266–7): *Wigra Ceastre – Weogerna ceastre*, *Wegerna ceaster – Wigerna cestre*. Obviously somebody altered something, and probably not all of the spellings cited represent local usage.

the reflex of OE *ea* to a sound resembling /e/, not /a/.[13] But these spellings in no way discredit the possibility that other speakers retained the diphthongal pronunciation, and they certainly suggest that the reflex of OE *ea* was not identical with that of OE *æ*. As evidence on the latter point, place-name spellings with *ea*, *e*, *i*, or *y* for the reflex of OE *ea* are as significant as those with *ia*, *ya*, *ie*, or *ye*. The existence of spellings with *a* (e.g. *Farnlegh*) may be used as evidence that an *a*-type of pronunciation existed, either in the dialect of some Southern speakers or in the dialect of the royal scribes at London or Westminster; but it cannot, in itself, discredit the evidence of spellings like *Fiern-* and *Fern-*. Some linguists may regard this discussion as too elementary for a journal like *Language*, but we wish to protest the way in which Stockwell and Barritt draw unwarranted conclusions from the ME forms which they cite.

We are puzzled by the reference to 'the consistent diphthongal indications that *ēa* reflexes show' and would welcome a further statement on the dialect and period in which the reflexes of *ēa* are consistently diphthongal, or consistently spelled in a manner suggesting diphthongal pronunciation.

We are aware that lengthening must have taken place in several of the forms which we cited (Paper 5 above, p. 47); in fact, our examples were selected with a view to showing the reflexes of OE *ea* in a variety of contexts.[14] In some cases, the lengthening occurred in Old English before certain consonant clusters; in others, one may assume that ME lengthening in the open syllable had taken place by the time the spelling was recorded. We note, however, that Stockwell and Barritt are forced to prop up their argument by assuming a special type of juncture in *Fiernham* and by promulgating a new sound law. They ask us to accept their view that *u* or *w* was lost in words like *bearu*, with compensatory lengthening but they offer no evidence or other support for this.

The importance of the lengthening clusters to us in this study is that they caused *ea* to behave exactly like *ēa*, which would suggest that OE speakers at the time of lengthening did not regard *ea* and *æ* (which was

[13] The phoneme which we label /a/ is that which Stockwell and Barritt call /ɔ/, inaccurately we believe.

[14] The shift in their argument is worth pointing out, since it suggests that the gap between their views and ours may be closing. They originally stated that OE *ea* and *æ* were identically treated in Middle English, further maintaining that 'when secondary influences [which would include lengthening] operate, they operate to affect *ae* and *ea* in identical ways when all other conditions are identical' (8). This is the sentence expunged by §2.11.

lengthened to *ǣ*) as phonemic 'sames'. Since this argument is self-evident, we shall pursue it no further but content ourselves with submitting some further forms in which the clusters have not hitherto been regarded as lengthening groups and from which no *h*, *u*, or *w* has been lost.[15] It would be of interest to us to know whether the various new types of lengthening posited by Stockwell and Barritt could cover the following: *Bylk* (< *bealca*), *Chealgraue* or *Chilgrave* (< *cealc*), *Helfacre* (< *healf*), *Sesealtre* (< *sealt*), *Spearkeheghes* (<*spearca*), *Wermelegh* (<*wearm*), *Scerphawe* (< *scearp*), *swierte leie* (< *sweart*), *Smyrt* (< *smeart*), *Bearwefeld* (< *bearu*, oblique *bearw*-). For the development before geminated *l*, which they seem to find more difficult than the others, we offer: *Dealleghe*, *Ganeshiall*, *Kockeswealle*, *Miellingetis* (< **Meallingas*), *Pealton* or *Pyawton*, and *Tunstealle*. The traditional explanation of breaking permits us to explain the relevant portions of all these forms without resort to any untested and improbable theories of lengthening.

§7.21. Stockwell and Barritt state that the spellings of MS Bodley 34 show no 'three-way contrast among the reflexes of OE *ǽ*, *ĕa*, and *ēa*', because the spellings used for the reflexes of the short diphthongs are similar to those used for the reflexes of the long diphthongs. Why must there be a three-way spelling contrast? In Old English, there was no such contrast of *æ*, *ea*, and *ēa*. As we have already pointed out, the long and short diphthongs were normally undifferentiated in spelling.[16] The macrons and circumflexes placed over the long diphthongs by modern editors and grammarians will not be found in the manuscripts.[17]

In their fn. 9, they present the evidence which supposedly contradicts our statements regarding the orthography of MS Bodley 34 (Paper 5 above, pp. 47–8). It is true that there are inconsistencies in the spellings of this manuscript and we have no desire to exaggerate the relative consistency of the writing. Any ME text is apt to contain some scribal errors and some eccentricities of the individual writer. The spelling of MS Bodley 34 is complicated by the fact that, while its dialect is basically Midland (< Mercian), it contains some admixture of Southwestern

---

[15] The spellings are not limited to the ME diphthongal types this time but include various types indicating that the reflex of *ea* was not identical with that of *æ*.

[16] This feature of the orthography is most clearly seen in the Nthb. portions of the Rushworth Gospels (Bodleian MS Auct. D.2.19), in which the long *ēa* (< Gmc. *au*) is frequently replaced by the spelling *eo*. The same spelling is also frequently substituted for the short *ea*.

[17] The uses of the acute have already been mentioned, cf. our fn. 5.

(< West Saxon) forms. But these rather minor inconsistencies are nothing in comparison with those which are made to appear by the authors' mode of analysis. They lift whole blocks of data from Frances Mack's phonology, with little or no rearrangement of the examples and apparently without realizing that her organization was designed to serve a purpose very different from their own. As a consequence, their paragraph entitled 'OE *ea*' includes reflexes of Merc. *a* (WS *ea*) *alle*, etc.; Merc. *æ* (WS *ea*) *strahte*, etc.; Merc. *ea* (WS *ea*) *dear*, etc.; Merc. *e* (WS *ea*) *sterke*, etc.; Merc. *e* (WS *ie*) *merren*, etc.; late Merc. *ǣ* (late WS *ȳ*) *welden*, etc.; late Merc. *ēa* (late WS *ēa*) *bearn*, etc.; and late Merc. *ē* (late WS *ȳ*) *ʒerce*, etc. Thus it is made to appear that the scribe spelled the reflexes of a single phoneme (to Stockwell and Barritt, only an allophone) in three different ways; whereas the three spellings actually represent reflexes of seven Merc. phonemes: /a/ and /æ/ (which normally fell together in ME times); /æː/, /e/, and /eː/ (which were often spelled alike in ME texts of the Midland area); /ea/ and /eaː/ (which were usually spelled alike even in Old English).[18] In short, the relatively consistent and logical spelling practices of the manuscript are completely misrepresented. The distortion is further aggravated by the fact that Miss Mack's lists are selective and that (as is apt to be the case in a phonology of this type) unusual spellings are much better represented numerically than are the majority spellings. The remaining paragraphs, 'OE *æ*', etc., show the same type of confusion as the one examined above, but we see no point in treating these errors in detail.

§7.4. Once again, we plead guilty to the charge of ignoring the lengthenings of OE *ea*. When we presented our evidence from the Cambridge University Library MS Ii.1.33, Stockwell and Barritt had not yet reversed themselves on the subject of 'secondary influences' (§2.11, cf. our fn. 14). Different examples could have been used, but in any case *cyealf* and *sielt-* have none of the recognized lengthening combinations, and there is little evidence to bear out the statement that the second grade of *weorðan* (our example was *wiarþ*) ever had a long vowel element. As to their claim that the '*ie* in *sielt-* is a spelling not of *ea* but of *ie*', we can make nothing of it; we would have thought that the WS form *sealt* ('salt') was amply attested and beyond controversy.

§7.5. It seems to us very unlikely that the reflex of OE *eo* was /ə/ in

---

[18] We may be misinterpreting the vowel system set forth in §§5.1–2, but it seems to us that Stockwell and Barritt analyse WS *ie*, *ȳ*, *ea*, and *ēa* as orthographic representations of four phonemically different vowel nuclei. We suppose that they would also regard Merc. *a*, *æ*, *ǣ*, *e*, *ē*, *ea*, and *ēa* as representing more than one phoneme.

Middle English, but discussion of this matter should probably be post-poned until Stockwell and Barritt have presented their phonemic systems in more detail.

Our argument based on the falling together of *eo* and *io* in some OE dialects (Paper 5 above, pp. 50f) seems to have been misunderstood. It was directed at the view that the *o* in each case was a consonantal dia-critic, and that the *e* and the *i* in breaking position remained unchanged. The argument was concerned, not with allophones, but with supposedly unchanged vowels.

§8.1. Stockwell and Barritt offer no positive support for their view that *i*-umlaut preceded palatal diphthongization. Their objections to *cȳse* as a test word are based upon several misconceptions and another ad hoc sound law.

There are many OE words which are not recorded in early West Saxon. *Cȳse* is one of these, because of the accidental circumstance that the thing called 'cheese' is not mentioned by the early WS writers whose works have survived. It is not surprising, therefore, that the spelling **ciese* cannot be found. The vocabulary referred to appears in British Museum MS Cotton Cleopatra A.3, and is assigned by Thomas Wright to 'the latter part of the tenth or earlier part of the eleventh century'. If this dating is correct, the glossary is a transition text – in so far as the shift *īe > ȳ* is concerned. As might be expected, it contains some forms spelled according to the earlier tradition, others spelled in the later fashion.

§8.2. The late WS *cȳse* requires no special sound law. Merely by applying in correct sequence the sound changes established on other evidence, one gets from *cāseus* (Popular Lat. **kāsju*) to *cȳse* without difficulty (Paper 5 above, p. 43). Every stage in the process can be tested and verified by reference to numerous other OE words; e.g. fronting, *strǣt* (< *ā*); palatal diphthongization, *cēace* (< *ǣ* < *ā*); *i*-umlaut, *nīed* (< *ēa* < *au*); monophthongization and rounding, *nȳd* (< *īe*). It is hard to find any one form that parallels *cȳse* throughout its entire history; hence, the importance of *cȳse* as a test word for determining (or dis-covering) the order of the changes.

It is unsound procedure to rely upon words like *giest* as evidence of the order of the sound changes, since forms like **gastiz* and **kafisa* could become *giest* and *ciefes* with either order of palatal diphthongiza-tion and *i*-umlaut (cf. Paper 5, p. 43). How can such ambiguous items, however numerous, outweigh an unambiguous item like *cȳse*? Zero multiplied by 1000 is still less than one.

In the final paragraph of this section, the authors introduce another of their new sound changes in order to account for *cȳse*. They assume a WS shift of *ǣ* (< *ā*) > *ē* in this one word, a change which is not paralleled elsewhere in the dialect, cf. WS *strǣt* (< Lat. *strātum*), etc. As in §7.12, the new sound law is presented as a bare and unsupported statement.[19]

Before we leave this subject, it may be well to remind ourselves that most of the chronology of prehistoric OE sound changes which we now accept and use was arrived at by means of 'test words', i.e. words whose OE shape would be of one sort if affected by the changes in one sequence, but something else if affected by the same changes in a different sequence. The relative chronology of breaking and palatal diphthongization is supported by several; e.g. if palatal diphthongization had been the earlier change, a prehistoric **kerfan* (cf. OFris. *kerva*) would have become **cierfan*, rather than the *ceorfan* which it actually became. Such test words may hamper us sometimes in our theoretical speculations, but we abandon them at our peril, for much of our chronology is supported by no other evidence.

§§9–9.4. We presented evidence (Paper 5 above, pp. 52 f) tending to show that OE *æ* and *ea* represented different phonemes.[20] Stockwell and Barritt confine their rebuttal to four of our nine minimal pairs, three of the analogous pairs (including two for the distinction *e:eo*), and a small portion of the evidence for non-complementary distribution.

§9. OE minimal pairs are all orthographic as far as a twentieth-century linguist is concerned. To prove that a pair is purely orthographic, without phonemic significance, one must do more than merely explain how the forms came into existence (by a metathesis, by analogy within a paradigm, or the like). Modern English *bed* and *bid* are due to various linguistic changes, which altered the shapes of OE *bed* (*beddes*, *bedde*, etc.) and of the verb *biddan*. Without those changes, there could

---

[19] We note a similar suggestion by Samuels: 'there is . . . nothing to show that the fronting in *cȳse* could not have been due simply to the combined influence of the initial palatal consonant and *i*-mutation' (36). We hesitate to enter into a detailed discussion of this point, since it is presented only incidentally and may not represent Samuels' considered view. Nevertheless, it should be observed that he has suggested a new sound change (a sort of combined palatal diphthongization, *i*-umlaut, and rounding), which must be assumed to have affected *cȳse* alone. Since the change in question did not affect other words, there is no possibility of testing or verifying it.

[20] Samuels arrives at the conclusion (43) that the breaking diphthongs became phonemic in the seventh century. Although absolute datings for prehistoric developments are hazardous, we believe that we can accept this view as a working hypothesis.

5

be no minimal distinction, yet we have never heard a linguist object to *bed*:*bid* as a minimal pair.

At the risk of being obvious, we may further point out that a highly inflected language with relatively few foreign borrowings and a vocabulary which is preserved only in part, e.g. Old English, cannot be expected to furnish the abundance of minimal pairs found in an analytical language of mixed origin and readily available vocabulary, e.g. Modern English. If Stockwell and Barritt continue to demand minimal pairs in large numbers for all of the phonemes of Old English, they may be forced to the conclusion that Old English had no phonemic distinctions at all.[21]

§§9.2–3. The phonetic deficiencies of OE spelling have long been known to historical linguists. Most of the latter are well aware that medieval scribes were not, as a class, expert phoneticians.[22] Very few linguists regard the OE writings as phonetic transcriptions of OE speech, although it is true that some linguists have occasionally fallen into this error when dealing with some specific problem. Stockwell and Barritt appear to fall into the opposite error, that of supposing that OE orthography was completely dominated by foreign traditions and unrelated to native pronunciation.

They object to our supposed use of manuscripts as 'informants' or as 'the records of methodical field workers'. We do not pretend to use an OE text as we should use a living informant or even as we might use a field record made by a worker whose ability and methods of transcription were already known to us. It would be more accurate to say that we treat the manuscript text as though it were a record made by a worker whose system of transcription must be puzzled out before anything can be done with the evidence. The reliability of the evidence must then be checked in various ways: by a study of its internal consistency, by comparison with other manuscript texts, by application of the findings of etymology, and by other equally standard procedures. Imperfect as most of the manuscripts are, it behooves us to treat them with respect. No other primary source of information exists. The only objective data bearing directly upon problems of historical linguistics appear in the manuscripts and other written records, and what-

---

[21] We have in mind especially such contrasts as those between /æ/ and /ɔ/, /o/ and /u/, /o/ and /ö/, all of which Stockwell and Barritt seem to regard as phonemic (§5.1). Similar difficulties arise in the analysis of dialects (e.g. Kentish) in which the materials for study are very limited.

[22] Cf. Brunner's remarks, *English Studies* 34.1.

ever one says about such matters as the phonetics or phonemics of a historical language must be inferred from ink marks on vellum or from comparable facts.

It is hard for us to believe that the chasm between our methods (which are not of our inventing but the outgrowth of generations of linguistic scholarship) and those of Stockwell and Barritt is so impassable as they suppose.[23] Their own data are admittedly drawn from 'standard secondary sources' (§2.44). The secondary sources, presumably grammars and dictionaries, contain manuscript materials, although they may be at second, third, or fourth hand, and subject to much selection and normalization. Each statement or example in them is ultimately derived from someone's examination of a manuscript text.

§9.4. The statement that *steal, weal, wear, fear* contained the 'front allophone of /æ/' prompts us to ask, How did it get there? The authors follow tradition in assuming that a WGmc. /a/ became /æ/ in certain environments during some epoch in history (24); hence, there must have been a time when no allophones of /æ/ existed anywhere. The presence in *steal* etc. of a vowel sound identical with that in *steallas* etc. (a diphthong to us, a 'back allophone' to Stockwell and Barritt) could be accounted for in either of two ways: (*a*) the onset of breaking may have preceded the loss of the ending in *a*-stem nominatives like Gmc. **stallaʒ*, in which case it must also have preceded simplification of the *ll, rr*, etc.; or (*b*) the diphthongal pronunciation of forms like *steallas* may have been analogically transferred to the forms like *steal*. In either case, we have a rational linguistic explanation, and pairs like *steal:stæl* are the minimal pairs which they appear to be.[24] But Stockwell and Barritt argue that *steal* had a vowel element different from that of *steallas*, and that the *ea*-spelling of *steal* is due to a spelling analogy unrelated to pronunciation. We might accept this view if there were any evidence to support it. Not only is there a complete absence of supporting evidence, but this explanation necessitates our assuming that *steal* and *stæl* (also *weal* and *wæl, wear* and *wær, fear* and *fær*) were completely homophonous. And this despite the consistency with which these pairs were distinguished in OE spelling. To suppose that OE scribes (working without Bosworth-Toller to guide them) could consistently differentiate sets of perfect homophones, is to credit them with powers of memory that seem to us improbable.

---

[23] Most of §§12.1–2 sounds like old-line historical linguistics restated in contemporary structuralist terms.

[24] For some additional minimal and analogous pairs, see Samuels (22–3).

Open juncture in *ælmesse* is also too improbable for ready acceptance. The Popular Lat. *alimōsina*, which evidently lies behind the Gmc. and Romance cognates of the OE word, can be traced to the OE form without resort to open juncture as an explanation. As far as the OE meaning is concerned, treating *ælmesse* as though it consisted of separable and formative elements in Old English, i.e. *æl* and *messe*, creates new problems, solves none. The discussion of juncture referred to[25] was specifically related to inflectional forms; it seems hardly analogous to the postulation of open juncture in a unit word like *ælmesse*.

It would be hard for us to accept the 'traditionalized spellings' explanation of metathesized forms like *fersc*. Are we to suppose that the scribes carefully noted the letter *e* of **fresc* in very ancient manuscripts, but overlooked the initial *fr*-cluster? Is it not strange that, in all of the metathesized forms, the tradition should preserve the ancient vowel and forget the order of vowels and consonants?[26]

We think that very few linguists could dispose of our evidence from the Vespasian Psalter (Paper 5 above, p. 52) with the casualness shown here. The only forms mentioned by Stockwell and Barritt are *hneapedun*, *steaðelas*, and *fearende*, which are labelled 'spelling analogy within the paradigm', as though that alone were sufficient to discredit them. Our examples also included forms like *gedeafenað*, *gongeweafre*, and *heolstur*, in which there is little likelihood that analogy within a paradigm produced the diphthongal spelling. These alone would be sufficient to convince some linguists of the phonemic identity of the sound represented by *ea* in the Vespasian Psalter.

If it is true that forms like *steaðelas* and *fearende* had the *ea*-spelling without the corresponding pronunciation, they are very weak evidence of the transfer of a conditioned diphthong to an environment in which it is not conditioned. But Stockwell and Barritt do not (and, we believe, cannot) show that it was the spelling alone that was transferred from forms like *steaðul* and *fearað*. The pronunciation may also have been transferred.

§9.5. In conclusion, the extensive correspondence and exchange of views which preceded publication of their rebuttal and this reply have cleared up some misunderstandings but have not materially altered our views. The OE minimal pairs seem as valid as ever and still suggest to us that OE *æ* and *ea* represented phonemically distinct sounds. These pairs are necessarily few in number, but they are more numerous than can

---

[25] That is, Paper 4 above.
[26] For a fuller discussion of this point, see Bazell, *Litera* 1.76.

be found 'in any single dialect' for the distinction between /o/ and /ö/, which Stockwell and Barritt regard as phonemic (§5.1). The evidence that OE *æ* and *ea* were no longer in complementary distribution has, for the most part, gone unchallenged in the rebuttal. Our argument that the two sounds did not develop identically in Middle English seems to have been conceded. In our opinion, the cumulative evidence of minimal pairs, contrastive distribution, and divergent history should not be dismissed merely because it conflicts with the formalistic criterion of simplicity.

The controversy, which has been so freely ventilated in the pages of *Language*, has been salutary and to some extent constructive. Partly through the modification of their earlier position and partly through further explanation of their views, it seems to us that the gulf between Stockwell and Barritt and ourselves has significantly narrowed. We reaffirm our belief that modern descriptive techniques have much to contribute to the solution of historical problems, but only when used with a due regard for the tried and tested principles of historical linguistics.

Seven

The survey of English usage†

1

When one reflects for how long and by how many and with what degree of attention the English language has been studied, it seems likely that English is one of the world's most thoroughly studied languages. The position is, however, that the masses of material compiled over the years prove quite inadequate to serve as the basis of even elementary teaching-grammars, a fact which has emerged rather suddenly and with particular starkness in recent years, when increasing attempts have been made to improve and extend the teaching of English as a foreign language. I say 'rather suddenly', but although a state of urgency has been recognized only since about 1950, the problem and projected solutions of it were clearly outlined in the years between the wars, and even earlier. Yet it remains true today that for no period in its history has the grammar of English been described with anything approaching systematic accuracy and completeness, and the writers of practical teaching manuals in consequence have no body of full and objective data from which to draw material or on which to build a structural approach or base dependable rules, and the inadequacy of current teaching-grammars used both at home and overseas is often recognized by none more clearly than by those who write them. These writers have still to rely upon their own uncertain impression of what is normally written or spoken by the educated (and therefore safely imitable) native speaker, and some are emboldened by the lack of reliable information to continue prescribing according to their own predilections. The extent to which prescription is seriously or pathologically at variance with ac-

† Based on an address to the Philological Society which was published in the *Transactions of the Philological Society 1960*, 40 ff.

tual usage (a matter which itself needs investigation) is in large measure a direct result of the continued absence of proper information, and it is at the same time a rebuke and a challenge to linguists.

By contrast with English grammar, the lexicon – the 'word-hoard' – of English has received magnificent treatment in the volumes of the *NED*, and this book, as a descriptive register of forms and meanings, has become the natural primary source for a series of 'practical' dictionaries designed for particular purposes and for particular educational strata. Indeed, it is more than that: it is the best primary source not only for lexical but also for a great deal of grammatical information, a fact which is sometimes overlooked by practising grammarians and also by theorizing linguists distinguishing between word-stock and grammar. It has become a commonplace to criticize lexicographers for treating the 'closed' categories of words on the same principles as the 'open' categories,[1] and there are several rueful comments in *NED* prefaces on the difficulties which are consequential to such treatment, and especially on the fact that – conceived as a primarily semantic unit – a word like *get* or *of* or *any* is vastly more difficult to edit than a word like *disposition*. But we also find, notably in his lively reports in the Society's *Transactions*, Dr Murray complaining of the collection difficulties and of his poor files for the closed category words: 'no more important help', he says in 1882, 'could now be rendered to the Dictionary than by the collection of modern instances of all uses and constructions of these little words' (*TPS 1882–4*, 7). So much had these tended to be overlooked and ignored by those engaged in reading and making out quotations for the Dictionary that he had often been forced to abandon the principle of basing the Dictionary upon recorded usage and instead 'to concoct sentences and phrases as illustrations' of them (*ibid.* 6), and he is clearly alive to the serious disadvantages of such a procedure. Two years later, we find him praising one of the helpers, Charles Gray, who had provided detailed information on 'the ordinary language of Addison and his colleagues', supplying many thousands of quotations 'for ordinary words, the constructions of verbs and prepositions, use of adverbs and conjunctions' which give a picture of literary usage in the eighteenth century but one which unfortunately had no analogue for earlier or later periods (*ibid.* 517).

This awareness on the part of Murray and later editors of the *NED* that the closed category words posed special problems should not tempt

---

[1] It was partly in this connexion that Sweet said 'Our . . . dictionaries err in trying to satisfy too many requirements at once' (*TPS 1882–4*, 586).

us (as do sometimes our intellectual inclinations) to the extreme of claiming an absolute distinction between lexicon and grammar which would endorse our drawing up a list of words or word-classes which have no place at all in a dictionary. Such distinctions as between 'lexical items' and 'function words', full words and empty words, open and closed categories, are convenient fictions of which we must all make good use for our several purposes, but they are ultimately relative. Some of the most fertile thinking by linguists in recent years has been on the interpenetration of lexicon and grammar, and on the extent to which phrasal construction and interpretation alike depend upon an indissociable complex of semantic analogy and grammatical analogy. This is something to which I wish to return but it may be said here that this line of thinking demands what Sweet seems to have had in mind in talking of the need for 'a sort of lexicographical syntax'; he mentions such examples as *get* which along with other forms that enter into phrasal verb complexes so troubled the *NED* editors, and he stresses the difficulty of drawing the line between lexicon and grammar, insisting on the need to treat many words both lexicographically and grammatically (*TPS 1882-4*, 585). The *NED* principle of taking a copious body of actually recorded usage as the starting point for treating these words too is not therefore in question.

2

Yet this is the first point at which the major descriptions of English grammar let us down and fail to give us that authority in grammar analogous to the *NED*'s authority in lexical matters which Mr R. A. Close of the British Council suggested as a desideratum in an article in *The Times* a good many years ago.[2] Our best handbooks have rather, Mr Close said, given us well-illustrated accounts of an English grammar which to a greater or less degree is hypothetical. By this he meant, as I take it, the disposition of even the best grammars (such as Kruisinga's or Jespersen's) to start from – remembering Dr Murray's expression – 'concocted' examples which suggest that the grammarian is describing primarily what is grammatologically received and what he expects to find. From such basic illustrations, the grammarian then radiates out to

[2] 'English in the Far East', From a Correspondent in China. 3 February 1937, 15–16. Already in 1935, indeed, after discussing the aims and achievement of the *NED*, J. R. Firth had suggested that the Philological Society 'might promote research into Present-day English by inaugurating a Dictionary of Spoken Usage and Idiom' (*TPS 1935*, 72).

deal with what he takes to be minor or variant constructions, either again via concocted examples, or sporadically via actual recorded instances, which again have only the status of *illustrations*. Here is a fundamental inadequacy of method which (as we saw a moment ago) Murray regarded as merely an unsatisfactory makeshift when applied to lexicographical purposes: to regard material only as 'illustrations' of distinctions and structures which have been made aprioristically or through the agency of accumulated grammatological tradition – or even intuitively, instead of causing the distinctions to emerge from the configurations which a body of natural material reveals.

An allied inadequacy is seen here in the mention of *sporadic* use of recorded material. All the major grammarians, who in the past half-century or so have given us our completest grammars, have from time to time, and some more than others, based statements squarely upon an examination of recorded material: but such instances are highlights in their work, not a basic principle, and the points at which such welcome moves have been made have been sporadic and eclectic, sometimes reflecting a given grammarian's special field of interest, sometimes merely caused by the urge to grapple with an oddity, an outstanding feature which has caught the grammarian's eye in reading. As E. A. Nida has said, the method of using source material 'has not been to note everything systematically but only to note those particular features which have struck the attention of the investigator. Accordingly exceptional patterns have been carefully analysed, but the great framework of patterns into which they fit has been neglected, and the result is a conglomerate picture'.[3] We are reminded again of Murray's difficulties in collecting data on the 'ordinary use of the little words' and in particular of his remark in 1884 that all the books which had been read for the Dictionary ought to be read over again, with instructions to the readers to make slips 'for all words that do *not* strike you as rare, peculiar, or peculiarly used' (*TPS 1882–4*, 516). Whether because of the almost preposterous magnitude of the task, or the reflection that many of its most obvious and immediate revelations would be excessively trivial ('*and* appears between adjectives *x* thousand times in the prose of Sir Thomas Browne'), the idea was not pursued. In syntactical description, a clearer knowledge of the actual and the normal remains a frequently mentioned desideratum.

Our grammars may be indicted on further counts, of course. It has

---

[3] *A Synopsis of English Syntax* (mimeo., Afghan Institute of Technology, South Pasadena, Calif., 1951), 13.

not been usual to attempt any rigorous separation of strata, either dia-chronically or synchronically. The 'illustrations' are culled from H. G. Wells and W. B. Yeats, *Punch* and *The Times*, Hardy and Quiller-Couch, with only sporadic labels indicating degrees of restriction to such strata as 'poetic', 'literary', and 'colloquial'. Moreover, it has to be remem-bered that even for so-called 'colloquial' English, the material used as authority or illustration usually comes from written sources,[4] and it is often taken for granted that pieces of writing between quotation marks in a novel *are* 'spoken English'. The comparable disinclination of some grammarians to distinguish historical strata purposefully (as when Shakespeare, Swift, Thackeray, and G. B. Shaw rub shoulders even in a book called *Our Living Language*)[5] often accompanies or is conditioned by a historical bias in explanation and classification which has long since been discredited. Some eighty years ago, after quoting Storm's criticism of standard grammars which confuse 'Tudor English, eighteenth- and nineteenth-century English in one chaotic mass', Sweet goes on to criticize historical explanation as a principle: 'What can historical philology contribute to the analysis of *will love, shall love, is loving*, etc. ...? The constant application of historical and compara-tive illustrations is often positively injurious from the disturbing influence it has on the purity and definiteness of the groups of associa-tions gained by the practical study' (*TPS 1882-4*, 578). We may note in passing, with reference to what has already been said, the almost pejorative connotations that Sweet here gives to 'illustrations'.

3

But, one may reasonably ask, if none of the existing complete grammars meets the rather exacting demands required of a source book for prac-tical manuals, cannot such a source book be now assembled by collating the results of theses, scholarly monographs, and articles which have accumulated over three generations and which have often incorporated the requisite standards of procedure? It would appear that little can be satisfactorily done on these lines.

Many recent studies, it is true, are purely descriptive and are based on usage, but not only are they inevitably fractional as regards strata examined and constructions analysed, but they are for the most part

---

[4] In 1935, Professor Firth noted that the study of conversational English had not yet begun (*TPS 1935*, 71); even today, the study is too little advanced.

[5] J. H. G. Grattan and P. Gurrey: first published, London, 1925.

mutually incommensurable: one cannot add together two studies in the use of phrasal verbs if 'phrasal verb' is differently delimited in the two works, or if the material for one is non-fictional prose before 1930 in the United States and the material for the other is prose fiction and drama written in Great Britain since 1950. Moreover, if – as usually – we have only the results and some examples from the material presented in such studies, there are other difficulties: not only must we accept the investigator's results without being able to check them (no great problem perhaps where we know his standards of accuracy), but, more seriously, we may be faced by the need to incorporate data on (say) the *'s* genitive which has been based on one body of material with otherwise adequately matching data on the *of*-phrase which has been based on quite different material. An example of several of these difficulties can be found in J. Ellinger's article, 'Substantivsätze mit oder ohne *that* in der neueren englischen Literatur' (*Anglia* 57 (1933), 78 ff.), the material for which is necessarily pre-1933 and in fact ranges over 200 years without any distinction, and the results of which depend upon the consideration of a single variable factor (the governing verb or phrase). Before Ellinger's data could be used at all, therefore, even as a check or source of useful comparison, his material – if still in existence – would have to be reanalysed in order to relate the selection of form to the total network of contextual variables. It is true, however, that these difficulties do not prevent our using modern descriptive studies in all cases: whatever other problems confront us with Fries's *The Structure of English* (not least the restricted contexts of situation), we are here in touch with a still accessible corpus of material and his examples are made verifiable by means of reference keys to this large and valuable body of material.

Many of the recent studies that have been helpful have been those suggesting structural analyses of various aspects of English grammar, and these have not been remarkable for the extent to which the proposed analyses are grounded upon the actual manifestations in usage. One might even say that they are as characteristically eclectic in their resort to usage as were the earlier grammarians. A single example must suffice. C. F. Hockett, who analyses *outside* as two words,[6] explicitly bases this on an actual speech event, a chance observation in which his previously erected criteria were satisfied. That such reaction to nonce-usage must lead us to abandon all idea of free and bound does not seem to have occurred to him; we have all heard some wag adding *-ly* to another speaker's 'Drive slow', or saying *un-* in response to such an inquiry as

---

[6] *A Course in Modern Linguistics* (New York, 1958), 167.

'Did you say friendly or unfriendly?' There is nothing so sacred about usage as such that we have to take the sporadic and – again let us note – the odd and memorable as the basis for a rule or definition. Many structuralist studies, however, make even less contact with actual usage. There has been until about a decade ago a passion for the artificially contrived minimal pair (*nitrate* and *night rate*, *not a tall man* and *not at all, man*), with microscopic examination for 'substantial' difference in isolation, as the phrases wriggle out their death agonies in a sound spectrograph or on spliced tape, regardless of how or whether they are distinguished in their natural environment in the stream of speech. More generally, linguists have taken a very small number of elementary invented examples to illustrate structural theory: Bloomfield's 'Poor John ran away', Bloch's 'John stumbled' and more recently Chomsky's 'The man hit the boy', which (as T. F. Mitchell told the Philological Society recently) 'still looks remarkably like a traditional subject-predicate proposition and only somewhat less likely than Sapir's "The farmer killed the duckling"'.[7]

To proceed from such concocted examples to permutations of them does not increase one's confidence that one is dealing with natural language, and one welcomes the recent emphasis in the transformational theory of Chomsky and others upon the distinction between the rules in their schematically most perfect form and the restrictions upon the realization of these rules in usage. As well as (if not indeed rather than) the bare rules for transforming *The man hit the boy* into *The boy was hit by the man*, we need to know about the analogous constructions for which the transformation does not obtain or is only restrictively permitted, and – if so – what the restrictions are. We need to know the environments in which either an active or a passive is more natural and what prompts us to select the one rather than the other. On the title page of his *Accidence and Syntax*, Kruisinga aptly quotes Aldous Huxley: 'Our most refined theories, our most elaborate descriptions are but crude and barbarous simplifications of a reality that is, in every smallest sample, infinitely complex.' It is that complexity of the reality that merits our attention. There is of course already complexity enough when Harris tells us that 'for any sentence like *Casals plays the cello*, we can find a sentence *The cello is played by Casals*', adding – rather less controversially – that 'we do not find *Casals is played by the cello*' (*Lg.* 28.19). But the lexical incompatibility of this last example or of *Matthews is played by football* is of less consequence, one might argue, than

[7] *TPS 1958*, 101; see also J. R. Firth, *TPS 1935*, 60–1.

the syntactical incompatibility (on which Harris is silent) of *The cello is played by Casals* with an important range of utterances in which *Casals plays the cello* is perfectly acceptable. At the least, one may feel, it would be worth stating 'we will not find' the sentence *Football is played by Matthews for Blackpool*. One further example may be cited: Harris's rather elaborate demonstration that modifier plus noun can be made into the predication 'noun is modifier', offering the pseudo-algebraic formula '*MN* is equivalent to *N* is *M*' (*Lg.* 28.20). The degree of generalization here, given meretriciously scientific precision, not only fails to distinguish pairs like *the criminal acts of Russia* and *the criminal courts of Russia*, but even obscures the lack of '*N* is *M*' transformational parity between simple *MN* pairs like *little room* and *refreshment room*. My point is that for all these very real problems and complexities, which are obscured or ignored in such work, descriptive statements are possible, though they are not easily made by introspection and invented examples; indeed, it is unscientific to attempt them by these means when they may be based upon the examination of publicly accessible raw material.

4

A collation of recent work, then, can hardly constitute the material basis that is required for new grammars: the fresh data provided in descriptive studies are not for the most part collatable, while the structuralist studies have tended to re-describe – albeit often in revolutionary and fertile ways – a handful of stereotyped examples such as have been handed down in elementary handbooks. If I have dwelt longer and more critically on the latter, it is because many of us have felt that there are dangers in basing imposingly symmetrical structural analyses upon imperfect, incomplete traditional accounts of English grammar or upon imperfect, incomplete impressions of English grammar, derived from introspection. This has nothing to do with the issue between the 'God's truth' and 'hocus-pocus' protagonists: even if one begins by believing that there is inherent or immanent structure, one ought not to begin by assuming *the* structures and their constituent elements, *the* systems and their constituent terms; these are end-products, whether one regards them as revealed or imposed by the linguist. One obvious danger is that any tendency to aprioristic structuring may obscure the functioning of language in failing to account for actual facts. Another is that, in making free use of the word 'descriptive' together with numerous references to the use of native informants (often apparently a purely theoretical and almost certainly unworkable use), they give the impression of a closer relationship to natural usage than their materials warrant.

Dwight Bolinger has had occasion to criticize some recent work for 'a certain proneness to skimp the specimen-gathering phase of our science and to base generalizations on insufficient data' (*Lg.* 37.366). C. E. Bazell has stressed that it is 'important to distinguish between the tasks of descriptive grammar and those of structural linguistics', and that 'the task of descriptive grammar is not that of describing a language-structure; it is quite simply that of describing a language'.[8] McQuown similarly has insisted that one should not 'prematurely synthesize inadequate materials. On the contrary, it is essential . . . to accommodate all the data . . . and to expand the size of the corpus indefinitely as the progress of the investigation requires. Admittedly there are practical difficulties in such a course, but if the linguist is to do his job these must be overcome' (*Lg.* 28.500).

One of the most obvious 'practical difficulties' in the way of assembling and analysing an adequate corpus of data is money. I am happy to say that the need to *assemble* as McQuown recommends and to *describe* as Bazell recommends has been recognized by some organizations which have generously made money available to launch a Survey of Educated English Usage.[9]

Some of the Survey's aims are implicit in what has been said in the foregoing discussion of where our needs remain unfulfilled in our progress over the years towards writing a grammar of English. The basis must be copious materials, made up of continuous stretches or 'texts' taken from the full range of co-existing varieties and strata of educated English, spoken as well as written, at the present time. For each stretch of material, account must be taken of *all* the grammatical data, distinguishing between the normal and the variant forms of each constructional type, and observing which constructions occur with which other constructions. Through the plotting of variables, full information will be sought on the factors which tend to prompt or which even demand a given variant.[10] Each text, moreover, must be seen in relation to its situational matrix which can therefore – along with other contextual

---

[8] *Linguistic Form* (Istanbul, 1953), 103.

[9] I gratefully acknowledge initial financial support from Naturmetodens Sproginstitut of Denmark, the Delegates of the Clarendon Press, and Messrs Longmans, Green.

[10] Cf. B. Ulvestad, 'An Approach to Describing Usage of Language Variants', Memoir 12 of *IJAL* (1956), 37–59, and my own study of relative pronoun selection (Paper 9 below).

variables, linguistic and otherwise – be called to account, where necessary, for whatever restrictions upon constructions appear to emerge. The data assembled from the examination of this 'primary material', organized as a Descriptive Register, will provide adequate information for precise, objective, and comprehensive statements to be made describing the *majority* of English constructions, and the conditions under which they and their variants occur naturally. Upon this Descriptive Register it will be possible to base authoritative and objective teaching-grammars and other handbooks, which must otherwise obviously vary according to their specific purpose.

5

Some discussion is necessary upon salient points that have been raised in the foregoing outline. The Survey is concerned with 'educated' English: that is, no account is taken of dialect or sub-standard usage. But it is necessarily acknowledged that these terms are relative and that the varieties of English so labelled are by no means entirely contained within hard and fast boundaries. It is an important feature of a language's 'style reservoir' that there should be a periphery of relatively dubious usage which the timid avoid, the defiant embrace, and the provocative exploit; we may compare our mild fun with 'he didn't ought to have ate it' or 'who-done-it'. The plotting and evaluation of this periphery are conceived as among the Survey's functions, and informant-reaction tests will be used to reinforce or clarify results from the basic material. For identifying the central core of educated usage, it is probably futile to erect rigid criteria; one cannot claim that a particular kind of degree of formal education is necessary to produce an educated speaker, nor even that all who have attained the highest degree of formal education necessarily speak educated English. On the other hand, it would seem true that a majority of people who have had a high degree of formal education and who are engaged in the professions are capable of (and perhaps prone to) assessing English that they hear or read as acceptable and educated or not, and that they would reach a large measure of agreement on these assessments. A working definition like 'Educated English is English that is recognized as such by educated native English speakers' is not as valueless as its circularity would suggest; it can be made the basis of reaction tests and in any case draws frank attention to the social basis on which such concepts as 'standard language' uneasily rest. One may also perhaps defend being cavalier on the delimitation of 'educated' for the following reason. If the expressions of a certain speaker or writer or writer's fictional character are *mistakenly* counted as educated at the stage of collecting material, any such expressions will show up as minority forms and will be duly recognized as uneducated at the analysis stage when these particular minority forms are investigated and explained in terms of their conditioning factors.

Three fundamental principles of the Survey's method in compiling a Descriptive Register may be summarized as follows:

1. The primary material will be *all* the grammatical data in selected continuous stretches of actual recorded (spoken and written) English. As already noted, for previous grammars (and for some modern structural studies), examples have often been assembled eclectically, a slip being made out by the grammarian when he came across an expression which happened to illustrate a required point or even which simply struck him as unusual. The Survey aims at viewing each grammatical feature, be it commonplace or rare, in the light of a statistical norm and at explaining the circumstances under which users of the language depart from that norm.

2. The Survey attempts to embrace the whole range of educated English usage, from learned and technical writing to the most spontaneous colloquial English. Special attention will be paid to the usage of natural speech (that is, unprepared talk, with no written original) in its chief educated varieties, ranging from learned discussion to informal conversation between friends, and these varieties will be distinguished from and closely compared with 'literary speech', that is, fictional dialogue which has a written origin.

3. The Survey is concerned only with present-day English, and will seek to avoid the eclecticism of many existing descriptions which present examples from Swift and Shaw side by side. For our purposes, 'present-day' will be taken to mean 'since 1950', a working rule made in the full realization that no arbitrary time-limitation will ensure absolute homogeneity and that even on the same day an educated man of sixty-five and an educated woman of twenty-five may differ in their usage; it is hoped that the chief linguistic variations occasioned by such factors as these, too, will be revealed at the stage of explanatory analysis.

The specimens of continuous English will be selected to represent as fairly as possible and as copiously as practicable the co-existing varieties of educated English. A single continuous stretch or 'text' will normally amount to about 5000 words, and it is envisaged collecting on slips something over 200 texts for British English alone. The texts will be taken, in what seems suitable proportions, from unscripted speech; novels; plays; poetry; criticism and other non-fictional prose; psychology and social sciences; philosophy; physics and other physical sciences; biological sciences; law; politics; religion; useful arts (such as cookery); newspapers; etc.

The slips thus enshrining the grammar of over a million running words will constitute the 'primary material', whose function will be to provide sufficient data on high-frequency features and most constructional norms. It is obvious, however, that low-frequency constructions and some variants of high-frequency ones will not be susceptible to adequate treatment on the basis of the primary material. That is to say, while interpenetrating sampling[11] can show with fair certainty when we have reached saturation point on one given construction, it can equally show that we have not reached this point on others. For these, it will be necessary to make supplementary searches, again taking account only of continual stretches of material but being able to survey a large amount of material relatively speedily since one would no longer be concerned with total grammatical description. Use will also be made of tests for informant-reaction and of techniques for eliciting the required features.

6

I have said elsewhere that to base description solely upon substitution techniques and similar work with informants is to investigate (and uncertainly at that) what is barely *possible* rather than what is *actual and normal* in linguistic behaviour.[12] It should be emphasized that the basic principle of the Survey is that radically different and more serviceable – though not necessarily or even probably neater – rules can be formulated from the patterns that may be seen emerging from a corpus of natural material, in which at the same time the co-occurrent factors may be observed and from which statements may be made not merely listing but *ranking* the factors conditioning variants of these patterns. The extent to which, as J. R. Firth put it, 'words are mutually expectant and mutually prehended',[13] I would see as of prime relevance to the

[11] Cf. F. Yates, *Sampling Methods for Censuses and Surveys* (London, 1953), 45 f.
[12] See Paper 15 below.
[13] *Studies in Linguistic Analysis* (Special Volume of the Philological Society, Oxford, 1957), 12.

6

Survey, and it would seem beneficial to one's procedure of description to bear in mind the Hjelmslevian register of dependences. A word or word-group might thus be seen as related to other words or word-groups by interdependence, determination, or constellation, or in terms of subclassifications of this triad which readily suggest themselves as a mode of handling anaphoric and other contextually dependent expressions, including elliptical and abbreviative ones.

Such a procedure seems to encourage an outward, radiatory direction of description, beginning – where relevant – from the word, and this seems to me well suited both to the analysis of English and specifically to the aims of the Survey. That is to say, we argue that the sentence is less satisfactorily definable as a unit than is the word, more particularly so in English where the word may be said to be fully institutionalized, and that it is in fact difficult to set up phonological or other criteria for the spoken sentence which will isolate any very useful or stable unit,[14] or which will enable different investigators to segment alike the same material, or which can even be applied consistently by a single investigator. Moreover, just as the word has relations in a specific context, so has a sentence – however defined – in its own context: its form and meaning are or may be importantly determined by outward reference in an ever-widening orbit. By the upward procedure from the word one may proceed as far as one likes to plot the chain of determinants, and this is congruent with the Survey's aim to widen the inquiry from syntax to style. The downward procedure, on this view, starts in some degree at an arbitrary point, turning its back on some features of relevance. This is clearly recognized by M. A. K. Halliday who speaks of 'the possibility, and even necessity, of making contextual statements about some larger unit' than the Chinese sentence. 'Such a unit might show a distribution of sentence classes, in which case it would be discussed in the grammar; alternatively a contextual unit might be shown to display a structure such that some sentences could be said to be contextually bound.'[15] So too W. Nelson Francis notes that the 'use of certain linguistic devices in the sequence-sentence recalls certain elements in the sentence which it follows', thus establishing 'retrospective links with it, both lexical and structural'.[16] Nor is it only a matter of

---

[14] Cf. *Studies in Communication* (London, 1955), 172–4.

[15] *TPS 1956*, 182, 184; we may note his remarks also on 'context of mention' and 'context of reference', *Studies in Linguistic Analysis* (Oxford, 1957), 61.

[16] *The Structure of American English* (New York, 1958), 410; cf. the discussion in R. Quirk and A. H. Smith, *The Teaching of English* (London, 1959), 27–30.

formally marked internal links; one may again mention Harris's example *Casals plays the cello*, which will not bear his transformational statements when placed in certain networks of contextual determinants. Moreover, while R. H. Robins adopts the procedure of describing downward from the sentence, he takes the view that the word in Sundanese 'is of more fundamental importance to the grammatical analysis of the language' than the phrase, clause, or sentence (his higher-level units), 'and has been assumed in making some of the earlier statements' about these (*TPS 1953*, 123). Elsewhere, Robins has defended the word as the unit in grammatical analysis in which 'phonological and grammatical exponents are maximally congruent'.[17]

Taking the word as our starting point, as exponent of a grammatical category and in its tension of dependences, puts us in a position to follow Sweet in his wariness, already mentioned, of erecting *a priori* barriers between the material of lexicography and the material of grammar and in his recommendation to provide for what he called 'a sort of lexicographical syntax'. Sweet draws the broad distinction between 'general' utterances, which are resolvable into frames permitting free production of new utterances having identical structure, and 'special' utterances (like *how do you do*) whose structure is non-productive (*TPS 1882–4*, 586). But we need at least one intermediary class of *restricted* utterances where substitutions of certain kinds and within certain ranges are permitted, but with statable (though not yet stated) limitations. It was frames of this sort that I had in mind earlier (p. 72) when I spoke of an 'indissociable complex of semantic analogy and grammatical analogy', and in any register of dependences these two sides must not be ignored. In the utterance 'He's an odd sort of man', there is decidedly more restriction upon occupation of the place filled by *sort* than there is upon the place of *odd*, and more upon the place of *odd* than there is upon the place of *man*. Moreover, semantic analogy as well as grammatical analogy will affect the replacement of *sort* and *odd*: the replacements will not merely be like *sort* and *odd* in being nouns and adjectives respectively, but will tend to be semantically like *sort* and *odd* as well – *type* and *queer*, for instance. The effectiveness of

---

[17] *Proceedings of the Eighth International Congress of Linguists* (Oslo, 1958), 380; still more recently: 'As a grammatical element the word is unique in its relative fixity of internal morphemic structure, its focal status in relation to syntactically relevant categories, and ... the stability of its paradigms' (*TPS 1959*, 137). To insist on the centrality of the word is by no means, however, to exclude 'downward' analysis altogether; in practice, it is convenient to have both directions of analytic procedure available.

a Dylan Thomas phrase like *all the sun long* derives its impact from forcing us to view *sun* as a unit of time because it is put into a restricted phrase in the position where lexico-grammatical analogy demands not merely a noun but a noun like *day, night, week.*

7

To adopt such a line of thinking is, of course, merely to follow the main stream of linguistics from Sweet and de Saussure to Mukařovsky, Vachek, Hjelmslev, Firth, and Pike, in attempting to make linguistic statements which take account of both form and meaning. Indeed, there are signs that even those American groups who have followed a different course in the name of Bloomfield are now realizing that only relatively coarse-meshed statements can be made if the consideration of meaning is rigorously excluded. Harris has shown recently that he wishes to take account of what he calls 'information content' (*Lg.* 33.290), and W. Nelson Francis, while carefully working within the constraints of mechanistic structuralism, admits at times to some misgiving, observing that there are some utterances which 'are distinguished by rather subtle formal indications, aided by lexical probability' (*op. cit.* 350). There is, as A. E. Sharp judiciously pointed out in Oslo, 'more near-ambiguity in language than it is always convenient to admit',[18] and we must acknowledge that a hunt for substantial differences· at such points (for example, distinctions of pitch, stress, or juncture) may be unrewarding or even misleading, if supposed or occasional 'subtle formal indications' (to quote the cautious words of Francis again) prevent us from observing that in the natural speech situation meaning in fact provides the clue.[19]

Many of us in recent years have found it useful in providing an insight into basic linguistic structures to filter off lexical meaning and to see how grammar functions without it. I first came across the technique in Carnap's *Logical Syntax of Language* (London, 1937, 2), but his example *Piroten karulisieren elatisch* is by no means the first instance of its use.[20] But the value of nonsense forms is rather strictly limited to the very simplest structures. That is, while accepting that *the blim ate the blom* is intelligible while *the blim the blom ate* is not, we are superficial

[18] *Proc. VIII Intern. Cong.*, 584.

[19] This point is touched upon in my review of Francis's book, *Archivum Linguisticum* 11 (1959), esp. 157–8.

[20] It was effectively used, for example, by A. Ingraham in *Swain School Lectures* in 1903; see *Psyche* 18.123.

if we go on to claim that *the blim the blom ate* is thereby demonstrated
to be un-English. SOV and OSV are comprehendingly accepted not
only from our poets but also from prose writers making even the slightest gesture towards the elevated: 'The women many soldiers fell to
raping, while others their very children pitilessly abducted'. 'God our
foes shall vanquish' or 'Our enemies God shall vanquish'. It is surely
worth investigating the extent to which in linguistic usage our reliance
shifts between grammatical and semantic signals: there is some evidence
that they are in complementary balance, semantic information having to
be present in greater concentration when grammatical information is
reduced. Thus our poetic tradition has conditioned a ready acceptance
of SOV, while instances of OSV seem often by contrast to require the
support of lexical probability and grammatical patterning in the neighbouring clauses. We may instance the following lines from Dylan
Thomas's poem, *When Like a Running Grave*:

> All, men my madmen the unwholesome wind
> With whistler's cough contages, time on track
> Shapes in a cinder death

or – a somewhat simpler example – the following from Pope's *Iliad*,
near the end of Book XIV:

> The Lance yet sticking through the bleeding eye,
> The victor seized; and, as aloft he shook
> The gory visage, thus insulting spoke.

Here, militating against the fact that 'the lance the victor seized'
would be a verse commonplace as SOV, plus the fact that in verse a
lance *could* be said to seize someone, we have the more powerful factors
of animate being more usually S than inanimate, plus the semantic hint
in *victor*, plus the congruence with the grammatical pattern of the subsequent clauses in which *victor*, through the substitute form 'he', is
undoubtedly S. Yet, where semantic probability is only slightly less
strong, the balance may well be seriously disturbed. In a recent Durham
examination, twenty candidates discussed the doggerel lines:

> In a trice the wretched man
> The closing gates squeezed flat.

Two accepted the OSV word-order as perfectly clear, but the remainder
found the order initially baffling or misleading (three in fact were so
misled as to suppose that the man was squeezing the gates), and there
were numerous comments to the effect that common sense pointed

disturbingly in the opposite direction to grammar; the grammar, said one, is no help and one has to rely on the probable sense; only the meaning of the verb, said another, gives the clue as to which of the two possible nouns is the subject. Clearly, there is room for some research into the ranking of factors which affect interpretation, and the notion of dependences may be useful here too.[21]

The discussion of this last point brings in a further aspect of the Survey to which only a slight allusion has so far been made (p. 79) and on which I should like to say a word before closing: the investigation of educated public opinion on linguistic matters. While it would seem obvious that natural usage provides by far the most valuable and important material for descriptive statements, I think one should aim at seeing educated usage as far as possible against the background of educated *reaction* to usage, a matter which is especially relevant perhaps for stylistic statements but by no means negligible for others. A distinction may further be made between 'believed usage' and 'preceptive usage'. What a person actually says may be different from what he believes he says, and this in turn may be different from what he thinks he ought to say. It seems likely that it is discrepancies between believed usage and actual usage which promote some of the sharp differences that have been observed between natural colloquial and the literary representations of colloquial speech in novels and plays. On the other hand, it is equally likely that preceptive usage influences us when we wish to speak or write formally. In recent years, much has been written about attitudes to 'correctness', but it is one thing to regard the prescriptively minded as pathologically inhibited and quite another to dismiss them as an uninfluential lunatic fringe living retired in Hove, Sussex, or Newport, Rhode Island. One must fully recognize how widespread and deeply entrenched among the educated – including language students and scholars – are concepts of right and wrong, good and bad, at all strata of linguistic usage. It is time we grew out of such naïvely anarchic views as those expressed by E. A. Nida (*op. cit.* 12) when he takes Sweet to task (*New English Grammar*, §2152) for calling 'ungrammatical' the sentence 'The captain with three of his men were taken prisoner'. There must be some investigation of what beliefs and precepts obtain;

---

[21] One thinks, for instance, of temporal adverbs functioning as both congruent with and supplementary to tense-inflexion; cf. also Firth's remark that 'Aspectival auxiliaries and particles necessarily lead to colligation with relevant adverbials and particles suitably grouped and classified', and his noting the co-operation of forms in aspectual expression in sequences like 'might have kept on popping in and out all afternoon' (*Studies in Linguistic Analysis* 18–19).

they cannot be sneered or shrugged away as the inheritance of prescriptivism, as though this were to demonstrate that they lack significance or influence. They are features of our linguistic morality, as deeply and as complicatedly entrenched as our licensing laws. Some experience has been gained over the past decade or so in investigating this morality and its impact, but much remains to be done, and it would seem fruitful to attempt this work in conjunction with the usage survey. When for example, a feature is found to be relatively restricted to certain styles or strata of actual usage, it may suggest a direct relation to precept reaction, and this can be put to the test with controlled groups. Some tentative experiments have been made on these lines, but methods of tackling this whole shadowy and prejudice-ridden area of belief and precept are still at a very primitive stage.

Eight

Research problems and the teaching of English†

[For all its informal tone and generality of content, it has been thought worthwhile to include the following contribution to a conference, since the conference itself was something of a historic occasion for the relation of linguistics and English language teaching in Britain and the Commonwealth. It was held in London in December 1960 under the auspices of the British Council but at the instance of the Committee of Vice-Chancellors and Principals of British universities in order to explore the needs in the field of teaching English as a second language. Many important developments both in teaching and in research have stemmed from the conference's recommendations.]

This conference has been convened in response to an urgent and immediate need for extended teaching of English and, in consequence, for extended teacher training. But urgent and immediate though the needs may be, the situation at all points is seen to demand extended *research* as a fundamental condition of our success in ultimately fulfilling all the needs satisfactorily. Each session of this conference has dealt with topics on which a vast amount of research is necessary, so much so that in a session which is devoted solely to research problems, the greatest problem is to know where to begin. The subject, for example, of our first session – the nature of the demand for English in the world today – itself resounds with problems which only research can answer. Research and exchange of information are needed on what English is actually used for in the world, and by whom and how it is used, what the standards are, and how they differ. J. R. Firth has rightly insisted that it is time to stop arguing about the merits of British or American or Ghanaian English and to start studying them. We must

† Reprinted from *English Teaching Abroad and the British Universities*, ed. H. G. Wayment (London 1961), 51 ff.

learn more about the nature and the variety of the demand for English and let our research face the implications of distinguishing an English-speaking world from an English-listening world, and an English-writing world from an English-reading world. We shall then be in a better position to apply the valuable concept of 'restricted language' in fulfilling the relevant needs. For restricted languages are not ready-made commodities waiting to be supplied to pupils; they have to be constructed in the light of two complementary factors: the nature of the demand for a restricted language on the one hand, and on the other hand the requisite isolatable features in the reservoir of what one might call total English. Such features having been isolated by linguistic research have to be systematized by linguistic science. Furthermore, we should not forget that the ultimate fulfilment of the demand requires research into the methods of teaching the various kinds of English to the various kinds of pupil.

Another of our sessions tackled the subject of English language and English literature. Obviously there, too, we have a relationship in pedagogy which is another urgent problem. Selection of the relevant literature to teach presumably involves enquiring not only into *English* literature but into the literature of our students' own cultures. We need to know the part that the literature in a given foreign language plays in the lives of that language's speakers before we can intelligently ask what kind of English literature can readily be appreciated in the cultural and social milieu of such students. We might also investigate how much and what kind of British and American literature is necessary to give foreign students the requisite grasp of our language's scope. Indeed, we must ask how one should teach literature and how one should edit a text for presentation to various age levels and cultural backgrounds.

But the session which raised most problems in the fields with which I am personally most concerned was that on contemporary English language and general linguistics. With this topic we reach the fundamentals, the very mechanics of our language, the features that have to be taught as a basic essential; and if we are to have the better teaching that is demanded on all sides, the better gradings of material that have been discussed by William Haas, the better structuring of the linguistic phenomena, then we must have vastly more research on the operation of our language itself, its natural operation by native speakers and writers, and its natural reception by native listeners and readers. Let me quote some recent words of Professor H. A. Gleason[1] on the need for

---

[1] *Lg.* 36 (1960), 250.

assembling data on the actual occurrence of English forms and on how we use them. He says: 'We have recently passed out of the *elevator-operator* period into a new era of *Flying planes can be dangerous.* And through it all, many of us seem steadfastly to resist looking at the language in its richness and variety as it is actually used.' One should, perhaps, forbear to point out that Gleason's idea of the new era seems as preoccupied as the old with minimal distinctiveness, and perhaps equally resistant in fact to what he calls 'looking at the language in its richness and variety as it is actually used'. But it is his demand for scrutiny of actual usage that I am concerned with. He goes on: 'This is the kind of groundwork which is needed in much greater volume if we are to make real progress in the analysis of English. We have reached a point where the needed constant checking and rechecking against text has become incredibly laborious, and the temptation is strong to rely on the easier route of introspective elicitation. But without check against text, English grammatical analysis may rapidly degenerate into a rather empiric-looking type of pure speculation.'

One would think that here was something of which one could say with Lear, 'Oh, reason not the need', but it has had to be reasoned repeatedly. Professor Firth called for the collection of data on English usage in 1935, and in 1937 Mr R. A. Close of the British Council did so again, in an article in *The Times* almost anticipating Gleason's very words in an indictment of existing textbooks as giving 'a meticulous plan of the *hypothetical* structure of the English language'.[2] I have referred to Gleason because he is one of the most prominent and currently influential of the American scientific linguists, and what he writes is an indication that there is a change of direction in their thinking. It is a criticism of the main theoretical work since Bloomfield:Bloch, Trager, Smith, Hockett, Harris, even Pike, even his own *Introduction to Descriptive Linguistics.* It comes at a time when, as an American correspondent put it to me in a letter last week, we are witnessing 'the breaking-up of the old orthodoxy'; at a time too, when there are signs of a new orthodoxy taking hold on the imagination of American linguists – that of Chomsky, Lees, and the transformation theorists, whose influence may well (in the opinion of many on both sides of the Atlantic) be to draw linguistics away from the description of 'raw data' towards the description of languages in some kind of ideal state.

I quote Gleason also, of course, because his words echo what it has

---

[2] *The Times*, 3 February, 1937.

been my lot to preach *ad nauseam* over the past five years, and because the Survey of English Usage which is now in progress at University College London is a full-scale attempt to supply the information on English that is needed for writing completer and more objective grammars.

The problem briefly, as we see it, is that previous descriptions such as Jespersen's let us down because they are eclectic (using material mainly only as illustration and often describing an oddity or a rare construction with more detail and precision than a more normal and important feature); because they observe no regular separation of strata either diachronically or synchronically (that is to say, *Punch* and *The Times* are allowed to rub shoulders not only with each other but with Shakespeare and W. B. Yeats); and because fictional dialogue is often taken to be spoken English, while the real spoken English is scarcely examined at all. On the other hand, as Gleason points out, the attempts of more scientific linguists of recent years to improve the situation have too often ignored the descriptive side in favour of devising structural statements of an English which is grossly over-simplified, statements which often account for little more than simple examples either taken over from our grammatological tradition or concocted on the spot. Our own approach, which we are using in the Survey, is to find the systems and structures which can best handle the data obtaining in corpus after corpus of actual English, as it is used throughout the wide range of situations, spoken and written, in which native English speakers communicate with each other.

But descriptive research must go hand in hand with the development of theory. Professor McIntosh has reminded us in this conference, that linguistics provides the theory for organizing the real data of English; but there is no adequate theory without the 'brute facts', as he put it, and he went on to say that at the present time we are more deficient in data than we are on the theoretical side. The descriptivist needs the experimental categories of the theorist, and the theorist needs the precise data exposed by the descriptivist. One could speak ruefully and at length about the vicious circle of this research problem in relation to English intonation and modulation, where those engaged in description are gravely in need of criteria and descriptive categories in order to handle the amorphous raw material, while it is acutely difficult to formulate relevant criteria and categories without a good deal of descriptive data.

This brings me to what may well be regarded as the thorniest research problem of all: how most efficiently and speedily to accomplish all the necessary research. There are three points I should like to make.

First, it must be obvious that, while all the various areas of research can be readily segmented so that pieces of work can be dealt with by individuals and in individual centres, they are vitally interrelated and interdependent. We need to extend facilities for the exchange of information between centres and between individuals, so that all can have the readiest possible access to basic research data. I should like to see explored the possibility of establishing an active information service for this purpose. This is something that I have felt strongly about for some time and I have been very pleased with the amount of support the idea obviously has at this conference.

Secondly, we need to extend facilities for practical collaboration. I am personally most grateful for offers of help in the Survey's work that have come from several scholars in this country and in the United States. We for our part at University College London will readily put the materials that we are collecting at the disposal of any scholars who need such information in the course of their own researches, one of the purposes of the Survey being to provide a public archive.

Thirdly and finally, the accomplishment of all these researches will depend on funds being provided for the payment of assistants. However wisely we use the energies of research students themselves (including foreign diploma students who may usefully be assigned tasks like the scrutiny of common errors and trial editing of literary texts, as exercises or dissertations), the bulk of the most vital research must be done by properly trained assistants who are working full time. I should very much like to reinforce what William Haas has just said on this. The research work that many of us are doing up and down the country has been widely acknowledged as necessary. We have received encouraging murmurs of support from the Ministry of Education and other Government and public organizations; but if this work is wanted, those who want it must realize that it cannot be done on a shoestring. It must receive the proper financial backing that is readily accorded by sources like DSIR to research of national importance in the physical sciences. In reply to Professor Gordon's plea for more published research, Professor McIntosh reminded us of the many demands on our time and energy from teaching, tuition, supervision, committee work, memorandum writing, administration, and so on. He did not mention the hundreds of hours that many of us have to spend literally begging from foundations and private firms for the money to *do* our research, let alone get it published. Our work is being demanded of us in the interests, we are told, of international relations; yet virtually all of it could be financed with the money spent by the Ministry of Defence in a single hour.

Nine

Relative clauses in educated spoken English†

After some three hundred years of continuous study, it is somewhat disheartening that so little is known about the systematic functioning of English grammatical forms, and much dissatisfaction has consequently been expressed in recent years about the aims and premises of grammatical study. A good deal of the dissatisfaction arose on the grounds that grammarians traditionally aimed at prescribing good usage instead of describing it. The prolonged wrangle over this issue has given rise to a good deal of misconception and done some harm in creating to some extent a climate of benevolent agnosticism and uninterest, but nevertheless it has had the beneficial result of making most grammarians regard it as axiomatic that at any rate descriptive work is primary and that normative, prescriptive grammars must only be based upon it. The leading grammars of English in the last half-century (Jespersen's *Modern English Grammar*, for instance) have in consequence been for the most part descriptive.

Another source of dissatisfaction has been the fact that even descriptive grammarians have confined their attention, or at any rate drawn their material, largely from written English, without always realizing the implications of this limitation. There is undoubtedly excellent reason for compiling full and accurate grammars of written usage; but there is

† This piece of research upon Spoken English was made possible by a grant from the University of Durham Research Fund and by the co-operation of the British Broadcasting Corporation in making available for grammatical investigation some of their valuable materials. A preliminary report on the present study, reprinted here from *English Studies* 38 (1957), 97 ff., was read at the Third Triennial Conference of the International Association of University Professors of English held in Cambridge in August 1956, and I am grateful for the comments offered in the ensuing discussion.

comparable reason for requiring that spoken usage, as the primary form of English, be given similar attention. What has been disturbing is the often implicit assumption that in describing the phenomena of written usage one is *ipso facto* describing the language as a whole, and that in so far as spoken usage has to be recognized as differing from written usage, the features in question can be observed in the dialogue of drama and fiction or in the trivia of small-talk sporadically and impressionistically noted. One result of this has been to exaggerate the importance in speech of a few outstandingly noticeable and distinctive features, and indeed to equate Spoken English with racy, ephemeral colloquialism. It is true that a remarkable corrective to this imbalance appeared in the writings of Henry Sweet before the close of the nineteenth century, but far too few have developed what he so brilliantly began. It is only within the last few years that the need for a thorough differentiation between the description of spoken and of written usage has been fully recognized in work such as that of C. C. Fries, which begins with the gross features of actual speech and which eschews the wholly inadequate and misleading process of introspection by the grammarian into his own usage.

Yet a third source of dissatisfaction with grammatical study has been its unsystematic nature. The major grammars have aimed at being encyclopedic in their description, rather than at establishing the dominant patterns and the systematic relationship of these to forms of less frequent occurrence. Not only is material of one period often presented without regard to distinctions in the levels of usage, but it is by no means uncommon to find data from one period ranged, without clear distinction, with data from another period. Again, while several grammarians have seen the value of examining the precise occurrence of a given feature in a sizeable, unified body of material (say, a hundred running pages of Dickens), there has been little attempt at a complete statement of English grammar on such a systematic basis. An admirable demonstration of what a treatment of written material on these lines could tell us appeared in 1940 in the *American English Grammar* of C. C. Fries.

There can be little doubt that the need for a thorough analysis of the English grammatical system has not yet been fulfilled and that it becomes increasingly great. On the one hand, there is the need in schools and among laymen for an assured and accurate statement of educated usage (together with the need, expressed by more than one literary critic, for precise linguistic data); on the other hand, an at least equally pressing need springs from the new importance of English as a second language and from the challenge of large-scale translation, including mechanical translation.

The present paper is an exploratory step towards a more satisfactory treatment and, concentrating on one minor segment of English grammar, attempts to establish the system governing the selection of relative pronouns in present-day educated speech. The material on which the analysis is based consists of the tape-recorded contributions of some fifty adults to what would amount to about sixteen hours of continuous, impromptu talk (equivalent to between three and four hundred printed pages). The speakers were English men and women, educated to university standard, and mainly between the ages of 25 and 50.

Impromptu speech can take place under sharply differing conditions, and although the 1300 examples of relative clauses found in the material are here analysed as a single group, they are taken in fact from three distinct bodies of material. The first kind of speech analysed consisted of impromptu conversation surreptitiously recorded under friendly and informal conditions; my own speech, where I was a participant, was excluded from consideration. The second body of material was also impromptu, but in this case the groups of participants knew that the proceedings were being recorded and that it was the intention that a shortened and tidied version should ultimately be broadcast; there were thus possibilities of tension and departure from normal usage that were absent from the first kind. The third class of material comprised impromptu discussion on a platform in front of an audience and simultaneously broadcast. Each body of material was analysed separately to observe the extent to which the different conditions produced different grammatical phenomena, and to see whether or not there was a continued emergence of new configurations which would invalidate the size of each sample. The three revealed a striking uniformity: no one group of examples added significantly to the variety of structures present in either of the others, nor (still more importantly) did any reveal a different pattern of distribution for these structures. In short, whatever differences these different conditions evoke in speech (and some differences there certainly appear to be), they do not lie in the formation of relative clauses; the patterns here presented would seem to be distributionally complete and accurate for any body of educated spoken English of comparable size.

There follows a selection of examples from the material, matching in order of patterns, though not in completeness, [1]the statistical Table on p. 104:

WH-

nr npsnif	using the living half of your own performance – which is the audience
npsim	the office administration department – which is the department I meant – comes in very much
npsoif	that science is a special form of knowledge – which I should have said was complete rubbish
npoif	it's all based on violence – which I hate
npcif	you're asking me to be introspective – which I'm not
npa*p*(f)if	what about a cold punch – which one is always reading about
psif	like politicians – who notoriously have no sense of humour at all
r npsif	you're living in a world which is in the main stream
npsnif	discussions about ideologies which may help to lessen the gap between East and West
nponif	interests outside the immediate work of aviation and its problems which you have found satisfying and of assistance to you
npoim	the ideas which the playwright is expressing are uncongenial
npa*p*(i)if	I do like an animal with which one can be on personal terms
npa*p*(i)im	is the line from which you start from which you begin a poem is that always the opening line
psnif	brought together peoples with a clash who had such diverse civilizations
psim	the very people who criticize the design now had never seen St Paul's Cathedral
psoif	I haven't served under many whom I didn't think were jolly good
poif	various of my colleagues whom I asked to volunteer
poim	virtues in a person who I was going to like were curiosity and courage

---

[1] For reasons of space, a more extensive presentation of the material is not possible, but the complete material remains intact and will continue to be made accessible to interested scholars.

| pa*p*(i)if . | people with whom he had to negotiate things |
| 'whose' (if) | after a lady whose name I certainly won't mention |

THAT

nr npoif	all he had in his tummy was raw turnip – that he'd taken from the fields
r npsif	it's not a thing that would disturb me in any way
npsnif	parts were indicated to me that showed quality
npsim	the policy that has to be followed has to be determined
nponif	the things to catch up on in the winter that I've neglected during the summer
npoim	I don't think anything that any critic ever says . . . is worthy of consideration
npaif	it's the first time that it's happened
npa*p*(f)if	cope with things that I've had no basic training for
psnif	as to who the chaps will be that will get to the top
poim	all the people that you like best really have one thing in common

ZERO

r npsnif	I don't think there's any fighting-service in any element is any good
npoif	the one you sometimes find in poetry books
npoim	the sort of self-confidence you learn in your professional job can be carried into life in general
npcif	they can pull every string there is to be pulled
npaim	the only place it's been officially faced is India
npa*p*(f)if	that's the thing you should compare it with
psnif	there's no architect if he's honest is ever satisfied with what he's done
poif	I was the worst lawbreaker he'd ever met
pa*p*(f)im	would you oblige the people you were fond of at the expense of your principles

The symbols used above and in the statistical Table are explained as follows:

r, nr	– the clause is restrictive or non-restrictive;
p, np	– the antecedent is personal or non-personal;
s	– the relative pronoun is subject of the clause;
so (co)	– the relative pronoun is subject (or complement) in a partially object environment;

o, c   – the relative pronoun is object or complement;

a   – the relative clause is a prepositional adjunct or is sub-
            stitutable for one;

$p(i)$, $p(f)$ – the relative structure has an initially or finally placed
            preposition;

i, ni   – the relative clause follows, or does not follow, the
            antecedent immediately;

m, f   – the relative clause is medial or final (i.e. is included in
            or follows the clause containing the antecedent).

Objection may be raised to certain functional categories used here. These have been retained deliberately where they correspond to formal categories, because it has been felt that the advantages of using traditional and well-known distinctions wherever possible are greater than those conveyed by using a formal, more precise, but idiosyncratic categorization. Misgiving may be greatest in the case of 'restrictive' and 'non-restrictive', but here too there is an important formal distinction though it is certainly difficult to draw in marginal cases. Leaving considerations of meaning aside, there are three features which mark off what are here called 'non-restrictive' clauses from the 'restrictive' ones: these are juncture, intonation, and prominence. Restrictive clauses (as in 'you're living in a world which is in the main stream') are linked to their antecedents by close syntactic juncture, by unity of intonation contour,[2] and by continuity of the degree of loudness. In contrast, non-restrictive clauses are characterized by open juncture (recognized, together with the following features, by a comma in written materials), a fresh intonation contour, and a change (especially a diminution) in the degree of loudness. For example:

that's the Haydn Seven Words from the Cross – which is an extremely
             2   24   p3
interesting work   (4 is low; p = 'piano')

It is by no means universally the case that all three of these distinctions are present (the closeness or openness of the juncture seems to be especially dispensable), but it is rarely difficult on the basis of these criteria to distinguish restrictive from non-restrictive clauses.

There are other formal characteristics of non-restrictive clauses, but none seems to be regular enough to rank as a distinguishing criterion. It is often possible, for instance, to substitute *and this* for *which*,[3] and

---

[2] W. R. Lee in *Lingua* 5.351 f. touches on this criterion.

[3] A substitution test involving the replacement of *which* by a conjunctive form such as *and this* can be misleading, because the substitution often involves a

another notable feature is that the antecedent of a non-restrictive clause is often a whole clause rather than a noun or noun-cluster; for example, 'I know that I changed schools several times – which sounds rather a doubtful thing.' Again, so preponderant is the use of the *wh-* pronouns with non-restrictive clauses that it might seem that a substitution test on this feature could rank as a means of classifying them. Out of 174 non-restrictive clauses in the material, only one was not introduced by a *wh-* pronoun: 'all he'd got in his tummy was raw turnip – that he'd taken from the fields.' Nevertheless, this use of *that* is not rare enough to make a substitution test effective; it is, for instance, by no means a rarity in literary English: one can find it in Graham Greene, and Tennyson's well-known dislike of *which* led to its partial exclusion from non-restrictive as well as from restrictive clauses. In a substitution test carried out on 80 of the non-restrictive clauses, there turned out to be more than a score in which *that* appeared to be idiomatically possible, that is to say, where one could retain open juncture and change of tone contour and prominence, and introduce *that* without the significant shift in vowel and stress from /ðət/ to /ðæt/ which would change its function from relative to demonstrative. For instance, with the example 'what about the incidental cruelty to the horses – which do get gored?', substitution as follows is not rejected as unidiomatic:

$$\ldots \text{to the horses} - /\eth\text{ət } {}^{\rm l}\text{du}/ \text{ get gored}$$
$$\phantom{\ldots \text{to the horses}}_{24} \phantom{- /\eth\text{ət}}_{3} \phantom{{}^{\rm l}}_{2} \phantom{\text{du}/}_{4} \phantom{\text{get}}_{343}$$

But substitution of *wh-* by *that* appears not to be possible when the antecedent is a whole clause, as in the following example: 'we may have exploded the Canal at the same time – which is going to be very unfortunate.' Moreover, although the informants on whom I tested these substitutions accepted *that* in a score of instances as idiomatic, when subsequently given the choice between the two forms they preferred

---

significant change which it is easy to overlook. One example from the material will illustrate this:

we may have exploded the Canal at the same time – which is going to be
$$_{4} _{4}$$
very unfortunate
$$_{4} _{4} _{3}$$

A replacement of the clause here by 'and that is going to be very unfortunate' makes idiomatic English, but the two utterances are not received as precisely equivalent. The change involves consequential differences in tone pattern, stress distribution, and degree of prominence, all of these constituting a linguistic means of distinguishing two types of relationship between the parts of the utterance. The choice between the two involves a deliberate indication of intention.

wh- in all cases. This, taken together with the fact that all but one of the non-restrictive clauses in the material were constructed with *wh-*pronouns, reduces one's confidence in the extent to which *that* is a genuine substitute. Indeed, this highlights the limitations of the substitution test technique as compared with the more laborious and time-consuming frequency survey. The substitution test is admirable in drawing attention to what is idiomatically quite impossible, but it does not readily distinguish between the merely and marginally possible and the actually normal, between what one will tolerate as a hearer and what one will produce as a user of the language (see Paper 15 below).

One category which calls for comment is that designated 'so' and explained (p. 98) as indicating that the relative pronoun is 'subject in a partially object environment': for example, 'the piece of eighteenth-century costume that I always thought was a sensible one ... is the nightshirt.' The justification for distinguishing this pattern, on the basis of the partially object environment, from other clauses in which the pronoun is subject without that complication lies in the fact that when a personal antecedent obtains, there is a notable tendency to use *whom* instead of *who* as the pronoun. Two surrenders to this tendency (as against one example of resistance to it) appeared in the material: for example, 'I haven't served under many whom I didn't think were jolly good'. Instances of this phenomenon have been recorded over hundreds of years. In *King John* IV.ii.165, the Bastard speaks of 'Arthur whom they say is kill'd tonight'; Keats writes of 'women whom I really think would like to be married'. And while recent examples in *The Times* and elsewhere confirm the persistence of the tendency,[4] there seems to be little basis for the view expressed recently in *English* (vol. 10, pp. 159–160) by Mr H. C. Duffin that this feature is on the increase; in connexion with examples in *The Times* and in the work of Richard Church and C. P. Snow, he claims that they would not have appeared 'in similar contexts thirty years ago' and that in fact this use of *whom* 'seems to have become the accepted norm'.

One consequence of the partially object environment (and another reason for distinguishing this form of relative construction) is that it is

[4] In an examination in the University of Durham, six candidates tackled the problem of commenting upon the following sentence: 'Yet these men whom we thought had died for their country have received no reward beyond newspaper sentiment.' Two of the six pointed out that *whom* is the subject of *had died* and is here attracted into object form by *we thought*; the remaining four commented upon various features, linguistic and moral, and suggested various changes, but they rewrote the sentence leaving *whom* unaltered and unmentioned.

usually possible in such cases to replace the pronoun by zero, an otherwise very rare possibility when the pronoun is subject. Thus instead of 'the piece of eighteenth-century costume that I always thought was a sensible one . . . is the nightshirt', the speaker could have said 'the piece of eighteenth-century costume I always thought was a sensible one . . . is the nightshirt'. That my examples do not include such a zero construction is probably because they mostly have (as in this case) a complex antecedent, and this as we shall see militates in general against the selection of zero.

Some comment may be welcome also on the category designated 'a' and explained as indicating that the relative clause is 'a prepositional adjunct or is substitutable for one'. This embraces clauses with *wh*- pronouns in which the pronoun is preceded by a preposition, as well as clauses of all three main types where the preposition follows the verb; for example, 'something in which you're . . . involved', 'cold punch – which one is always reading about', 'the only thing that they disapprove of', 'the thing you should compare it with'. But it also embraces some constructions from which not only the relative pronoun but also the preposition itself may be absent; for instance, 'the first year that American literature was on', 'I'm always fascinated by the way other people work'. Clauses of this type are properly included in this study where the *that* or zero will readily admit of substitution by a prepositional *which*-construction. In one instance in the material, such a substitution was demonstrated in the actual exchange between the participants thus:

> 1st speaker: I don't see how else she could do it . . . not . . . the way she . . . does
> 2nd speaker: What do you mean . . . the way in which she does
> 1st speaker: Well she manages to make it. . . a very interesting story
> – the way she does

The clauses of this type included here turn out in the majority of cases to relate to the antecedents *time* and *way*.[5]

[5] This appears to indicate a sharp limitation upon the construction as compared with the situation in the eighteenth century when the grammarians (for example Ash, Lowth, and Lindley Murray) found it necessary to reprove their contemporaries and predecessors for such examples as Addison's 'in the temper of mind he was then' and Swift's 'in the posture I lay'. How compelling was the tendency to use this idiom can be seen in the amusing fact that Lindley Murray, who firmly proscribes this and indeed any use of the zero construction in 'all writings of a serious . . . kind', falls to using it himself in that most serious of writings, his *Grammar*: 'learning to read, in the best manner it is now taught' (*English Grammar*, edition of 1808, I.340). It may be of interest to point out too that all the prepositionless 'a' examples in my material were introduced by

Attention may be briefly drawn now to the whole body of restrictive clauses as analysed in the Table (p. 104), and to some of the dominant patterns that this analysis demonstrates. The last two columns, m and f, show that the majority of relative clauses are placed after the completion of the clause containing the antecedent; this means in effect that relative clauses normally qualify the object or complement rather than the subject of a main clause. Where relative clauses are placed medially – in particular, where they qualify the subject of the main clause – speakers have a strong tendency to anacoluthon, and one finds many examples like the following:

> anyone in this world who cannot be moved to change their views in the light of what has been what has happened in Hungary well it it's a shocking commentary upon human thought

The two columns i and ni point to an equally marked tendency to avoid separating the antecedent from the relative clause; examples like the following are in a distinct minority: 'to find how problems were dealt with of which you have spoken.'

If we look at the Table horizontally, we find some further predominating features. When the pronoun is subject of the clause, we have the well-known restriction on the zero construction, nps i and ps i, whereas with *that* and the *wh-* pronouns there are many examples in subject function, – at any rate of nps. For ps, however, we see a decided difference as between the *wh-* form and *that*; with *wh-* there are 200 examples (psf 149, psm 51), whereas there are only 19 with *that*. The restriction upon *that* for referring to personal antecedents is, in fact, far greater than has been generally supposed.[6]

Indeed, one of the most striking revelations in this Table is the preponderance of *wh-* forms for restrictive clauses as a whole, in view of

---

that or zero; this is to say, I have not recorded any instance of a type which Poutsma found in a modern literary source: 'on the day which he should have been born' (*A Grammar of Late Modern English* XVI.15).

[6] It is rarely difficult in practice to distinguish between p and np antecedents, though with the pronouns *whose*, *that*, and zero there are theoretical difficulties where the antecedents are words like *audience, government, country*. In such cases it is usually possible to tell from the speaker's use of reference pronouns or neighbouring relative constructions containing unambiguous forms whether he is using a given antecedent 'personally' or 'non-personally'. In the present material, antecedents and usage were unambiguous in the vast majority of cases, and the problem scarcely arose. Vacillation was interestingly observed with one speaker (a biologist) who twice referred to animals 'with *which*' he was 'on *personal* terms' and once to females among them '*who*' had the reprehensible habit of eating their mates.

	p	np	s	so	o	c	a	$p^{(1)}$	$p^{(f)}$	i	ni	m	f
WH- nr npsf		77	77							66	11		77
npsm		10	10							7	3	10	
npsof		14		14						13	1		14
npo (1 × nim)		19			19					13	6	1	18
npc		3				3				3			3
npapf (5 × p(f)i)		11					11	6	5	6	5		11
'all' ⎫ npapm		2					2	1	1		2	2	
'each' ⎬ 'x of which'		4					4	4		2	2		4
2 × 'one' ⎭ np- (incomplete)		2										1	1
psf	19		19							16	3		19
psm	6		6							4	2	6	
'whom' pso	1			1						1			1
po	1				1					1			1
pa (1 × im)	4						4	4		3	1	1	3
nr 173	31	142	112	15	20	3	21	15	6	135	36	21	152
r npsf		128	128							101	27		128
npsm		11	11							6	5	11	
npsof		7		7						7			7
npof		65			65					57	8		65
npom		7			7					7		7	
npapf		68					68	56	12	53	15		68
npapm		9					9	9		8	1	9	
'as a result of which'		1					1	1			1		1
np- (incomplete)		2								2			2
psf	149		149							127	22		149
psm	51		51							49	2	51	
1 × 'whom' pso	2			2						2			2
2 × 'who' pof	9				9					7	2		9
1 × 'who' pom	2				2					2		2	
papf	5						5		5	4	1		5
'whose' (2 × nim)	6						6			3	3	2	4
r 522	224	298	339	9	83	0	89	71	12	435	87	82	440
THAT nr 1 npoif		1			1					1			1
r npsf		125	125							112	13		125
npsm		27	27							24	3	27	
npso (1 × im)		5		5						4	1	1	4
npof		94			94					82	12		94
npom		41			41					40	1	41	
npc (2 × im)		4				4				3	1	2	2
npa (1 × im)		9					9			7	2	1	8
npap (4 × im)		30					30		30	24	6	4	26
np- (incomplete)		2								1			2
ps (1 × im)	19		19							14	5	1	18
pof	7				7					6	1		7
pom	3				3					2	1	3	
pc (1 × conif)	2					2				2	1		2
pap (1 × im)	4						4		4	3	1	1	3
r 372	35	337	171	5	145	6	43	0	34	324	48	81	291
ZERO r npsf		1	1								1		1
npof		89			89					89			89
npom		48			48					47	1	48	
npcf		5				5				5			5
npaf		17					17			16	1		17
npam		11					11			11		11	
npapf		31					31		31	30	1		31
npapm		7					7		7	6	1	7	
psf	1		1								1		1
po	11				11					11		2	9
pcf	3					3				3			3
pap	4						4		4	4		2	2
r 228	19	209	2	0	148	8	70	0	42	222	6	70	158
	p	np	s	so	o	c	a	$p^{(1)}$	$p^{(f)}$	i	ni	m	f

the persistent observation in grammars since the time of Sweet that in spoken English *that* and zero constructions are preferred to the *wh*-forms. In my material there turned out to be more *wh*- clauses than *that* and zero clauses put together.[7] A substitution test carried out on about one third of the material may have helped to explain the discrepancy (if discrepancy there is and not a change in usage), by showing that it was idiomatically easier to replace *that* and zero by *wh*- than it was to replace *wh*- by *that* or zero.[8] Thus, if, as is reasonable to suppose, an impressionistic grammarian notices more readily features in which an actual choice exists for users of the language (especially if this correlates with distinctions between styles of usage), he will regard with some reason the colloquial occurrence of *that* and zero as of great significance.

But the substitution test leaves unexplained in the majority of cases both the preponderance of *wh*- and the basis on which speakers select their forms. For example, it makes it appear that the majority of *wh*-clauses could equally well be expressed by *that* and the majority of *that* clauses by *wh*-, and a conclusion based on this test alone would be that personal choice dictated the selection in upwards of 90 per cent of cases, that there was almost complete free variation. Thus, where the antecedent is personal and the pronoun is subject of the clause, *that* is a possible substitute for *who*: 'the people who came' – 'the people that came'. Yet the frequency survey, as we have seen, shows that *who* is in fact preferred in the proportion of ten to one, a proportion which indicates not so much personal choice as predictability on the basis of environment.

The frequency survey points to other factors too which help to determine the selection of one form as against another. As already pointed out, relative clauses normally follow their antecedents immediately, but there are times when this is inconvenient and when a certain distancing of the parts is required. This turns out to be one of the circumstances that tend to call for the use of *wh*- in preference to other forms, as can be seen by examining the i and ni columns for the three types. With *wh*- we find 87 distanced clauses, with *that* (where the

---

[7] The preponderance of *wh*- is at its greatest in the cases of double restriction (as in 'there are certain activities which are not scientific which are very important to the human race' where the second clause has *wh*- 15 times as against *that* 5 times and no examples of zero.

[8] The percentages were as follows:

    Zero clauses: 100 per cent could have *that*, 86 per cent *wh*-.
    That clauses: 95 per cent could have *wh*-, 42 per cent zero.
    Wh- clauses: 90 per cent could have *that*, 25 per cent zero.

distancing is also usually slighter) there are 48, while with zero there is a still sharper curb on this phenomenon or indeed on any clustering which makes the antecedent complex. On the other hand, where speakers depart from the norm in another way and introduce medial as opposed to final relative clauses, the columns m and f show them reacting proportionately against *wh-* in favour of *that* and still more in favour of zero. The total of 82 for *wh-* may obscure this tendency until one notices that 51 of these 82 are in the ps line where zero is practically inadmissible and where, as we have seen, *that* too is largely avoided. The reaction against medial *wh-* comes out most clearly in comparing the npom lines for the three forms: *wh-* has only 7, *that* has 41, and zero 48. The importance that this medial zero structure has in English expression is noticed by Mr Donald Davie, when he cites Pope's line 'The Rights a Court attack'd, a Poet sav'd' and speaks of 'syntactical closeness and rapidity, which is delightful and significant in its own right'.[9] To be most successful, a medially placed relative clause requires the closeness and rapidity of the zero construction where idiom allows it, and npo constitutes one of the notable sets of circumstances in which idiom does allow it.

It has been pointed out that *wh-* is the overwhelmingly preferred pronoun where it is subject in a clause relating to a personal antecedent. The position is markedly different where, with a personal antecedent, the relative pronoun is object of the clause; the lines containing the po data show that 11 such clauses have *wh-*, 10 *that*, and 11 zero. These are slender figures on which to base any conclusion with confidence, but in the drastic shift in the selection of pronouns as we pass from ps to po we probably see evidence of a reluctance that has been noticeable for some generations to use *whom* in spoken English. Even the 11 *wh-* examples show three cases of *who* instead of *whom*,[10] but this clearly is not an expedient that can commend itself to most educated speakers, and rather than use the *whom* form about which they are apparently self-conscious, they will use zero or even *that* despite the tendency away from the latter form with personal antecedents.[11]

[9] *Articulate Energy* (London, 1955), 80.

[10] Compare the following from *The Daily Telegraph*, 19 July 1956: 'He told her he had reason to believe that she had a man there who he knew as Fred Harmsworth and who he wished to interview'.

[11] It is of some interest to note how rarely po in any form occurs in the material. Of the clauses relating to personal antecedents, only about 8 per cent are po, whereas of the clauses relating to non-personal antecedents, over 40 per cent are npo. This is perhaps a matter less for linguistic than philosophical speculation, but it is not impossible that embarrassment over *whom* on the one hand and the

To a lesser extent, with non-personal antecedents too, *that* and zero are preferred to *which* in object function, even where the clause is final. The three npof lines for restrictive clauses show 65 *which* as against 94 *that* and 89 zero, and it would appear that English conditions of stress and rhythm favour a lighter pronoun than the *wh-* series to introduce any relative clause in which the second element is the subject of the dependent verb. Even so, in spite of the proportionate tendency away from *which* in the npof construction, the figures 65, 94, and 89 still seem to leave considerable scope for personal choice, and it would be well to see if there are other conditioning factors apart from those noted so far. One such factor is the form-class of the subject in the relative clause. In all three types of clause, the majority of the subjects are personal pronouns, as in 'the one you sometimes find in poetry books'. Indeed, in the zero clauses all but 2 per cent of the subjects are personal pronouns. With the *that* and *which* clauses, however, a significantly higher proportion of the subjects are other than personal pronouns; heavier subjects such as nouns or personal names appear in nearly 24 per cent of the *that* clauses and in precisely 25 per cent of the *which* clauses. We cannot of course on this evidence distinguish between *that* and *which*, but we are shown conditions under which either of these is preferred to zero.

Another factor which has a marked significance is clause length. For the npof clauses under consideration (where we can make a convenient three-way comparison over a fair body of material) the position is as follows. The majority of the zero examples have only two or three words (characteristically a subject pronoun and a verb nucleus), with a sharp fall away then to six words, and with very few clauses longer than this. With *that*, there is a fairly even spread of examples having from two to five words, with a gradual decline then to nine words, and only a few clauses longer than this. With *which*, the peak is reached at five words, but there is a fairly even spread between two and nine words, with only a gradual decline in the number of longer clauses thereafter. There are no zero clauses of more than nine words, whereas 3 per cent of the *that* clauses and 11 per cent of the *which* clauses are longer than nine words. The absolute averages show the zero clause as being four words, *that* clauses five words, and *which* clauses six words.[12]

The length factor is significant also in considering the npsf clauses

---

np associations of *that* on the other induce to some extent a reorganization of our utterances to achieve ps relative clauses.

[12] The relative pronouns themselves were not of course counted in this comparison of clause length.

and diminishes the impression of free variation that we get from the figures in the table: 128 *which*, 125 *that*. The *that* clauses here too occupy a narrower band as regards length, and the thickest concentration comes between three and seven words, while greater freedom is shown in the *which* clauses which spread evenly between two and eleven words. In absolute terms, the *that* clauses have an average length of 4·9 words and the *which* clauses 6·3 words.

All this points to a quite drastic limitation on the extent to which a truly unconditioned free variation can be said to exist in the construction of relative clauses. We have seen that it is important to distinguish between the variation that a native hearer will tolerate and the much narrower limits of variation which on the basis of the frequency survey we can predict from that native when he is speaking. Even from the comparatively unrefined analysis to which this body of material has been subjected, there emerges a network of conditioning factors each of which functions in a series (or perhaps a scale) of biases, influencing our selection of relative form according to the linguistic environment. It becomes possible to envisage, whether for critical or translation or normative teaching purposes, the attainment of a descriptive and objective grasp of processes formerly private, intuitive, and obscure.

Ten

From descriptive to prescriptive: an example†

After a generation or so during which 'prescriptivism' has become a thoroughly bad word, a title like that of the present essay may appear to herald a perversely retrograde movement. We do not always sufficiently realize that the teaching grammars of English, particularly those directed at foreign students, must be – and the best have always been – rather solidly prescriptive. There is little value to the learner in being presented with a collection of features observed from the lips (or pens) of natives: he wants to be told which features to learn. It is not for their prescriptivism as such that the older teaching grammars stand condemned (as they have been splendidly indeed condemned by dozens of modern writers, most notably perhaps by S. A. Leonard in *The Doctrine of Correctness in English Usage*): it is for the fact that their prescriptions have not been based upon a sound foundation of description.

All recent grammars of English as a foreign language have naturally taken their normative function for granted, and have explicitly or implicitly sought to present rules of structure, compliance with which will produce English of the kind used by educated natives. In the best recent grammars, this aim has gone along with rejection of the old grammarians' bias towards seeking authority in logical and universal language concepts, and acceptance of a scientific description as the primary authority. Now, the scientific description of English has so far been virtually restricted to the phonological and lexical levels. That is to say, there are impressive analyses of the phonetics and phonemics of English, the structure of sound clusters, and to some extent the patterns

† Reprinted, with small alterations, from *English Language Teaching* 12 (1958), 9 ff.

of stress and intonation; and there are valuable word-counts which give a clear picture of the relative importance of specific words in our total lexicon. At these levels, the writer of a teaching grammar is able to draw on good material so as to create precise rules and graded exercises. But at the grammatical level he is almost entirely without a body of systematic descriptive data, and so, with varying degrees of success, he has to rely largely on a hesitant and uncertain introspection into his own usage or his intuitive knowledge of the gross phenomena of English grammar, checked against such a grammatical encyclopedia as Jespersen's, which expounds historical trends rather than descriptive patterns. What we undoubtedly need is descriptive analysis – systematic and as complete as possible – of English grammatical usage, so that a body of data can be available for a new and objectively based prescriptivism.

It is hoped that the next few years will see increasing attention being paid to closing this important gap in the description of English, and the notes which follow seek to give an example of the kind of rules that can be readily abstracted from a fairly full account of a small segment of grammar. They concern the construction of idiomatic *restrictive relative clauses* and are based on an examination of all such clauses (over 1100) as occurred in a large body of impromptu speech of educated English adults.[1] By 'restrictive' relative clauses is meant nonparenthetic clauses in nominal group structure, that is, those clauses that are linked to their antecedents by close juncture, unity of intonation contour, and continuity of prominence.

In cultivating idiomatic English as spoken by educated natives, learners should note the importance of placing such clauses immediately after the antecedents which they qualify and at the same time of having the clause follow the completed main clause. This means in effect that relative clauses should qualify an end-placed noun (usually the complement), and one should be encouraged to reformulate sentences that would contravene this. Thus instead of either of the following:

1. The book has a page torn out which came from the library this morning.

2. The book which came from the library this morning has a page torn out.

---

[1] Details of the descriptive survey have been given in Papers 7 and 9 above. I am limiting my remarks here to restrictive clauses because they constitute nearly 90 per cent of the relative clauses used in speech and because they offer interesting varieties of pronoun and structure.

one might have

> 3. There is a page torn out of the book which came from the library this morning.

This is not to say, of course, that (1) and (2) are unidiomatic, still less 'incorrect'; but they do not conform to the dominant native pattern, and it is the dominant native pattern that the foreign learner should primarily be taught.

The dominant pronoun to be taught is the *wh-* series (especially *which* and *who*; *whom* and *whose* are rarer and less important), which is most frequent in educated speech and has fewest restrictions upon its use. It is particularly important when the pronoun is subject of the clause, and indeed with a personal antecedent in these circumstances *who* should be regarded as virtually the only permissible pronoun. Models: (3) above, and

> 4. One sees hundreds of people who appear to have nothing to do.

Having stated the broad norm, one may turn to special cases, exceptions, and stylistically permissible variations. It is frequently desirable to have the relative clause qualify an antecedent at or near the beginning of a main clause. In such cases, the relative clause should be kept short and the pronoun *which* avoided. If the antecedent is non-personal and the pronoun subject of the clause, *that* should be used; if the pronoun is complement, zero should be used if the subject is a personal pronoun, *that* if the subject is 'heavier' than a personal pronoun. If the antecedent is personal and the pronoun subject, *who* should be used. Models:

> 5. The book that's on the desk was sent me by a friend in Germany.
> 6. The book I mentioned was sent me by a friend in Germany.
> 7. The book that Robert mentioned was sent me by a friend in Germany.
> 8. The man who spoke is employed by a firm of solicitors.

On somewhat rarer occasions, what we wish to say comes out best if the relative clause is separated from the antecedent; when this is the case, the pronoun should generally be of the *wh-* series, regardless of its grammatical function or antecedent. Models: example (1) above, suitably contextualized, and

> 9. I have interests outside my immediate work and its problems which I find satisfying.

Provided the clause is short, *that* is slightly preferable to *which* in complement function even where the non-personal antecedent is at the end of the main clause:

> 10. He reminded me of many things that most people have neglected.

In similar conditions, zero is also preferable to *which* provided also that the subject of the clause is a personal pronoun:

> 11. He reminded me of many things they have neglected.

Where the antecedent is at the end of the main clause and the relative clause is short, *that* is a permissible variant of *which* even where the pronoun is subject:

> 12. The desk was covered with books that had been published recently.

Where the relative pronoun is governed by a preposition and the antecedent is non-personal, the primary pattern to teach is *which*, preceded by the preposition:

> 13. It's a service for which even the very poor seem always willing to pay.

An admissible alternative, especially if the clause is short, is to use *that*, with the preposition coming after the verb:

> 14. It's a service that people are willing to pay for.

Provided also that the subject is a personal pronoun, zero is permissible:

> 15. It's a service they are willing to pay for.

Finally, we come to the cases in which the antecedent is personal but where in contrast to (3) and (8) the pronoun is complement or governed by a preposition. These appear to be fairly rare in speech, and usage is divided between the three possibilities (*to*) *whom, that* . . . (*to*), and zero . . . (*to*), with a slight preference for the latter which it would therefore probably be best to teach:

> 16. He's a man I've always liked.
> 17. That's the man I gave it to.

But where the clause is long or has a subject heavier than a personal pronoun, zero should give way to *whom* and *that* respectively.

Thus one can see emerging from descriptive data a pattern of reliable and systematic prescriptive rules which can be summarized as follows: With non-personal antecedents and end-placed clauses, *which* is the general-purpose pronoun (3) and is especially important when the clause is long, is separated from its antecedent (9), and has a preposition governing the pronoun (13). *That* is preferable with medial clauses of which the pronoun is subject (5), or of which the subject is a 'heavy' word (7); in a final clause which is fairly short, it is preferable as complement (10), and permissible as subject (12) or when governed by a subsequent preposition (14). When the subject is a personal pronoun, zero is preferable as complement in medial clauses (6) and in short final clauses (11), and when governed by a subsequent preposition (15). With personal antecedents, *who* is required when subject of the clause (4, 8), but while *whom* is permissible in other functions, zero is preferable where the subject is a personal pronoun (16, 17), *that* where the subject is heavier.

Eleven

Co-existing negative preterite forms of *dare*†

Not only in its history as a preterite-present verb but also in its modern use, the verb *dare* shows a marked resistance to conformity. Like *need*, it can operate both as a 'full' verb ('he'll dare anything') and as an auxiliary element in a complex verb expression. In the latter capacity, again like *need*, it occupies an uneasy place between wholly regular verbs like *begin* ('he does not begin to fight' – 'he does not dare to fight') and the 'modal auxiliaries' which have no 3rd person singular present in -*s*, which lack also an infinitive (thus excluding the possibility of the *do*-periphrasis in negations and questions), and which enter into construction with a 'bare' infinitive ('he may not fight' – 'he dare not fight'). But *dare* is of decidedly rarer occurrence than *need* and is more restricted to being an auxiliary element in negative expressions; unlike *need*, moreover, its morphology is complicated by its preterite-present history and the partial survival of the form *durst*.

The general picture of the morphology and syntax of *dare* in written usage was usefully investigated in a series of articles in *Englische Studien* over half a century ago by A. E. H. Swaen, J. Ellinger, and W. Sattler (vols. 20, 21, and 26 respectively), and more recently in a valuable study by G. Mulder in vol. 22 (1937) of *Neophilologus*. In consequence, modern grammars can be much more accurate and specific about the use of *dare* and one might especially mention the precision achieved by R. W. Zandvoort.[1] In contrast with previous studies which have aimed at giving a generalized account of *dare* in the language as a whole and over a more or less wide time-span (even Mulder's survey, the nearest we have to a

† Written in collaboration with A. P. Duckworth and reprinted from the A. M. Jensen Festschrift, *Language and Society* (Copenhagen, 1961), pp. 135 ff.
[1] *A Handbook of English Grammar* (London, 1957), §§203–9.

synchronic one, covers literary materials over a period of forty years), the present modest contribution is narrower in several respects. It reports the results of an experiment to investigate the range of usage in the grammatical sphere of '(1st pers.) preterite negative', in a single context of situation (an examination in the written translation of Old English poetry), in a single age and education stratum (British Honours students of English, mainly between 19 and 21 years), at a single time (June 1960). The 55 students (28 women, 27 men) translated a passage from *The Dream of the Rood* which contains within the space of six lines (ll. 42–7) three occurrences of *ne dorste* (*ic*) plus infinitive. The relevant lines are:

> Bifode ic þā mē se Beorn ymbclypte; ne *dorste* ic hwæðre būgan tō eorðan,
> feallan tō foldan scēatum, ac ic sceolde fæste standan.
> Rōd wæs ic āræred; āhōf ic rīcne Cyning,
> heofona Hlāford; hyldan mē ne *dorste*.
> Þurhdrifan hī mē mid deorcan næglum; on mē syndon þā dolg gesīene,
> opene inwidhlemmas; ne *dorste* ic hira ǣnigum sceððan.

One was thus able, at a blow, to achieve a bigger collection of negative preterite forms from a larger number of informants than Mulder records from his forty-odd authors writing over a like number of years.[2]

The forms used by the students have been summarized in the accompanying table. Since each of the 55 students used a negative preterite three times, it has been thought useful to indicate in parentheses, where it is not otherwise obvious, the number of students who used a given form. Thus, for example, we may immediately dismiss as a casual idiosyncrasy the three instances of *darest*, tentatively classed in the table with the archaic *durst*, at which the student was no doubt aiming. At the same time, it can be seen that *durst* (also relatively rare) was distributed among the papers of a comparatively large number of students who, either reacting mechanically to the original or deeming it fitting to the stylistic occasion, used it as at least one of their three forms. It was indeed most striking in the results as a whole to find, within four main groups, such a wide variety of different forms. It is immediately apparent that the dominant forms are *dared* and *did+dare*: two-thirds of the students,

[2] The relative rarity of *dare* may be indicated as follows: Mr D. Kalogjera of Sarajevo University found that in some considerable stretches of recent prose fiction that contained about 1200 instances of *can/could* there were only 34 occurrences of the verb *dare* (including its use in set phrases like *I dare say*).

in fact, used one or other of these at least twice. But it is also obvious that the individual's natural repertoire of negative preterite forms freely comprehended all combinations of the main forms, and that this could be exploited for stylistic reasons by those who preferred not to repeat the same sequence of forms three times in succession. For while 16 students did indeed use a single form three times, and 13 more kept to variations within one of the four main groups, there were 22 who, deliberately or otherwise, used forms from two main groups, and 4 who selected a different main form for each of the renderings. In other words, almost half the students showed a distinct tendency to variation.

dared	I dared not V	50 (26)	59 (27)	60 (27)
	V I dared not	2 (1)		
	I dared V no one	1		
	neither/nor dared I V	3 (3)		
	I dared not either V	1		
	I neither dared V	1		
	I dared neither V	1		
	I dared not at all to V	1	1	
dare	I dare not V	21 (13)	22 (14)	34 (18)
	V I dare not	1		
	nor dare I V	9 (5)	12 (7)	
	I dare by no means V	1		
	dare I not V	2 (2)		
did + dare	I did not dare to V	34 (19)	36 (19)	56 (31)
	nor did I dare to V	2 (2)		
	I did not dare V	19 (12)	20 (13)	
	nor did I dare V	1		
durst	I durst not V	10 (7)	11 (7)	14 (8)
	nor durst I V	1		
	I darest not V	1	3 (1)	
	nor darest I V	1		
	V I darest not	1		
	not daring to V	1	1	
Total				165 (55)

An artificially high level of conservatism must be expected here by reason of the context of style and situation in which the students were writing and which undoubtedly prompted the use of *durst* and the sporadic inversions.[3] Whether or not this accounts for the density of non-periphrastic *dared* (in '*I dared not* V') is another matter. Mulder's materials, largely in the stylistic stratum that we may call 'literary colloquial' (the dialogue of novels, for instance), yield a higher proportion of *dared not* V as against the periphrastic *did not dare (to)* V: 59 *dared*, 33 *did not dare*.[4] In the present material, the fairly evenly balanced *I dared not* V and *I did not dare (to)* V seem to be of equal stylistic status; *dared* does not correlate with obviously formal, 'literary', or archaic features in the translation, nor (more importantly) does *did + dare* correlate with colloquial ones. It would therefore seem likely that periphrastic negation with *dare* has increased since the early part of this century when most of Mulder's materials were written.

Another discrepancy between Mulder's results and the present ones lies in the proportion of preterite *dare* forms: where both materials have almost the same number of occurrences of *dared* (Mulder 66, the present 60), he found 13 instances of *dare* as against the 34 used by the students. All of his, moreover, are in the sequence *dare not* (9 are written as one word, *daren't*) which according to Jespersen[5] constitutes the environment in which *dared* lost the preterite dental, allegedly as a purely phonetic change; in the present material, over a third of the instances occur independently of this environment (especially in the sequence *dare I*) and no written abbreviated form *daren't* is to be found. Again, not merely does the general context of style dissuade us from regarding preterite *dare* as colloquial, but we have positive evidence of its formal status in the non-colloquial expressions in which it frequently appears (*nor dare I* V, V *I dare not*, *dare I not* V).[6] No doubt, the difference between Mulder's results and our own arises from the normative influence of the printing house on his material.

[3] The rarer inversion pattern 'V *I* . . .' seems to have been prompted by the form of the OE, since of the 4 examples 3 are translations of 'hyldan mē ne dorste', the only example in the OE where the infinitive precedes.

[4] *Neophilologus* 22 (1936–7), 33 ff. Our figures here and elsewhere for Mulder are based on his material and not on his tables, since the latter are drawn up on a somewhat different principle of grouping from that used here.

[5] *Modern English Grammar* IV.1.8(1).

[6] One may note in passing that the present material lends no support to those grammarians who relate preterite *dare* primarily to indirect speech, as, for instance, A. Gabrielson who notes specifically that such forms 'äro vanliga i indirekt anföring' (*Engelsk Grammatik* (Stockholm, 1950), §223).

Note is taken in our table of the extent to which, in the present material, there is divided usage between V and *to* V after the negative preterite of *dare*. Only in the case of the periphrastic preterite does there appear to be any real possibility of choice,[7] and this raises some interesting points. Alongside the increased acceptance of periphrasis which we have already noted (a development in the direction of 'regularity' in conjugational structure), we find an apparently tenacious resistance to regularization in the matter of connecting *dare* with a following verb. That is to say, if 'he dared not fight' be regarded as the unregularized form in respect of two structural features, exactly as with 'he could not fight', the treatment of *dare* as regular in respect of one feature (periphrasis) does not carry with it automatically the regularization of the other feature (through the introduction of *to*) which would bring the whole verbal expression into line with 'he *did* not begin *to* fight'. In the present material, periphrasis co-occurs with *to* in 35 cases, but *to* is absent from 20 further periphrastic expressions; Mulder's material yields similar results with 20 *did not dare to* V as against 16 *did not dare* V.[8] It would seem that the regularizing tendency, powerfully manifesting itself (no doubt by reason of the relative rarity of *dare* as mentioned on p. 115, note 2) in the number of subjects who freely use the auxiliary *did* to form the negative preterite, is opposed to a correspondingly powerful conservative tendency to leave *dare* in construction with the 'bare' infinitive. This latter tendency in turn, no doubt, derives its power from the persistence in everyday English of the non-periphrastic negative preterites *dared* and *dare*, thus preserving a familiarity with a sequence *dare(d)* V.

But while it is clear that there is this ratio of free variation to the

[7] The single occurrence of negated *dared* followed by *to* seems to have been idiomatically possible to the writer only because he used the expanded and emphatic negative phrase *not at all* rather than the simple *not*. One has therefore little reason to quarrel with Zandvoort's flat statement (*A Handbook of English Grammar*, §204) that in negative sentences with *dared not* 'the plain infinitive is always used', although A. E. H. Swaen (*Englische Studien* 20.286 ff.) found four examples of *dared not to* in his nineteenth-century material. With *durst* and preterite *dare*, the question of *to* does not arise; Jespersen quotes a single example of *durst* with *to* (from Defoe) and says that preterite *dare* is 'always with the bare infinitive' (*Modern English Grammar* V.12.2(3); so too Mulder, *Neophilologus* 22.44).

[8] If the earlier results of Swaen and Sattler were known to be representative in showing a much lower ratio of *did not dare* V to *did not dare to* V, Mulder's and the present material would indicate a significant strengthening of the former variant in the past three-quarters of a century. See *Englische Studien* 20.271 ff., 26.50, and *Neophilologus* 22.42 f.

extent of about 3:5 as between *did+dare* V and *did+dare to* V in the *langue*, the present material would strongly indicate that no such ratio of free variation exists in the individual's *parole*. On the contrary, the material suggests that in the *parole* the two constructions are almost mutually exclusive. Out of the 31 students who used the periphrastic expression, only one used both *did+dare to* V and *did+dare* V. Of the 19 who used the former, 6 did so exclusively, while 12 used it beside *dared*, *dare* or *durst* (i.e. forms that do not have *to*); combinations with each of these forms occur and one student had as his three forms *did+dare to*, *durst*, and *dare*. Of the 13 who used *did+dare* V, 3 did so exclusively, while 9 used it beside one or more of the other main forms, and again combinations with each of the forms *dared*, *dare* and *durst* occur; in other words, these 12 students used no negative preterite form which had *to* in the verbal expression.

Thus, while the grammar of negative preterite *dare* can be quite economically and accurately stated despite the variations that occur, we are very far from having a simple monolithic system.[9] Nor, in view of the persistence of patterns fairly evenly balanced in mutual opposition, is it easy to predict the speed or indeed the course of any future developments towards regularity.

[9] The results of further research, showing more of the complexity of the system, have since been published in R. Quirk and J. Svartvik, *Investigating Linguistic Acceptability* (The Hague, 1966), 90 ff. See also Paper 17 below, especially Table 2 on p. 199.

Twelve

Studies in the correspondence of prosodic to grammatical features in English†

As K. L. Pike has said, 'In each language . . . the use of pitch fluctuation tends to become semi-standardized, or formalized, so that all speakers of the language use basic pitch sequences in similar ways under similar circumstances'.[1] The present paper reports an experiment in the use of a computer to correlate data on intonation and grammar, conducted within the framework of the Survey of English Usage. The limited aims of the experiment have been to investigate the extent of relationship between types of nucleus and types of grammatical unit; the grammatical relevance of the elements bearing nuclear tones; the grammatical junctions that occur between units of intonation; and the kind and degree of correspondence between units of intonation and units of grammar.[2]

The material used in the experiment consisted of two texts, each of 5000 words, of continuous unscripted speech, transcribed from recordings of panel discussions. There were four speakers and a chairman in each discussion, making ten different speakers in the material as a whole; they were all university-educated men of middle age or over, well accustomed to speaking in public. In each discussion, the panel was asked to comment on questions of general interest; speakers in Text 1

† This report on research conducted in the course of the Survey of English Usage in collaboration with J. Svartvik, A. P. Duckworth, J. P. L. Rusiecki, and A. J. T. Colin, was presented at the 1962 International Congress of Linguists held at M.I.T. It is reprinted here from the *Proceedings* of the Congress (The Hague, 1964), 679 ff.

[1] *The Intonation of American English* (Ann Arbor, 1945), § 3.1.

[2] Space forbids a consideration of previous work in this field—for example, D. L. Bolinger, 'Intonation and Grammar', *Language Learning* 8.31–7; 'Contrastive Accent and Contrastive Stress', *Language* 37.83–96; F. Daneš, 'Sentence Intonation from a Functional Point of View', *Word* 16.34–54.

were broadcasting from a hall in the presence of an audience, those in Text 2 were televised in a studio.

The textual samples given below illustrate how the material was transcribed and reproduced on the 6″ × 4″ slips on which all the Survey texts are filed. In general, orthography is used, but incomplete words are given in phonetic notation in square brackets, whereas the sounds of voiced hesitation are indicated only approximately by the use of ə, əː, əm, without square brackets. Each slip has a number in the top left-hand corner: the first symbol indicates the type of material, the second is the number of the text within this category, and the third is the number of the slip. Capital letters in the left-hand margin identify the speakers; continuation of speech from a previous slip or after interruption by another speaker is shown by enclosing the speech heading in round brackets. The two consecutive slips 5b.1.21 and 5b.1.22 show how an overlap of four lines is given on each slip in order to provide adequate linguistic context for each feature analysed: the starred lines at the top and the bottom of each slip are not treated as part of the material on that slip, but are analysed when they appear without stars on neighbouring slips. Interruptions of one speaker by another, and passages where two or more people are speaking at once, are marked by paired asterisks and crosses, as on slip 5b.2.56.

The system of discriminations in terms of which we make the present report has been formulated under the pressure of specific practical needs. We have aimed at a system which could be applied with reasonably high speed to large bodies of material and in which the distinctions were sufficiently broad to be heard with a high level of agreement by the team engaged in analysis. Since we wished to investigate the relation of grammatical categories to categories of intonation, we had to avoid using grammatical criteria in setting up our intonation units. We favoured a set of discriminations based on phonetic substance, which suggest their phonological status chiefly by promoting least disagreement in their recognition.

In common with most of our colleagues in this field, we find ourselves unable to use instrumental assistance to any more than a minor extent, and our work is based on auditory analysis. Play-back at half speed has, however, proved valuable, and of course a loop repeater has been quite indispensable.

It may be convenient if we state our intonation categories with some reference to those set up by K. L. Pike[3] in what is probably the

[3] *Op. cit.*

best-known treatment of English intonation. Our basis is the TONE UNIT (cf. Pike's 'Total Contour', 3.5.3), marked as the stretches between the sign '#' (cf. Pike's 'Ending Point', 3.5.2). Minimally, the tone unit comprises a NUCLEAR SEGMENT[4] containing the NUCLEAR TONE (cf. Pike's 'Primary Contour', 3.5.2), but may have:

(*a*) a PRE-ONSET, terminating at the ONSET, marked '/' (cf. Pike's 'Beginning Point', 3.5.2); (*b*) one or more PRE-NUCLEAR SEGMENTS, in addition to (*c*) the NUCLEAR SEGMENT. A segment consists of at least one stressed syllable (which bears some correspondence to Pike's 'Key Point', 3.5.3). After the first segment, which begins with the onset, a new segment begins where a stressed syllable is uttered on a higher pitch than the preceding syllable; this point is called a BOOSTER and is marked ':'.[5] When such a syllable is uttered on a higher pitch than the first syllable of the preceding segment, this point is called a HIGH BOOSTER and is marked '!'. Either type of booster may also obtain at the beginning of a nuclear tone. The basic nuclear tones are as follows: the simple fall (`\`), rise (`´`), fall-rise (`ᵛ`), rise-fall (`ᵃ`), and level (`⁻`); and the compound fall-plus-rise (`\+´`), and rise-plus-fall (`´+\`). Tone units with simple nuclei are here called 'mononuclear', those with compound are 'binuclear'. STRESS (with its variant HEAVY STRESS: cf. Pike 4.4.7) is recognized in contrast with absence of stress, which is never marked. Tonetic marks are indications also of stress, and so stress as such (`ˈ`) is only marked when it does not occur at a nucleus or at the beginning of a segment. Heavy stress (`ˈˈ`), however, is marked wherever it occurs. A post-nuclear syllable bearing stress and continuing the nuclear tone is marked by a raised period (·).

The system is illustrated in the specimens of material given below (p. 123: the corresponding recordings were available for conference

---

[4] Our *segment* is by no means the same as that of W. Jassem, *Intonation of Conversational English* (Wrocław, 1952). Although like him we work in terms of pitch-direction instead of pitch-level, there is less obvious correspondence between our units and his than between ours and Pike's. To some extent, our *tone unit* resembles Jassem's 'tone group' and our *nuclear tone* his 'tone unit'; in some cases our *nuclear segment* corresponds to his 'nuclear tune', but the latter term has apparently a much wider reference than the former: cf. '"I suppose", observed Lord Mansfield', which has for Jassem (p. 59) two nuclear tunes but for us only one nuclear tone. We obviously cannot attempt here to correlate our system with that of other linguists, for example G. F. Arnold and J. D. O'Connor, R. Kingdon, W. R. Lee, M. Schubiger, nor can we consider important contributions to intonation theory by M. A. K. Halliday, L. S. Hultzén, A. E. Sharp, R. P. Stockwell, and others.

[5] Cf. Pike on 'centers of attention', 4.1.2.

Specimens of Material (actual size of each slip is 6" × 4")

5b.1.21

(TL) *:group of cóuncillors# . /in Cróydon# en/tirely on
*their own bát# without /reference to :anybody :else
have decíded to :"dó# - a I /just don't believe#
that it's/trúe# a that they're going to /hurl a#
everybody into the :street tomórrow# . that /clearly
couldn't be ríght#
(?) /six months nôtice . they're . 'giving . them# /bfil#
(TL) /six [man] are you :sure of 'that# is /that what it
says in the páper#
(?) /yés# I /think só# /yes#
(TL) /six months notice# . /wéll#. a/?gáin# I /don't

again know [ðə ðə] /that would depend on :how many houses
(RQ)   a:vailable. there :are in . Cróydon# whether that's
/fair or nót#. I /don't know thát# and /neither do
any of us# - /out [ɔ:] the :"principle of "surely of
* :"people :"paying . :what they can af:ford to páy#
* an /economic rent#. is /"surely :"right# . and I

[right margin] m = narrow & rhythmic

5b.2.29

G *oh /déar# ə ə - /this is :quite im:póssible# /cer-
*tainly for me to :answer# - /but - :if one :tries to
draw an a:nalogy from ánimals# - - /their :acts .
which :look . thóughtful# - m such as the :spider's
:spinning of a :wéb# m# or a m :bird :building of a
:nést# m# - am . are /?ot really thoughtful in 'our
sense# that they're. /concepts :drawn óut# . of
a /large number of individual . ?ítems# - [an] .
they're /concepts built in through a heréditary
:mechanism# . and I /think in the be:gínning# .
/man# . /must háve#. ao in in/verted cómmas# ao#
/thôught# - /in this sense of he :did certain
things with:out knowing the reason :whý# . /such as
am a :child suckling its :móther# am# - with/out
knowing :whý# . /but . the :mínute# /he was .
* :capable of :réal :thought# . he was /also capable
* I'm súre# of com/municating that thought# by / some

[right margin] items
m = narrow & rhythmic
m = rhythmic & narrow
pre-nucl.

5b.1.22

(TL) */fair or nót# . I /don't know thát# and /neither do
*àny of us# - /out [ɔ:] the :"principle . :"surely of
. :"people . :"páying . :what they can afford to páy#
an /economic rént# . is /"surely :"ríght# . and I
/would have thought# as /we've had here in . :"Bristol
for . "many yéars# . a /differential :rént# - because
/one of the great :problems# of of pro/víding#
/subsidized?housing# or /subsidized anything :élse#

(JS) housing - one of the /great problems of the :Welfare# :Státe
non-nuc.   :is# - that we :tax ourselves up the :hilt# to [prə]
to pro/vide benefits . :quite indis:criminately# for
/those who nééd# /and those who :don't nééd# - /with
the result that the :whole benefit is :spréad so
"thinly over the community# . you /can't :really do
enóugh# for /those who :really :"are in :nééd# . and
*/housing :subsidies is a :classical example :óf
*.that#

5b.2.56

(M) 'is /'that a Robertson óne# + + and and am . the ə ə
?F + yes +
(M) there /'are . 'these. 'things# that ap/péar to be
*sexlinked# on the /Y chromosome# ** but . ... /see it
(M) *yes*

gap in   :éven'a more stróngly# because they're /'all inter-
recording ?F related in Scot'land# it's it's a /small country# and
we've /'all intermarried for a :long time# a# and
/yet . there are the m :Campbell character'istics# m#
there are . the a /main Campbell characteristic was
their great :courage# a# . am if you /take the m
:Cawdor Campbells# . /three Victoria Crósses#
un/limited M m# ' Cs# . the m /Lindsays# - /always
very civilized# /they write plays# m# . they . ɔ
/Lord :Cráwford# is a very /good ex:ámple# ɔ# - they
*they're /very artístic# . and /yet they're all
*intermárried# - and I've /always wanted to :táckle

[right margin]
(M) = high
narrow
(M) = narrow
m = narrow

members to hear). A question mark placed before a syllable bearing a tone-mark indicates a doubtful reading: in some cases an alternative reading is suggested in the margin. The symbol *m* in the text, used to indicate a modification in voice quality, is amplified each time in the margin. It will be noticed that our system (*a*) regards pitch primarily in terms of direction rather than levels, and (*b*) takes account of pitch movement as such only at 'nuclei'. Several further intonation distinctions (observed, for example, by Pike) are handled in terms of the segment distinctions, together with the notation of tempo, prominence, pause, modification, and 'extended tone',[6] features which may receive only a bare mention here, since they were ignored in the limited computer experiment now being reported.

The material was described for the purposes of computer analysis in terms of nine sets of data, hereafter referred to as columns.

Column 1 was assigned to the description of the nucleus in a system of 27 terms – the basic seven already discussed, distributed over a number of sub-categorizations (for example, interrogation) that do not concern us here. In the 1880 tone units examined, simple falling nuclei were by far the most numerous (958); there were half as many rising nuclei (451). The next most numerous were the binuclear fall-plus-rise (170), the mononuclear fall-rise (125) and rise-fall (72).[7]

Column 2 registered the length of tone units (measured simply by the number of institutional words). It was necessary to have as many as 23 terms, but in fact only one unit was as long as 23 words, and only for lengths up to 14 words were there as many as ten units, while there were over a hundred units consisting of a single word. The overall average length of a tone unit (c. 10,000 words, 1880 units) was 5·3 words, and in fact 61 per cent of the units were found to have lengths fairly evenly distributed between 2 and 7 words, but the highest number of occurrences clustered between 3 and 5: there were 251 units of 3 words, 248 of 4 words, and 252 of 5 words.

Column 3 registered in a system of 16 terms the form-class of the word bearing the nuclear tone. Six classes accounted for 95 per cent of the nuclei. In 847 cases, the nucleus fell on a noun – and this class did not include the 'proper name' which accounted for a further 153 nuclei. The next most important form-class was the finite verb (310), followed

---

[6] We lack, however, the useful distinction observed by some other linguists between a '2-3' and a '2-4' fall (Pike, 4.1.2).

[7] Minor categories: 38 level, 11 rise-plus-fall, 9 extended, 46 doubtful.

by the adverb (262), the adjective (221), and the pronoun (126). Among the minor items, it is of interest to mention that prepositions bore the nucleus 25 times when the phrase-head was a pronoun, but only six times when it was a noun or name (though the latter types of phrase were more than five times as numerous as the former).

Column 4 dealt with two distinct systems with a total of 47 terms. First, a grammatical description of post-nuclear parts of mononuclear units: this phenomenon occurred in less than an eighth of the tone units, and the commonest form for 'tails' of this kind was a pronoun (as in ' ... sàw him#'). Secondly, a registration of the number of inter-nuclear words in binuclear units: most frequently (71 times) the tones were borne by consecutive words; there were 46 units with one inter-nuclear word and 28 units with two; there were few internuclear stretches of more than two words.

Column 5, in a system of 23 terms, handled the principal types of group structure into which the nucleus-bearing form-class of column 3 entered. About three-fifths of all nuclei fell on some part of a nominal group structure, and nearly 60 per cent of these were on the heads of 'simple' nominal groups (' ... the hèad#', a fall of course here repre-senting any type of nucleus). About 20 per cent of the nucleus-bearing nominal groups had the nucleus on a non-clausal postmodifier (' ... the head of the rìver#'); about 8 per cent had the nucleus on the head of a postmodified nominal group (' ... the hèad of the river#'), and a further 8 per cent had it on the premodifier of a simple group (' ... the ònly head#'). Something over 350 tone units (18 per cent of the total) had the nucleus on a part of the verbal group. Of these, 157 were 'simple' (one-element) groups: ' ... he wàlked#'. Where groups had more than one element, the nucleus was usually on the final element: there were 123 cases of the type 'he was wàlking#' beside 15 of the type 'he wàs walking#'; there were 25 of the type 'he had been wàlking#' as compared with 5 of the type 'he had bèen walking#' and none of the type 'he hàd been walking#'. There were 14 cases of nuclei on anaphoric verb forms ('he dìd#').

Column 6, in a system of 18 terms, dealt with the place in clause-structure[8] of the form-class and group-structure (columns 3 and 5)

---

[8] Although the abstraction here referred to as 'clause' includes what is commonly understood by the term, it also comprises units with non-finite verbal groups ('*Walking slowly*, he ...') and verbless units ('*His coat on his arm*, he ...').

bearing the nucleus. Of the 80 per cent of nuclei that did not fall on the verb, three-quarters fell on elements that were post-verbal in the clause structure. Whereas subjects bore the nucleus 170 times, adverbial phrases did so 457 times, and complements 553 times.

Column 7 categorized in a 27-term system the clause-structure in which the nuclear element operated. The most important clauses numerically were the 'free', e.g. 'He came yèsterday#'; 'independent terminal', e.g. '(He came yésterday#) and we had lùnch#'; 'independent nonterminal', e.g. 'He came yésterday# (and we had lùnch#)'; 'bound as complement with *that* or zero', e.g. '(He said) he was tìred#'; 'relative', e.g. '(the man) who was thère#'; and 'bound as adverbial with the main elements of clause structure following', e.g. 'After he cáme# (he had lùnch#)'. No other type occurred with as many as one hundred instances, though three came near it: 'bound as adverbial with main elements preceding', e.g. '(He had lunch) after he càme#'; 'non-finite verbal postmodifier in nominal group', e.g. '(the man) having lunch in the còrner#' (cf. 'relative' above); and 'verbless free', e.g. 'A pèn# pléase#'.

Column 8, in a 45-term system, assigned a grammatical description to the contents of the tone unit. This was primarily (and where relevant) done with reference to column 7, since, as we shall see, clause limits and tone-unit limits coincided in a large number of cases. Additional terms had however to be brought in to accommodate the several types of 'clause fragment' that were found co-extensive with tone units. The commonest of these were prepositional phrases with adverbial value in a clause occupying a preceding tone unit (150), nominal group as subject (82), and verb with post-verbal elements (109: this type was obviously, in the main, correlative to the preceding type).

Finally, in *column 9*, a system of 41 terms categorized the grammatical junction that obtained between tone units. About a quarter of the tone units terminated at the end of grammatical units which had no grammatical relation with what followed in the next tone unit (486). A further 97 might be added to these, since any grammatical link at the tone-unit junction was very weak and even questionable. A further 206 tone units ended at points of major grammatical break where the linkage was only through 'sentence co-ordination'. Thus about 800 of the roughly 1900 tone units terminated at points of grammatical junction no more binding than that between the two following clauses: 'we were

together befóre# and we're together nòw#'. Other statistically important unit-terminals were as follows: between co-ordinate bound clauses
(75); between co-ordinate nominal groups as complement (71);
subject and verb (108); between the head of a nominal group (not
operating as subject) and a clausal postmodifier (93); between the main
elements of a clause and a following non-clausal adverbial (125);
between the main elements of a clause and a following clausal adverbial
(80); and between a preceding clausal adverbial and the main elements
of a clause (82). No other type of grammatical junction was represented
more than fifty times.

When each tone unit had been described with reference to these nine
sets of variables, the total data were coded and transferred to punched
tape in the University of London Computer Unit. The material was fed
into a Ferranti Mercury computer and subjected to analysis by means
of a sorting and counting programme, the first output being a simple
inventory from which was abstracted the quantitative information so far
presented. The inventory itself is enough to show areas of strong
relationship between intonation and grammar, but is not enough to
show the terms of such a relationship. This can best be done, we would
claim, by carefully plotting the *co-occurrence* of variables,[9] a task which
is greatly facilitated by the use of a computer.

The programme involved the computer in noting and measuring
severa lthousand co-occurrences among the many variables in the nine
columns,[10] and the notes that follow draw attention to some of the
significant co-occurrences that were revealed and to the conclusions
that may be drawn from them.

Comparison of *columns 1 and 3* (with supplementary comparison
with *columns 4, 5, 6, and 7*) shows that in general the nucleus types
occurred on the same range of form-classes in the same proportions.
We would draw attention to certain exceptions which are presented in
the table below:

> (a) a relatively high proportion of rising tones on names; this is
> explained by the study of columns 3 and 7 which shows that the

[9] See Paper 7 above, p. 78.
[10] Since some analytic categories depend on correlation between columns, and
since for practical reasons it was necessary to cut out the computation of numerically small co-occurrences (less than ten in two-column comparisons, and less
than five in three-column comparisons), it has been necessary on stated occasions below to give figures which are approximations.

greatest clustering of nucleus-bearing names was in address-forms: 'Jóhn# what do you sày#';

(b) a relatively high proportion of rise-fall nuclei on adverbs, as in utterances like 'Rêally#' and 'He does it bêautifully#';

(c) a relatively high proportion of falling nuclei on premodifying adjectives in fall-plus-rise units, as in utterances like 'The òld man ísn't#'; comparison of columns 1, 3, and 4 shows that out of 71 instances of fall-plus-rise on juxtaposed words, the first of these was an adjective in 24 cases;

(d) a significant correlation between the falling nucleus in fall-plus-rise units and a pronoun as subject, as in utterances like 'Hè doesn't wórk#'.

Nucleus Type	Nucleus on					
	Noun	Name	Adverb	Adj. premod. Head of Nom. Gp.	Adj. not in Nom. Gp.	Pronoun as Subject
Fall	382	56	103	29	57	13
Rise	202	50	47	(<10)	22	(<10)
Fall-rise	55	(<10)	17	(<10)	10	(<10)
Rise-fall	20	(<10)	17	(<10)	(<10)	(<10)
Fall (of `+´)	25	(<10)	18	27	(<10)	17
Rise (of `+´)	82	14	16	(<10)	(<10)	(<10)

We shall return to the association of nucleus types with features of grammar in considering columns 1 and 9 below (pp. 133–5).

In view of points (a) and (d) in the preceding paragraph, it is of interest to point out (from columns 3, 5, and 6) that:

1. 10 per cent of nucleus-bearing subjects had a name as exponent, but only 3·5 per cent of nucleus-bearing complements; and that
2. 25 per cent of nucleus-bearing subjects had a pronoun as exponent but only 9 per cent of nucleus-bearing complements.

Columns 3, 5, and 7. In most types of clause, the nucleus fell within a nominal group structure in a ratio of between 2:1 and 4:1 as compared with the verbal group. In a few clause types the position was reversed:

Type 1: *I think* that he did it.

Type 2: He did it, *I think.*
Type 3: I wondered *how he did it.*
Type 4: I asked about *what he did.*

The figures in the material are given below, and for comparison we add those for a

Type 5: I think *that he did it.*

Nucleus on	Clause Type				
	1	2	3	4	5
Nominal Group	13	< 10	11	< 10	150
Verbal Group	26	19	15	12	24

Columns 2, 8, and 9. Whatever the type of grammatical unit, there was a considerable correlation between the length of tone units and their grammatical contents. The length tended to be a single word with certain types of adverbial contents; 3-4 words when the tone unit was co-extensive with end-placed prepositional phrase as adverbial or with nominal group as subject; but tone units consisting of verb plus post-verbal elements tended to be longer, 4–5 words. Tone units co-extensive with one full clause averaged 5–6 words, and the length increased to 8 words when the tone unit was co-extensive with two clauses. The dominant clause pairs were of the type 'Clause having a clause as complement'. The study of co-occurrences indicates some tension between (*a*) the tendency for such clause sequences to occupy single tone units, (*b*) the tendency for the end-point of a tone unit to be the end-point of a clause, and (*c*) the tendency for tone units to maintain a roughly constant length. Clause sequences of the type in question are of course sometimes longer than even the 8 words prosodically 'allowed' them, and this may explain why tone units comprising a clause plus a clause fragment occurred in the material 20 times with a nucleus on a clause having a clause as complement but did not reach double figures with any other grammatical type. For example: 'Everyone knew that his concentrà-tion# was the secret of the man's succèss#'. (See further p. 132.) The Table below shows the major correlations between the length of the tone unit and its contents:

Two Clauses (8 words)

I really think that he will come tomòrrow

9

One Clause (5-6 words)

| He will arrive by train tomòrrow |

Verb. Gp. plus Adverbial (4-5 words)

| will arrive at ten thìrty |

Nom. Gp. as Subject (3-4 words)

| The train from Lóndon |

Prep. Phrase as Adverbial (3-4 words)

| at this plátform |

Miscellaneous Nom. Gp. (2-3 words)

| and the Sóuth |

Adverbial (1 word)

| ŏbviously |

Columns 5, 6, and 8. Another indication that a tendency to constant tone-unit length was in conflict with the tendency for tone unit and clause to be co-extensive is shown by the study of columns 5, 6, and 8. Two types of nucleus-bearing nominal groups were most frequent: (1) 'the hèad', (2) 'the head of the rìver'. Clauses with the nucleus on a nominal group were more frequently co-extensive with the tone unit when the nominal group was type 1 than when it was type 2.

Nucleus as in	Tone Unit Co-extensive with Clause	Tone Unit Co-extensive with Nominal Group as S or with Prep. Phr. as A
Nominal Group (1)	342	123
Nominal Group (2)	90	82

This distribution reflects the fact that complex nominal groups (type 2) were generally longer than those of type 1 and might often therefore make a tone unit longer than normal; they thus tended to be separated off into separate tone units.

Nominal groups of type 1 were always numerically predominant, whatever the place in clause structure occupied by the nominal group; but the proportions differ, revealing a tendency for type 1 nominal groups to be used in prepositional phrases as adverbial, while type 2 had a higher ratio than usual when the nominal group was subject:

	As Subject	As Complement	In Prep. Phr. as Adverbial
Nominal Group (1)	60	201	265
Nominal Group (2)	46	99	76

Columns 6 and 8. Where the nucleus fell on the verb or complement, the tone unit in a large majority of cases was co-extensive with the clause. Where it fell on a prepositional phrase with adverbial value, over a third were in tone units co-extensive with a clause, while a quarter of the prepositional phrases themselves were co-extensive with the tone units. Where the nucleus was on the subject, only a small minority of the tone units were co-extensive with a clause, and a majority were co-extensive with the subject (having a nominal group as exponent). Salient points of distribution:

Nucleus on	Total Nucleus-Bearing	Tone Unit Co-ext. with Clause	Tone Unit Co-ext. with Nom. Gp. as S	Tone Unit Co-ext. with Prep. Phr. as A
Verb	366	200	—	—
Complement	553	296	—	—
Subject	170	19	76	—
Prep. Phr. as Adverbial	457	169	—	115

Columns 7, 8, and 9 show that free clauses were co-extensive with the tone unit in about half their occurrences and that a large number of clauses of various types were so in about one-third of their occurrences. Two clause types deserve a special comment. Sequences of 'Clause plus clause as complement' ('I think he came', 'I know how he did it', for example) were the only clause-pairs with frequency (61) of more than 10. The figures make clear that the clauses which operated as complement had a distinctly lower than average co-extensiveness (about 1/7). Moreover, since we know from the material that there were 177 clauses as complement, it is very likely that there were almost as many clauses having such clauses as complement ('almost', allowing for co-ordination of complements). It must therefore be remembered that when Table 1 gives one-third of such clauses (18) as co-extensive with a tone unit this does not mean one-third of all such clauses in the material. There would be a much smaller proportion of co-extensive instances if we were not restricting our comparison to those clauses (54) which had a nucleus.[11]

Comparison of *columns 8 and 9* shows the relation of unit contents to inter-unit breaks. As can be seen from Table 2, units co-extensive with one clause (879) or two (55) end in 422 cases at a point which had no overt grammatical relationship to the next. In a further 174 cases, the only grammatical link was clause co-ordination. There seems to be a tendency for a tone-unit break to come before an adverbial postmodifier in clause structure (109). In 16 cases, a clause co-extensive with a tone unit and operating as subject had a unit break before the verb (as in 'What worries me móst# is his làziness#'). When a tone unit was co-extensive with a nominal group, the group in the majority of cases (50) operated as subject and the tone-unit break was between subject and verb.

A unit co-extensive with verb plus complement had a break before a postmodifier as often as at a point of no overt relationship.

Clauses operating as postmodifiers in nominal groups and clauses operating as complement in another clause showed a tendency to have inter-unit junctions thus:

The man I knów# is over thère#
I think this mán# will dò it#

In all, 46 per cent of the total number of tone units ended at points where overt grammatical relationship ceased or with the only gram-

---

[11] Since, through our tone-unit orientation, we register a clause's existence only if a nucleus falls within it, our totals for all types of clauses are inevitably incomplete. The disparity, therefore, between a 50 per cent clause tone unit co-extensiveness (in the case of free clauses) and a 14 per cent co-extensiveness (in the case of clauses as complement) may be in part illusory, since the former permits no inference as to the existence of clauses which do not bear a nucleus. It is unlikely, however, that many clauses of other kinds occur without a nucleus, though no doubt the phenomenon occurs with the parenthetic type.

TABLE I

Clause Type	Total Clauses Bearing a Nucleus	Total Clauses Co-ext. with Tone Unit	Pro- portion
Forms of address	46	38	3/4
'Clause + Clause as C' sequences	79	61	3/4
Verbless free	75	46	2/3
Free	160*	95	3/5
Parenthetic	36*	16	1/2
End-placed Fin. Vb. Clause as A	82*	35	1/2
Front-placed Fin. Vb. Clause as A	101*	39	2/5
Indep. non-terminal	263*	104	2/5
Indep. terminal	120*	49	2/5
Clause as S	15	5	1/3
Clause having Clause as C	54*	18	1/3
Front-placed Verbless Cl. as A	34	12	1/4
Cl. as postmodifier in N. Gp.	162*	35	1/4
End-placed Verbless Cl. as A	22	6	1/4
Cl. correlative to anticipatory *it*	19	5	1/4
End-placed Non-Fin. Vb. Cl. as A	22	<5	<1/5
Cl. appos. to N. Gp. or comp. to. Adj.	30	<5	<1/6
Clause as C (*that* or zero)	134*	19 ⎫	1/7
Clause as C ('dep. question')	43	<5 ⎭	
Non-Fin. Vb. Cl. postmod. in Nom. Gp.	86	<5	<1/17

* Approximate: see footnote 10.

matical relationship being clause co-ordination. Only 5·6 per cent were at points of group or phrase co-ordination. Breaks between major elements in clause structure (subject, verb, complement) occurred in only 8·4 per cent of all cases (tone-unit breaks within nominal group structures represented almost as high a proportion of the material), whereas breaks between subject-verb-complement on the one hand, and adverbial on the other, constituted 18 per cent of the tone-unit junctions.

Columns 1 and 9. While the data examined in this experiment would offer no evidence that a particular type of nucleus has a specific gram- matical function, the Table below shows that particular nuclei occur with particular types and degrees of grammatical relationship in sig- nificantly different proportions. There is most notably an association

TABLE 2

Inter-unit Break Occurs Between	Two Clauses	One Clause	Nominal Group	Verb plus Complement	Prepositional Phrase	Special Fragments	Other Minor Categories	Inventory of Each Type	Percentage of Tone Units in Material
Units with no overt grammatical relationship	40	382	13	30	39	—	79	583	46
Co-ordinate Independent Clauses	15	115	10	—	22	—	44	206	46
Co-ordinate Dependent Clauses	—	44	—	—	—	—	31	75	46
Co-ordinate Complements	—	34	12	—	—	—	25	71	5·6
Co-ordinate Adverbials	—	14	—	—	—	—	20	34	5·6
Subject and Verb	—	16	50	—	—	24†	18	108	8·4
Verb and Complement	—	24*	—	—	—	11‡	15	50	8·4
Nominal and Postmodifier	—	58	15	14	27	—	27	141	7·5
SVC and End-placed Adverbial	—	109	—	15	—	—	81	205	18
Front-placed Adverbial and SVC	—	68	—	—	21	—	43	132	18
Clause and Parenthetic Clause	—	15	—	—	—	—	4	19	1
Totals	55	879	100	59	109	35	387	1624	

* 18 of type SV and Clause as C, e.g. 'I think he's going'.
† 12 of type N.Gp.+Rel. Cl. and 12 of type SV½C, where the '½C' is the S. of a Cl. operating as C, e.g. 'I think this man# will do it'.
‡ Chiefly SV or VS.

Nucleus Type	Total shown in Correlation of Columns 1 and 9	Units with no Overt Grammatical Relationship	Co-ord. Independent Clauses	Co-ord. Dependent Clauses	Co-ord. Subjects, Complements, or Adverbials	Subject and Verb	Nominal and Postmodifier	Front-placed Adverbials & SVC
Fall	907	365	122	22	54	30	53	37
Rise	424	97	43	22	34	30	36	41
Fall-rise	123	13	(<10)	(<10)	(<10)	16	17	(<10)

(a)   (b)

of a falling nucleus with a termination in the chain of grammatical dependence. Group (*a*) represents the tone-unit terminals corresponding with greatest grammatical independence; it will be seen that this group accounts for over *half* the falling nuclei, but only a *quarter* of the rising ones, and only a *sixth* of the fall-rises. In contrast, group (*b*), which comprises the remainder of the frequently occurring categories, represents unit terminals at points of close grammatical relationship, and the proportion of falls to rises and fall-rises is considerably lower.[12]

To judge from the present limited material and limited analysis of it, it would seem that:

(*a*) there is in some measure an association between certain nucleus types and certain form-classes (pp. 127 f.), and between certain broad categories of grammatical relationship and tone units having certain nuclei (pp. 133 ff.);

(*b*) there is a very considerable connexion between the point of nuclear tone and specific items of grammar, whether as regards form-class, group, phrase, clause, or clause-sequence (pp. 124, 125 f., 128 ff.);

(*c*) there is a tendency for certain constants to be observed in the length of tone units according to the types of grammatical content (pp. 129 f.) ;

(*d*) there is a high degree of co-extensiveness between tone units and grammatical units of group, phrase, and clause structure (pp. 130 ff.);

(*e*) the point at which one tone unit ends and the next begins tends to be one of a fairly small number of grammatical junctions (pp. 132 f.).

[12] Among the numerically minor categories not shown in the Table, one might mention the tone-unit break between non-co-ordinate adverbials: falling nuclei 4, rising nuclei 12.

Thirteen

On scales of contrast in connected English speech†

If we were to ask a group of native English speakers whether

    (*a*) Throw it into the garden

was more like

    (*b*) Throw it from the garden

or more like

    (*c*) Throw it in the garden

we can assume that more would equate (*a*) and (*c*) than (*a*) and (*b*), and that this would constitute evidence that there was a scale of importance within the differences between 'different' prepositions. Whatever difference there may be between *into* and *in*, we could say, there are environments in which they come together in contrast with *from*, and we might postulate within the 'system' of prepositions such a 'sub-system' as

$$\text{from} \quad :: \quad \text{in(to)}$$
$$\text{in} \quad : \quad \text{into}$$

In an attempt to see whether there was a scale of importance for some of the many possible types of difference manifest in the prosodic features of connected speech, we recorded the utterance:

A few minutes later, the fellow came; he walked up slowly, and said 'Oh, it wasn't you that I wanted'.

† This paper reports work done in collaboration with D. Crystal in 1962–3. Some years elapsed between our writing it and its publication in the volume *In Memory of J. R. Firth* (London, 1966), 359 ff.; we have therefore seized the opportunity to revise it at numerous points for the present occasion.

TABLE 1

Showing the distinctions relevant to the experiment and the extent to which the 46 informants observed them

'A few minutes later, the fellow came; he walked up slowly and said "Oh, it wasn't you that I wanted".'

		1	2	3	4	5	6	7	8	9	10	11	12	13	14
Tone Unit	I	•	•	♩	•	♩	♩	•	•	♩	♩	♩		♩	♩
	II	•	•	•	•	•	•	•	•	•	•	•		•	•
Tonicity	III	/	#	/ #		: # •	/ # •	n.a.	'	\ / #	/\ #	/\ # /		\ /	/ #
	IV			34		4		n.a.		41		42			
Tonicity	V		2	33	16	34 (+4S)				41		42	43	40	38 (+5S)
Onset	VI		46		34		4 (+4S)	46			32 9 43				1 (+5S)
Nucleus	VII		1\ 1\(+/)	28 3\ 2\		32 14\ 2\(+3S 1S−)				17 12\ 12\	10 29\ 2\ 1\			29(+/) 2\(+/) 9\	29 (/+) (/\+) 2 1\ 6\ (+5S')
Stress	VIII		15												
Stress replacing nucleus	IX													3	
Stress plus nucleus	X					1						19		2	
Booster	XI			5(/ or \)		21				11		33		23	1(/)
Booster replacing onset	XII				10										
Pause	XIII			1				n.a.	5	3			26		
Range	XIV			15 17N\ 1N\		28 4N\ 2N\			29 2N\ 7N\ 3N\			38 2N\ 7N\ 1N\		39 1N\	30 7N\ 1N\

Braces: rows I–IV grouped under **Model**; remaining rows under **Informants**.

Notes: The italicized numbers show agreement with features in the model; unitalicized numbers are deviations.

n.a. = 'not applicable', since informants reacted to a recording of the model in two parts bounded at these points.

S = 'subordinate', on which see p. 142 below and note 5.

Range in line XIV refers only to a contrast between 'not narrow', and 'narrow' (N); that is, a range equal to or greater than that of the model is here regarded as agreement and distinguished from instances of narrowed range in (non-subordinate) nuclei.

A transcription of this recording, narrow enough to register all the features relevant to the experiment, is given in line II of Table 1. Forty-six native English informants in turn heard the recording twice, first as a whole and then in two parts; they were asked simply to repeat it in the same two parts, the break being at point 5 (Table 1, line I). Their versions were recorded and transcribed in the same type of notation, and these were then scrutinized for the various kinds and degrees of similarity and dissimilarity to the original version (hereafter referred to as the 'model') in terms of the following key features:[1]

Points 3, 5, 9, 10, 13, 14 as 'nuclei', similarity being noted in terms of occurrence, location, pitch height at beginning of nucleus, pitch range, and direction of pitch movement;

Points 1, 4, 7, 10, 12 as the first points of pitch prominence ('onset') after beginning of utterance and after each nucleus, points 13 and 14 being considered correlative and interdependent, forming a complex without the possibility of an intervening onset;

Points 2, 8 as points of syllabic prominence without a step-up in pitch ('stress');

Points 6, 11 as pauses, similarity noted simply in terms of 'pause' or 'no pause', regardless of precise duration.

For example, the following is a selection of agreements over a stretch of the utterance up to the first nucleus, 'A few minutes later':

1. (a) 3 out of 46 informants had: onset on *few*; stress on first syllable of *minutes*; rising nucleus (with same range as model) on *later*.

   (b) 11/46: onset on *few*; rising nucleus (with same range as model) on *later*.

   (c) 28/46: onset on *few*; rising nucleus on *later*.

   (d) 33/46: onset on *few*; nucleus on *later*.

   (e) 34/46: onset on *few*; nucleus within the stretch.

To illustrate the fact that the two conditions remaining in 1(e) are not universally liable to equal agreement, we may give the comparable points in the selection for another stretch, admittedly least typical in

---

[1] The recordings of the model and of the informants' versions are filed in the Survey of English Usage and may be heard at University College London. The technical terms and the type of transcription used here are explained in the preceding Paper, and with more detail in Crystal and Quirk, *Systems of Prosodic and Paralinguistic Features in English* (The Hague, 1964).

the amount of disagreement over the placing of the onset, 'and said "Oh"':

2. (d) 7/46: onset on *oh*, nucleus on *oh*.
   (e) 42/46: nucleus on *oh*.

Applying such tests of agreement throughout the material, it was found, as we see in Table 1, first that different substantial criteria produced sharply different amounts of agreement, and secondly that the same substantial feature produced differing amounts of agreement at different points in the utterance. These two factors taken together suggested that we were dealing with different systems and not merely expansions of a single system. It was further found that the series (a)–(e) given for one particular stretch above had regularity and consistence in the correspondence of agreement to substantial features when compared with the series set up for the other stretches. Since, therefore, there was non-randomness in the kind of feature noted and the agreement observed, it is possible to re-state generalized forms of these series, accounting for all the data in the test material, as inverse hierarchies of systems.

The systemic statement which accounts for the highest level of agreement concerns what is common to 1 (e), 2 (e) above: the occurrence of an unstipulated nucleus at an unstipulated point within a stretch of speech. That is, the barely delimited 'tone unit'[2] or what Trim has called 'tone cum rhythm group'.[3] There was 85 per cent agreement in this respect, though such a level was not evenly spread over all tone units, yielding a point of subsidiary interest to which we shall return.

The next highest level of agreement, 82 per cent, was to be found in 'tonicity', the abstraction that relates to the location of the nucleus, without regard to the range or direction of the pitch movement.

The third highest level of agreement, 77 per cent, concerned the onset location – the first point of pitch prominence in the tone unit.

When we come to the exponent of nucleus, we find more difficulty in deciding what we should regard as agreement. In terms of a widespread typology that is based on direction of pitch movement alone, we have in the model five types of nucleus: rise (at Point 3), fall (5), fall-rise (9), rise-fall (10), and fall-plus-rise (13, 14). Examined in the light of this typology, the data of the experiment yield 62 per cent

[2] See Paper 12, pp. 122 ff. Cf. also M. A. K. Halliday, 'The Tones of English', *Archivum Linguisticum* 15 (1963).
[3] *Le Maître Phonétique* 112 (1959), 27.

agreement. This is a sharp drop from the agreement reached in respect of the previous feature considered, and probably most speakers would agree that they are intuitively aware of less randomness in nucleus selection than this figure would imply. Our uneasiness is confirmed when we examine the grossly uneven way in which agreement is registered in the test material by means of this typology. At one extreme, in the tone unit 'the fellow came', we find (with tonicity at *fellow* or *came*) that there is 95 per cent agreement on the nucleus type 'fall'. At the other extreme, in the tone unit 'and said "oh"', we find only 22 per cent agreement on a rise-fall nucleus. But scrutiny of the area of disagreement in the latter case reveals significant regularities. Where the model had a rise-fall on *oh*, 39/46 informants registered a step-up in pitch at this point, and of the 32/46 who did not repeat the rise-fall, no fewer than 29 made a fall nucleus here, 26 of them with a 'high' step-up in pitch (that is, to a point higher than the level of the previous pitch-prominent syllable), followed by a wide-range fall. It would seem, therefore, that an essential feature of a rise-fall is the attainment of a high pitch level (not at all necessarily by means of a pitch glide), and that even conservatively we can equate a high step-up plus wide fall with a rise-fall nucleus. Thus:

model: ôh   informants: ôh 10 ×   !ôh 26 ×

If we now bracket !$^\searrow$ with $^\frown$ as variant exponents of the 'same' nucleus, we find we have an agreement figure of 74 per cent for nucleus types.

Agreement levels of the four types so far noted may now be summarized as follows:

(*a*) Tone Units:
.......#.......#.......#.......#.......#   85%
(*b*) Tonicity:
... Ton.. (#) ... Ton .. (#) ... Ton .. (#) ... Ton .. (#) ...
Ton..(#)   82%
(*c*) Onset:
./. (Ton.. #) ./. (Ton .. #) ./. (Ton .. #) ./. (Ton .. #) ./.
(Ton..#)   77%
(*d*) Exponence of Nucleus:
.(/)Nuc(#).(/)Nuc(#).(/)Nuc(#).(/)Nuc(#).(/)Nuc(#)   74%

Since a high starting point plus wide range would seem to be significant features capable of distinguishing between a fall and a rise-fall, it is worth looking at the distribution of range characteristics elsewhere in the material. It is possible that we should associate range with the relatively low agreement found at another nuclear point, the fall-rise in 'he walked up slŏwly'. The fall-rise is repeated here by only 17/46 informants, while 12/46 had a rise and a further 12/46 a fall. But this scatter of results is perhaps not as random as such figures might suggest. Of the 24/46 repeating a nucleus but not a fall-rise, 10 had narrow range and 7 of these had the narrow range with a rise. Although the evidence from this particular experiment is slight, it seems possible that in a given grammatical environment a narrow-range unidirectional nuclear tone – especially a rise – may operate in a system of variants of fall-rise; further investigation may be expected to reveal the terms of such a subsystem and the conditions under which they are selected. In one of the unscripted texts in the Survey of English Usage collection (5b.51), for example, we find several examples like the following:

(a) the Advisory Council to which you re*ferred*# expressed an opinion#

(b) and in*deed*# flies# in the face# of the very considerable body of factual evidence that exists#

(c) have any crimes# in *prac*tice# been punishable by judicial beat-ing#

(d) in nineteen forty-*eight*# judicial beating was abolished#

In each of these, the italicized syllable bears a narrow-range rising nucleus (N′). The first terminates a postmodified nominal group operat-ing as subject, the other three a preverbal adjunct, that in (b) being followed by a similar one uttered by the same speaker a few seconds later, 'in actual fact', with a nucleus ∨ on *fact*. It is probable that if informants were asked to repeat these utterances (a)–(d), they would frequently replace N′ by ∨.

The part played by range is seen less equivocally in the data for the first tone unit in the experimental material, 'a few minutes later'. In the first place, it is to be noted that while the model had a full-range rise on *later*, 12/46 informants did not observe a tone unit at all in this instance. This is perhaps not surprising in view of the relatively low predictability that a front-placed verbless adjunct (as opposed to a finite or non-finite verb adjunct) should constitute a tone unit.[4] More importantly, while 28/46 not merely observed a tone unit but repeated a rise on *later*, 17 of these informants gave the rise a narrow range. In view of what was said in the previous paragraph, it is worth adding

---

[4] See Table 1 in Paper 12, p. 133.

that a further three informants gave a fall-rise on *later*. Even if this constitutes little additional evidence on the relation of $\vee$ and N′, it surely indicates that N′ has a place in a subsystem of nuclei, grammatically conditioned: that, in other words, the rise of yes-no questions is characteristically different from the rise of front-placed adjunct exponents.

Range has an evident relevance to the phenomenon of tonal subordination.[5] In the experimental material, subordination chiefly occurred when informants moved a nucleus forward from its place in the model; for example, from *came* to *fellow* in 'the fellow came'. A quarter of those who thus moved the nucleus retained a nuclear tone on *came* but gave it a narrower range than that of the fall on *fellow*. For example:

● ❨ ❩   transcribed as   `ˋ[ˋ]#`

In one case, the exponent of the subordinate nucleus was level, and interestingly enough it was an instance when the superordinate nucleus was itself narrow. Thus we might postulate a parallel series

● ❨ ❩   =   ˋ N ˋ systematized as   `ˋ[ˋ]#`

● ❨ ⊶   =   N ˋ⁻ systematized as   `Nˋ[ˋ]#`

where the final pair of transcriptions has reduced the substantial differences to a single determining distinction. It is clear that we might further generalize to the point of equating these as both

`ˋ[ˋ]`   in contrast with   ˋ

or, at a still higher level of abstraction, as both

ˋ   in contrast with   ´, ´[´], [´]´, etc.

But this is not to say that a 'level' nucleus is to be related solely to 'fall' in systemic description. Although our present materials offer much evidence for linking level with fall, an alternative link with rise is also suggested. Levels seem undoubtedly to have a place in a subsystem of rising nuclei, though perhaps rather in prosodic co-ordination than subordination. To illustrate again from the Survey text 5b.51:

(*a*) with having their trousers taken dōwn# and backsides bírched#
(*b*) between eighteen nīnety# and nineteen thirty-fòur#

---

[5] See further, Crystal and Quirk, *Systems of Prosodic and Paralinguistic Features in English*, 52 ff.

(c) it is subject to the final prerōgative# of mērcy# of the Home Sēcretary# who may recommend a reprìeve#

In these instances, the level nuclei seem more readily replaceable by rising nuclei than anything else and might ultimately be best viewed as exponents of narrow terms in a subsystem of rise relatable to a particular rhetorical register of speech.[6]

Finally, a narrowed range seems to be commoner than merely random in the second nucleus of the correlative pair in the sequence

it wasn't yòu that I wánted#

where 7 of the 29 informants who repeated a rise on *wanted* made it narrow. This may indeed suggest an affinity between the sets of 'correlative nuclei' (rise-plus-fall as in 'he walked áll the way hòme', fall-plus-rise as in 'the òld men tríed') and the phenomenon of 'subordination'. It is worth mentioning that, in the first tone unit, one informant gave such a correlative pair on *few* and *later*, making the rise of narrow range. There are several examples of ˋ+Nˊ in the Survey text 5b.51 from which other supplementary materials have already been quoted. For example:

(a) if they dìd these dreadful Nthíngs# they might . . .
(b) the plàin fact of the matter Nís# they have not . . .
(c) the vast majòrity of Nmúrderers# are . . .

The area of minority disagreements is, in its own way, as informative as that of majority agreements. Thus in the tone unit 'the fellow came', the fall nucleus of the model is repeated by 44/46 informants, while two substitute a rise. In the unit 'a few minutes later', 28/46 repeat a rise and three substitute a fall, while a further three substitute a fall-rise. In the unit with correlative nuclei, 'it wasn't you that I wanted', a fall on *you* is repeated 38 times and the only alternative nucleus type that occurs is a rise-fall in two cases, and these – as we have seen – should be treated as variants of a fall. The correlative rise on *wanted* presents a very different picture. While 32 repeat a rise (31 completing the fall-plus-rise correlation), no fewer than 11 informants substitute a fall. These 11 can be seen as two important groups. The first, numbering five, make the fall subordinate to that on *you*:

. . . yòu that I [wànted]#

[6] See further the doctoral dissertation of D. Crystal (*Studies in the Prosodic Features of Educated British English*: University of London, 1966), especially p. 388. Dr Crystal's thesis is shortly to be published by the Cambridge University Press in the new series of linguistics monographs.

The other six make the fall the primary nucleus, usually of the whole original unit (' ... you that I wànted#'), but in one case with the formation of a new unit (' ... yòu# that I /wànted#'). In the unit 'he walked up slowly', as we have already noted, the fall-rise is twelve times replaced by a rise and twelve times by a fall. Finally, we have the unit, 'and said "Oh"', in which – again as already noted – the principal disagreement is a majority one: 29/46 informants substitute a fall for the rise-fall; the minority disagreements here are a fall-rise twice and a rise once.

It is clear from the previous paragraph that the polarity is most extreme between fall and rise: the distinction between these two has clearest phonological status, with a contrastiveness most resembling that between, let us say, voiced and voiceless consonants in English phonology or between singular and plural in English grammar. A fall may be replaced by a rise-fall or it may even be ignored occasionally (at any rate in the correlative fall-plus-rise sequences); but it is very unusual to find it replaced by a rise. The other pole, the rise, has slightly less stability, and it can be replaced by a fall fairly readily as the second part of a correlative sequence, though such replacement seems rare elsewhere.[7]

By contrast, the fall-rise admits replacement by both fall and rise quite frequently, and we find it three times replacing a rise, twice replacing even a rise-fall,[8] and being introduced a further twice where there was no nucleus in the model:

$$\text{the} \quad \text{/fĕllow\#} \quad \text{/càme\#}$$

Its phonological status seems to be indicated most by its apparently strong tendency to co-occurrence with 'contingency' or close grammatical relationship with what follows.[9] Contingency is even more obvious, of course, in the correlative nuclei of fall-plus-rise units in contrast (not infrequently neutralized) with fall units.

Further study is required to validate the hypotheses suggested by the present material, but it would seem that systems of nuclei operate

[7] Compare the Table given at the end of Paper 12, p. 134, which shows that falls are not only twice as common as rises but that they frequently occur in similar environments, presumably indicating an area in which the contrast between fall and rise is neutralized.

[8] Both irregularities, however, occur with informants who seem to be unusual and unreliable in some of their other responses as well, ignoring or replacing the nuclei on *slowly, you* and *wanted*.

[9] Cf. Paper 12, pp. 128 f., 134 f.

in a set of relationships somewhat in the manner postulated for the present limited material in the two-dimensional model represented in Table 2.

TABLE 2

A brief comment may be of interest on some further disagreements relating to tone-unit limits, tonicity, and onset location. Four informants make a new tone unit begin with *came* (Table 1, line IV), thus tonally separating subject and verb, three making the exponent of subject alone ('the fellow') constitute a unit. The rarity of this type of break in clause structure (where the subject is a simple nominal group) is to be contrasted with the situation in which 42 informants follow the model in tonally interrupting the exponent of complement in 'and said . . .' where, however, the complement itself has clause structure in which the tonal interruption is between adjunct and SVC. As to tonicity, it was noted in Paper 12, p. 125, that a nucleus fell only rarely on an element preceding the head in group structure. In the present material, it is noteworthy that there are only two disagreements with the model in this respect: the placing of a falling nucleus on the pre-modifying *few* in the adverbial group 'a few minutes later' (Table 1, line V), and one of these appears less exceptional when it is pointed out that the fall is correlative to a rise on *later* (Table 1, line VII). Disagreements on onsets are in some cases unimportant: thus the relatively low agreement figure at *fellow* is a simple consequence of the relatively low level of agreement on the first tone unit's limits (Table 1, line IV). The shift of onset from *oh* to *said*, however, is very striking. In the model, it happened that the onset fell in four cases on the verb exponent or on the first lexical item in group structure (alternatively, but doubtless trivially, on the second syllable of each tone unit). The one exception was, so to say, 'regularized' by many informants:

and said /oh   9 ×   *but*   and /said oh   32 ×

The experimental material yielded little information on other aspects of agreement and disagreement. The pause at point 11 was repeated 57 per cent of cases, the booster[10] at point 5 in 46 per cent, and the stresses (prominence without step-up in pitch) at points 2 and 8 in 22 per cent. The chief interest that these features presented was their co-occurrence with others. Thus new pauses were introduced in several cases but only at tone-unit limits. New boosters were introduced liberally. Apart from those already mentioned which co-occurred with a fall replacing (and thus jointly representing) a rise-fall, forty were introduced before falls and fall-rises and it would seem that : or ! plus ˋ or ˇ can be regarded as variants of ˋ or ˇ respectively with a distinctiveness of an utterly different (and 'lower') order from the distinctiveness of ˋ and ´, ˋ and ˇ, ˇ and ´, or even ´ and Nˊ. On stress there is very little to say: in a few cases it was found replacing a nucleus at *you*, and in a few it was itself replaced by a booster at *up*; extra stress (ǁ) co-occurred with nuclei on a few occasions: *came* 1 ×, *you* 2 ×, *oh* 19 ×.

To conclude, it is clear that there is high predictability as to what will constitute a tone unit. This will be grammatically determined in two ways – internal structure, and the external relations of this structure. There is a comparably high predictability in tonicity, but this is not directly related to the predictability of tone unit. Tonicity is again grammatically determined primarily, but probably chiefly in respect of the internal grammatical structure of the tone unit. There is rather less predictability over the selection of nucleus type, but it is still high. But while certain subsystems seem certainly to be determined primarily by internal relations, the selection for the most part seems certainly to be determined by the external relations of the tone unit. Survey of English Usage materials show several kinds of pattern in tone-unit sequences. For example, there is a high expectation that a tone unit with fall-rise nucleus will be followed by one with a high-boostered fall nucleus, and that tone units of the latter type are equally expected after sequences of tone units with rising nuclei. Similarly, a rise-fall tone unit is more frequently than random followed by a fall unit, while a

[10] A booster is a step-up in pitch; see further, *Systems of Prosodic and Paralinguistic Features in English*, 46.

rise-plus-fall unit is more frequently than random followed by a fall-plus-rise unit and almost never by a fall-rise unit. These are matters at present being intensively studied by Crystal, Davy and others, and one may provisionally refer for further discussion to pp. 450 ff. of the doctoral dissertation by Crystal already mentioned.

Fourteen

Complex prepositions and related sequences†

It is obvious that sequences of the form *Preposition + Nominal Group + Preposition + Nominal Group* (hereafter referred to as $P^1N^1P^2N^2$) are of great importance in English grammar and of great complexity:

> on the table near the door
> with the slightest hint of suspicion
> at the west front of the cathedral
> by repeated exclamations at her stupidity
> in grave need of support
> in spite of his very considerable charm

It is equally obvious that there is considerable variation in the degree of interdependence between the four elements of such sequences. In most of the above examples, the P^1 is not obligatory and the $N^1P^2N^2$ can thus operate separately as complex nominal groups having N^1 as head:

> The table near the door (has been reserved . . .)
> The slightest hint of suspicion (was enough . . .)

In at least one of them, the P^2 can be independently selected also:

> on the table by (*or* furthest from) the door

But we cannot usually vary P^2 (**with the slightest hint for suspicion*) and sometimes we are debarred from varying P^1 (**with spite of his charm*) and from treating N^1 as the head of a nominal group (**The spite of his charm was* . . .). The history of the language shows that, in several instances where the elements have developed interdependence, $P^1N^1P^2$

---

† Written in collaboration with Joan Mulholland and reprinted here from the R. W. Zandvoort Festschrift Supplement to *English Studies* 45 (1964), 64 ff.

sequences can become fully institutionalized as complex prepositions, the P^1 or N^1 or both losing identity (*because of, ahead of, instead of*), and the P^2 in some instances becoming optionally deletable, as in *alongside (of), on board (of)*.[1] It is clear, however, that without by any means reaching the stage of interdependence at which the P^1N^1 sequence can be written as one word, the N in a $P^1N^1P^2$ sequence can be sharply divorced from its use outside the sequence both lexically (so that in the sequence *in spite of*, the N cannot be replaced by *spitefulness* or any other member of the lexical set to which it belongs outside the sequence) and grammatically (so that we cannot use a determiner or adjective with *in spite of* as we can with *in the comfortable lounge of* or with *The considerable spite he showed surprised everyone*). This lexical and grammatical isolation is important both as a symptom of the PNP's highly unified status as a quasi-preposition and also – it would appear – in part a condition of it.[2]

What may not be so clear is that, while the polarity of the highly interdependent (*in spite of*) and the freely dissociable (*on the table near*) is clear-cut, we are not here dealing with a simple binary classification. However convenient sharp distinctions may be between grammar and lexis, closed system and open class, it is important to realize here as elsewhere that, between the poles realizable in $P^1N^1P^2N^2$ sequences, there is a continuum or gradient, and that in fact it is largely through the productive power of these sequences that we keep the form-class 'preposition' open-ended in English. It is our purpose in this paper to explore the 'more grammatical' end of this continuum and to determine the typological features of some points at which major PNP sequences have been formed.

By comparing 'in the lounge of the hotel' (A), 'in spite of the hotel' (B), and 'at the sight of the hotel' (C), as representing points on the

[1] The *NED* cites an example of *ahead* used similarly without of (1596). On the deletion of P^2, see also Kruisinga, *A Handbook of Present-Day English*, §1423.

[2] This is not the occasion for a historical excursus on the subject, but it may be noted that the noun *lieu* seems to have been little used in English outside the sequence *in lieu of* (in which it has been current since the thirteenth century): we may compare *à propos of, apropos of*. The fact that *à bord* seems to underlie the English use of *aboard (of)*, which was then expanded (according to the *NED*) to *on board of* suggests that native speakers have deepseated powers to recognize the lexical and grammatical features of the unified PNP sequences and that, regardless of etymology, the process of analogy which we refer to as 'serial relationship' contributes to the clustering of *ahead of, aboard (of), inside (of), apart from, aside from*, and similar sequences. (On 'serial relationship', see Paper 16 below and other publications of Quirk, Svartvik and others associated with the Survey of English Usage.)

continuum, it is easy to see the kinds of variable that are relevant as parameters.[3] We may add 'because of the hotel' (D), as a known representative of the grammatical pole by reason of its formal (phonological and graphic) dissociation from 'by + cause + of'.

	A	B	C	D
P^1 can be replaced	A+	B−	C−	D−
P^1 can be deleted showing N^1 is head of Nom. Gp.	A+	B−	C+	D−
N^1 has definite article	A+	B−	C+	D−
N^1 is concrete	A+	B−	C−	D−
N^1 can take different deictics	A+	B−	C−	D−
N^1 can be premodified by adjective	A+	B−	C+	D−
N^1 can show number contrast in the PNPN sequence	A+	B−	C−	D−
N^1 is used as a member of a lexical set	A+	B−	C+	D−
P^2N^2 can be deleted	A+	B−	C+	D−
With P^2N^2 deleted, N^1 can show number contrast	A+		C−	
P^2N^2 can be replaced by genitive pronoun premodifying N^1	A+	B−	C−	D−
P^2N^2 can be replaced by a demonstrative (*that, such*) premodifying N^1	A+	B−	C+	D−
There is no transformation relation between N^1-N^2 and a V-C structure respectively	A+	B+[4]	C−	D−
N^2 must be concrete	A+	B−	C−	D−

Without attempting to present an exhaustive list of such potential characteristics, it is clear that A is more different from B than either is from C, and that B is more like D (i.e. is nearer the grammatical pole) than C is. Working on the assumption, therefore, that a total positive reaction (as with A) was the 'most lexical' (least grammatical) pole and of no further interest in the present connexion, we selected for further study a set of current sequences (using the Survey of English Usage materials) in which there were at least four negative reactions. The number was of course arbitrary but seemed adequate if our task was only

---

[3] The restriction on the use of articles is discussed by Kruisinga, §1363, and several of the characteristics appear in Poutsma's excellent treatment in *A Grammar of Late Modern English*, II.i.A.681 f. and II.ii.719 ff.

[4] We are concerned here, of course, with synchronic statement only.

to embrace the grammatical end of the continuum. The sequences so selected amounted to 130.

Some general notes on this corpus of material may be of interest. By far the majority were found to be operating as Adjunct (non-local, non-temporal) in sentence structure; contrast 'He delighted in the view of the sunset' and 'He was delighted, in view of the sunset'. Again, the vast majority were found to have an abstract noun as head of the nominal group N^2. Of similarly obvious significance is the high degree of invariability in P^1 and P^2 throughout the material. Less important as a diagnostic feature, no doubt, but of significance in considering the relative analogical power of patterns, is the exponence of P^1 and P^2; *in – of* are the most frequently linked, occurring in 47 of the sequences (more than one third of the total); *in* also occurs with *for* (1), *to* (6), *with* (11). The most frequent P^2 is *of*, occurring in 106 sequences; as well as with *in*, it is linked to *at* (10), *on* (15), *by* (13), *for* (6), as well as sporadically to *from*, *under*, *of*, *to* and one or two others. There are very few sequences that do not involve either *in* as P^1 or *of* as P^2: *by (reference) to, on (exposure) to, at (variance) with,* and *with (a view) to.*[5]

It may not be surprising that the last mentioned sequence, rare in its P^1-P^2 pairing, is equally rare in having the indefinite article. The article here is, however, invariable, a feature this example shares with the majority of the other sequences in the material, whether the article is *the* (48) or zero (66). This proportion is not maintained as between individual P^1-P^2 pairings: *in – of* has 18 *the*, 28 zero; *by – of* has 4 *the*, 8 zero; with *in – to* and *in – with* there were no *the* examples, while *at – of* has no zero examples.

It would appear that no single characteristic of sequences at the grammatical pole is diagnostic. Thus the absence of a number contrast (*by dint of, by means of, *by dints of, *by mean of*) can be paralleled trivially by *with scissors for (his mother)*. Correspondingly, the ability to delete P^2N^2 (*he was in the lounge of the hotel→he was in the lounge*) is far from being diagnostic of the least grammatical pole since this is a property of more than a quarter of sequences in the corpus being considered. Thus *he is in favour of the plan→he is in favour*; so too *by force (of arms), by order (of the council), in addition (to his work),* etc. An important subclass allows the deletion when the sequence (usually *in – with*) is in a reciprocal construction; thus *he has this in common with her→*he has this in common* but *→they have this in common*. This reci-

---

[5] It will be noted that when P^2 is not *of* it is often in a relation of determination with the lexical item, N^1; cf. 'on exposure *to*' – 'he exposed it *to*'.

procity condition also affects (if to a lesser degree) *in agreement with, in contact with, in conformity with, at variance with* and one or two others.

The position is similar with the criterion of replacing P^2N^2 by a genitive (*in its lounge* but **in its spite*). Some 27 sequences in the corpus (all having *of* as P^2) will allow this P^2N^2 replacement, and these include sequences whose nearness to the grammatical pole is suggested by the fact that the N^1 occurs only in the P^1N^1 sequence: *for the sake of John→ for John's sake (his sake); on behalf of this man→on his behalf.* Indeed, one example may be said to be actually *at* the 'most grammatical' end since it is one whose P^1N^1 is written as one word: *instead of the book→ in its stead.* Most of the examples are of the form P^1 *the* $N^1P^2N^2$, but, besides *on behalf of* N^2, *instead of* N^2, we find several with zero before N^1: *in favour of, in place of, in defence of, on account of.*

Nor is the other type of P^2N^2 substitution (*in that lounge* but **in that spite*) necessarily remote from the grammatical pole. Several sequences, whose proximity to this pole is suggested by the lexical isolation of the N^1, permit the substitution: for example, *in case of fire→in that case; in respect of superannuation→in that respect.* As with the genitive substitution, however, most of the 46 sequences in the corpus permitting the substitution have *the*+N^1; a dozen are without article.

In nine of the corpus sequences both genitive and demonstrative substitutions can be made (*in the case of John→in his case; in the case of oil being found→in that case*), but in general the acceptability of the one substitution seems to preclude that of the other: *for the sake of* N^1→*for its sake* but **for that sake; with the exception of* N^1→**with its exception* but *with that exception.*

As for the potentiality to premodify N^1 with an adjective (*in the large lounge of the hotel* but **in large spite of the hotel*), a moment's reflection on examples like *in great need of attention, by sheer force of habit, with due regard to the circumstances* is enough to be assured that one can come close to the grammatical pole without precluding the possibility of adjective premodification. On closer scrutiny, however, it would seem that sequences nearest the grammatical pole (e.g. with lexical isolation of N^1, as in *with regard to*) allow only a narrow range of adjectives: *in (close, . . .?) connexion with; in the (capable, . . .?) hands of; on the (immediate, vexed, . . .?) question of; with the (sole, . . .?) aim of,* etc. With some sequences (e.g. *for lack of, from want of, by virtue of*), the choice of adjective seems virtually restricted to one which is in any case syntactically atypical, *sheer.* Certainly, there would appear to be interdependence (to the extent of mutual exclusiveness) between two of the parameters we have been considering: free selection of adjective[6] before N^1 and lexical isolation of N^1.

If there are no uniquely diagnostic features in 'grammatical' PNPN sequences, we may follow up the hint of the last paragraph by seeking, through the interrelationship of variables, a specification of points along the continuum. Of the types of variable we have so far discussed, we found that a matrix-presentation of nine provided a useful taxonomy of the sequences in our corpus.[7]

The nine in question (in order of the total number of positive reactions) are: (1) invariability of P^2; (2) N^1 having no number contrast; (3) N^1 being invariable as to article or zero article selection; (4) invariability of P^1; (5) non-replaceability of P^2N^2 by genitive; (6) non-deletability of P^2N^2; (7) non-replaceability of P^2N^2 by demonstrative; (8) lexical isolation of N^1; (9) N^1 not admitting free premodification by adjective. By considering the material in relation to the number and similarity of restrictions observed, we found that the sequences fell into five broad classes as shown below.

[6] Testing the potentiality for adjective selection raises difficulties, however, since one is often aware that the admission of an adjective, though idiomatically permissible, modifies the PNP sequence by moving it nearer the lexical pole. We may compare:

> In the case of Mr Johnson, we have failed to trace his order (= As for or With Mr Johnson, . . .)
> *and*
> In the regrettable and very peculiar case of Mr Johnson, we have . . . (= In the regrettable . . . circumstances in which Mr Johnson has found himself, . . .)

Note also 'for the present purpose', acceptable without P^2N^2, whereas *sole* but not *present* may premodify *purpose* in the fully realised $P^1N^1P^2N^2$.

[7] Space, of course, forbids examination here of all the variables that are relevant to a greater or lesser degree for taxonomic purposes. One involves the potentiality for number contrast with N^1 when N^1 is modified by an adjective *and* when P^2N^2 have been deleted; this provides an interesting subclass among the sequences in which a number contrast is disallowed in the full basic PNPN sequence. Note 'in the case (*not* cases) of lives and reputations'→'in such cases' *beside* 'at the cost (*not* costs) of lives and reputations'→'at such a cost (*not* costs)'. A variable which, unlike this last, can be applied to the entire corpus is the potentiality for the $P^1N^1P^2$ to be postposed, N^2 being replaced by a preposed interrogative word. Poutsma goes so far as to say that complex prepositions with the form $P^1N^1P^2$ differ from ordinary prepositions in being insusceptible to post-position; he cites only a rare instance from Dickens (*op. cit.* II.ii.719). In fact, a fair number of sequences can take up this position ('He's in favour of going; what are you in favour of?'), and these are in sharp contrast with others which can not; for example, *'What is this by dint of?' *'What is this in the event of?' Unfortunately, between these extremes, the genuineness of the potentiality is hard to assess, even when care is taken to exclude the possibility of 'recapitulation questions'.

Classes	Restriction Parameters								
	1	2	3	4	5	6	7	8	9
I	+	+	+	+	+	+	+	+	+
II	+	+	+	+	+	−	+	−	+
III	+	+	+	+	+	+	−	−	−
IV	+	+	+	−	+	+	−	−	−
V	+	+	+	−	−	+	−	−	−

The registration of restrictions in this Table is generalized from the numerical preponderances in the subclass matrices on which it is based, and these in turn are a numerically based abstraction from the total matrix recording the restrictions observed with each PNPN sequence individually. It follows that not all – not even a majority – of Class III sequences, let us say, are negative to all of the restrictions 7, 8, and 9; what the Table tells us is that Class III sequences have six restrictions and that these are mostly distributed over the parameters 1 to 6.

CLASS I has 47 members in the corpus, of which we may regard 'in spite of' as the type; they are positive to at least 8 of the 9 restrictions. In all of them, N^1 is without contrast in article and number; N^1 is lexically isolated in 38 cases and without article in 32. There are six subclasses:

(a) in view of, in face of, by way of, by dint of, on pain of, on the strength of, etc.; 14 members; positive to all restrictions.

(b) in aid of, in quest of, in relation to, by reference to, etc.; 9 members; negative to parameter 8 (i.e. N^1 is not isolated).

(c) in terms of, in the light of, at the expense of, with a view to, etc.; 7 members; negative to parameter 7 (N^2 can be replaced by demonstrative plus N^1).

(d) in lieu of, in common with, in return for, etc.; 6 members; negative to parameter 6 (P^2N^2 can be deleted).

(e) in place of, on behalf of, for the sake of, etc.; 6 members; negative to parameter 5 (P^2N^2 can be replaced by genitive$+N^1$).

(f) in regard to, with respect to, etc.; 5 members; negative to parameter 4 (P^1 is variable).

Class I		1	2	3	4	5	6	7	8	9
Subclasses	a	+	+	+	+	+	+	+	+	+
	b	+	+	+	+	+	+	+	−	+
	c	+	+	+	+	+	+	−	+	+
	d	+	+	+	+	+	−	+	+	+
	e	+	+	+	+	−	+	+	+	+
	f	+	+	+	−	+	+	+	+	+

CLASS II has 31 members, of which 'in search of' can be taken as the type; they are all positive to 7 of the 9 restrictions; all are without number contrast, and all but 2 are without article contrast; 26 cannot have P^2N^2 replaced by genitive; in 18, N^1 is lexically isolated. It is convenient to distinguish 3 subclasses:

(*a*) in advance of, in search of, by means of, to the point of, at the cost of, in addition to, etc.; 18 members; all are negative to parameter 8; 2 additionally to parameter 9, 6 to parameter 7, and 10 to parameter 6.

(*b*) in case of, in favour of, at the hands of, with reference to, at the instance of, etc.; 10 members; they are negative to parameters 7 or 5 or 4 or 3, plus one other which is never parameter 1 or 2.

(*c*) in respect of, etc.; 3 members; negative to parameter 1 and one other.

Class II		1	2	3	4	5	6	7	8	9
Subclasses	a	+	+	+	+	+	−	+	−	+
	b	+	+	+	+	−	−	+	+	+
	c	−	+	+	+	+	+	−	+	+

CLASS III has 24 members, of which 'in praise of' can be taken as the type; all are positive to six of the restrictions; 21 have no number contrast, 20 no article contrast, 19 cannot have P^2N^2 replaced by genitive; very few have an isolated N^1. We may distinguish four subclasses:

(*a*) in the sense of, on the occasion of, in defiance of, in the event of, in the absence of, etc.; 9 members; all are positive to parameters 1, 2, 3, 4, and about half of them also to parameters 5, 6, and 7.

(*b*) in comparison with, under the pretence of, by force of, in the middle of, etc.; 7 members; all are positive to parameters 4 and 9; most are positive to parameter 7; nearly all are negative to parameter 6.

(*c*) for want of, on top of, in process of, etc.; 6 members; almost all are negative to parameters 3, 4, and 8.

(*d*) with the aim of, etc.; 3 members, all negative to parameter 2.

Class III		1	2	3	4	5	6	7	8	9
Subclasses	*a*	+	+	+	+	+	+	−	−	−
	b	+	+	+	−	+	−	+	−	+
	c	+	+	−	−	+	+	+	−	+
	d	+	−	+	+	+	+	−	−	+

CLASS IV has 19 members, of which 'in need of' may be taken as the type; all are positive to five of the restrictions; almost all are negative to parameter 8, and most to 7 and 9. We can distinguish four subclasses:

(*a*) in need of, in the region of, in defence of, etc.; 5 members; all are positive to parameters 1, 2, 3, and 4; all are negative to parameters 8 and 9; only one is positive to parameter 7.

(*b*) at the sight of, etc.; 3 members; all are negative to parameters 4, 7, and 8; most also to 9.

(*c*) by order of, etc.; 3 members; all are negative to parameters 3 and 8; most also to 6.

(*d*) with the exception of, for the purpose of, in the case of, in time of,

Class IV		1	2	3	4	5	6	7	8	9
Subclasses	*a*	+	+	+	+	+	−	−	−	−
	b	+	+	+	−	+	+	−	−	−
	c	+	+	−	+	−	−	+	−	+
	d	+	−	+	+	+	+	−	−	−

etc.; 8 members; nearly all are positive to parameters 3 and 5; nearly all negative to parameters 2 and 8.

CLASS V has 8 members, of which 'at the request of' may be taken as the type; all are positive to only four of the restrictions; all are negative to parameter 8, and almost all to 5, 7, and 9. We can distinguish three subclasses:

(a) at the request of, etc.; 3 members; none are positive to parameters 4, 5, 7, 8, and 9.

(b) by the use of, etc.; 2 members; none are positive to parameters 3, 8, and 9.

(c) in the name of, etc.; 3 members; none are positive to parameters 2, 5, and 8.

Class V		1	2	3	4	5	6	7	8	9
Subclasses	a	+	+	+	−	−	+	−	−	−
	b	+	+	−	−	−	+	+	−	−
	c	+	−	+	+	−	+	−	−	−

It is not unfitting that we should have, in the foregoing classification, a decreasing precision in characterizing the classes and subclasses. Since there is an accompanying decrease in the class-membership, we should in fact expect characterizing features to be less in evidence; as we move from the grammatical pole, in fact, we naturally find both fewer and a more random distribution of the features characteristic of this pole.

The matrix classification, however, cuts across some features of the PNPN corpus which may be regarded as taxonomically relevant. For instance, since $P^1 - P^2$ are expounded more often by *in – of* than by any other pair of prepositions, this feature may well have analogical power; yet in the above matrix classification, *in – of* sequences are distributed with remarkable evenness throughout the five classes (in each of which *in – of* examples account for one third of the material). A more important principle which results in a cross-classification is the relationship obtaining in PNPN sequences to finite verb predications. Since, as we have already pointed out, the PNPN structure is open-ended, providing for indefinite extension of the inventory of quasi-prepositions, a generatively-based classification is obviously of interest.

Though N^1 in PNPN sequences may belong to one of several lexical classes (general concrete as with *board*; body parts as with *face, hands*; general abstract as with *time, strength*), the greatest single class is that of verb-related abstract – a class which in fact accounts for more than half of the N^1s in the corpus. The first three types in our predication-based classification should therefore deal with those sequences in which N^1 is related to a verb.

TYPE I: 'objective'. N^1-N^2 corresponds to $(\pm \text{conj} + S+) V + C$, with direct order;[8] thus we may say that 'By the use of steel, we could ...' corresponds to 'If we used steel, we could ...' Other examples: in answer to, for lack of, in aid of, in favour of, at the sight of.

TYPE II: 'prepositional object' variant of Type I, retaining the P^2. $N^1P^2N^2$ corresponds to $(\pm \text{conj} + S+) V (+C) + P^2 + N^2$, with direct order: 'In relation to steel, we should greatly expand production' may be seen to have a correspondence with 'If we may relate (what we are saying) to steel, we should ...' Other examples: in connexion with, by/ with reference to, on exposure to. From a generative viewpoint, we should no doubt relate many of the examples of Type II primarily to a passive finite construction (' ... is related to N^2') since the currency of an active form is sometimes dubious.

TYPE III: 'subjective'. N^1-N^2 corresponds to $(\pm \text{conj}+) S+V (+C)$, with inverse order;[9] thus 'by order of N^2' corresponds to 'N^2 orders ...' Other examples: with/by the help of, at the request of, etc.; historically also: by dint of, at the instance of. The selection of *the* before N^1 is of structural significance here as we can see by noting that the ambiguity of *in John's favour* (either 'it is in John's favour'='it favours John', or 'he is in John's favour'='John favours him') is resolved in the PNPN structure by the obligatory absence or presence of *the* respectively: 'he is in favour of John', 'he is in the favour of John'.[10]

In the remaining four types, N^1 and N^2 have nominal characteristics in the related finite-verb predications.

---

[8] Cf. R. B. Lees's type of compound represented by *birthcontrol* (prepositionally, *control of birth*), *The Grammar of English Nominalizations* (*IJAL* Publication, 1960), 148 ff.

[9] Cf. the compound type represented by *heart-failure* (prepositionally, *failure of the heart*) in Lees, *op. cit.* 138 ff.

[10] Another example is 'in charge of' beside 'in the charge of'. Cf. Kruisinga's discussion of *in control of, in the control of, op. cit.* §1363.

TYPE IV: 'factive equational', with direct order; $N^1P^2N^2$ corresponds to $S+(BE+)$ C: '(on) the question of morality' $\sim$ 'the question is morality'. Other examples: for the purpose of, by means of, on pain of, of the order of, in case of, in terms of, under cover of,[11] etc.

TYPE V: 'factive equational', with inverse order, where N^1 corresponds to C and N^2 to S; thus we may regard 'On the basis of his hunch, he worked out an elaborate plan' as corresponding to 'His hunch was the basis . . .' rather than to 'The basis was his hunch'. So too 'by force of (necessity)', corresponding to '(necessity) was the force', the alternative being to see this as Type III, also with inverse order, '(necessity) (en)forced (it)'; 'by reason of'; 'with the aim of', etc. The need to set up Type V, even if its class membership is dubious in individual cases, is indicated by the similarity to Type VI and to the nominal group type 'a pig of a man' (= 'The man is a pig' rather than 'The pig is a man').[12]

TYPE VI: 'adjectival', with inverse order, where N^1 corresponds to adjective as C and N^2 to nominal group as S; thus 'in the absence of the chairman' corresponds to 'the chairman is absent'. So too 'in the presence of'.

TYPE VII: 'possessive', with inverse order, such that $N^1P^2N^2$ corresponds to $C+(HAVE+)$ S $=$ S$+(+HAVE)$ C. Thus 'In consequence of his death, the family had to . . .' corresponds to 'His death had this consequence, namely, the family had to . . .' Ultimately, a very large number of PNPN sequences are of this type, including most of those whose N^1 is concrete (*on board (of)*, *in the teeth of*, etc.), though by reason of lexical isolation, the correspondence is now often of historical interest only; thus *sake* in 'for the sake of' gained currency originally as N^1 because it meant 'case, cause'.

It is impossible in a brief paper to explore all the questions raised by the study of PNPN sequences. Further work is clearly needed on the extent to which the foregoing seven types are productive in current

---

[11] With this last as with several others, it is possible to see N^1 as primarily verb-related: 'under cover of darkness' $\sim$ '(when) darkness covered (them)', Type III. Since Type IV is a more numerous class, however, and therefore presumably exerts more analogical influence, it is probably both less devious and less 'counterintuitive' to class sequences here if they can go in both. Note, moreover, that 'under cover of' does not present the objective/subjective contrast through the presence or absence of *the*.

[12] Compare the discussion in Lees, *op. cit.* 126, 178, of inversion compounds like *fighter plane* = 'the plane is a fighter', rather than 'the plane fights' or of course 'the fighter is a plane'.

English, and on the relation between these types and the parameters set up for the earlier matrix classification. Enough has perhaps been done here, however, to present the main structural typology of PNPN sequences and the crucial features which accumulate towards the 'grammatical' end of the continuum at which the $P^1N^1P^2$ act as a complex prepositional unit.

Fifteen

Substitutions and syntactical research†

Substitutability is a concept fundamental to grammatical analysis and is thus traditional in linguistics. It is implicit in the setting up of paradigms and in the classification and definition of the parts of speech (as we have them in Dionysius Thrax), which constitute a clustering of elements as functional 'sames', partly at least on the criterion of what is now sometimes called 'slot' filling.[1] It is implicit too in the arguments of the Greek 'analogists' and 'anomalists', and is explicit in the term 'pronoun'. In modern times the concept can be seen in the work of several of the more scientific early grammarians, such as John Wallis,[2] and the analogous ideas of expansion and abbreviation of a segment in a frame were explored by the Gentlemen of Port Royal, Dalgarno, and others in the seventeenth century.[3]

With the development of modern structural linguistics, the formal character of substitutability has caused its importance to be enhanced as the keystone of analysis and has encouraged linguists to give it its present pseudo-scientific status. The substitution test is something we all use in our work, consciously and explicitly, and it is beyond question a most powerful and valuable tool. But its formal character appears to have encouraged a belief that it can be applied mechanically and

† This essay (reprinted with slight alterations from *Archivum Linguisticum* 10 (1958), 37 ff.) is based upon a paper read at the Eighth International Congress of Linguists at Oslo, August 1957, a shortened version of which was published in the *Proceedings* of the Congress.
[1] So K. L. Pike, *Language in Relation to a Unified Theory of the Structure of Human Behavior*, Part I (Glendale, 1954), for example p. 153.
[2] *Grammatica Linguae Anglicanae* (Oxford, 1653).
[3] See further R. H. Robins, *Ancient and Mediaeval Grammatical Theory in Europe* (London, 1951); O. Funke, *Studien zur Geschichte der Sprachphilosophie* (Berne, 1928); and I. Poldauf, *On the History of Some Problems of English Grammar Before 1800* (Prague, 1948).

11

promiscuously at all levels of linguistic analysis with no fear of the results being other than structurally true. Moreover, there has been something of a glib assurance as to the ease with which it is applicable, and this can mislead the unwary practical analyst. The practical problems of its application are, indeed, completely disregarded (or assumed to be non-existent) by some theorists. Thus, in *An Outline of English Structure*, G. Trager and H. L. Smith imply a practical observation which is very difficult to envisage: 'Utterances having only one vowel are found to be said always with a loudness equal to the greatest loudness found in larger utterances – under the same conditions of style, emphasis, and so on' (Norman, Okla., 1951, pp. 35 f.). But, as David Abercrombie has asked in a paper delivered in Hull in 1958, *how* are they to be found so? J. H. Greenberg mentions practical procedures only in a very general way and without betraying any awareness that they present fundamental problems and difficulties,[4] or as conceivable only 'if enough years were in the life span of the investigator and if he had at his command sufficient calculating machines', as K. L. Pike put it at the Oslo conference of 1957.

Zellig Harris is somewhat exceptional in the attention he has given to the nature and problems of the substitution test, both in its theoretical and practical aspects. He takes into account use of the test not merely at the phonological level (where problems are grave enough) but also at the morphological and syntactic levels, the latter of which particularly concerns us here. We may therefore dwell with some profit upon his procedural definition as given in *Methods in Structural Linguistics*:[5] 'The test of segment substitutability is the action of the native speaker: his use of it, or his acceptance of our use of it.' It must be noted at once that the two alternatives offered here demand procedures of the linguist which are quite distinct and which may in fact yield results that are partially incompatible – especially if we were to take the first alternative in the wider (but presumably not intended) sense of observing a native's total usage, outside set test frames.

One way of testing the informant's usage (Harris's first alternative) is to construct a frame that is presented direct to the informant with a blank piece left for him to fill with the required segment. This is widely used in the questionnaires of linguistic geography and with considerable success, but as a technique it leaves much to be desired since it draws

---

[4] *Essays in Linguistics* (Chicago, 1957), for example p. 8.

[5] Chicago, 1951, p. 31. See also his article, 'From Morpheme to Utterance', *Language* 22.16 ff.

special and unwelcome attention to the feature being investigated, thus seriously tending to make a sophisticated informant self-conscious and perhaps induce him to consider what is expected of him or even what he may have been taught as a 'correct' form. Thus I found that the frame 'Everyone would do it if . . . could' produced *he* and *he or she* frequently and *they* relatively rarely, but on the basis of a frequency survey of educated speakers' usage, *they* appears to be the clearly dominant form. Even with the so-called 'naïve' informants of folk-speech investigations, Hans Kurath notes that 'memory, politeness and the desire to appear to the best advantage plays tricks with informants' and that sometimes 'an affirmative answer is given to a suggestion merely to get the matter out of the way. . . .'[6] In this latter remark we have a reference to the procedure which is Harris's second alternative (informant's acceptance of an item), and there is no doubt that the method discussed so far of using frames with blanks is superior to this second one of seeking an informant's approval of a whole frame with a blank filled by the test segment. Yet it is the substitution test on these lines that is most widely taken as the more practicable, on the grounds that one can proceed straight to a yes-or-no answer to the problem at issue instead of eliciting forms or the still more tedious process of waiting for the feature in question to crop up naturally in the informant's usage. Here one might just interpose the point that we are deceiving ourselves if we think that the short cut commonly and rightly allowed[7] of admitting the linguist's 'own knowledge' of the language he is investigating is anything other than Harris's second alternative. One's own knowledge of a feature is information only on one's acceptance of it and not on one's normal production of it; such information is of course both admissible and valuable, but its precise nature must be recognized.

It seems to be the acceptance form of the test that Harris has in mind[8] when he speaks of substitutability as that modification of an utterance that can be made 'without obtaining a change in response from native speakers who hear the utterance before and after the substitution'. The crucial points are how to establish and measure a change in response and what is to be taken as indicating identity of response. Such problems have been raised by P. L. Garvin[9] and more recently they

[6] *Handbook of the Linguistic Geography of New England* (Providence, 1939), 46.
[7] For example by C. C. Fries, *The Structure of English* (New York, 1952), 74, note.
[8] *Methods in Structural Linguistics*, p. 20.
[9] For example, in *Language* 29.475.

have been discussed in *Archivum Linguisticum* by T. B. W. Reid who critically examines statements similar to Harris's made by K. Togeby.[10] To take one English example, it is frequently said that many non-restrictive relative clauses in English are substitutable for co-ordinate structures, and it is difficult to find an informant who will deny it in a given case. Yet the substitution involves consequential differences in tone-pattern, stress-distribution, and relative prominence, and careful examination of contexts in which either form occurs naturally indicates that a significant choice has been made – that at some level of analysis they *mean* something different.[11]

It is unnecessary to repeat here the cogent warnings that have been made by others against an uncritical reliance upon the substitution test. Several scholars have discussed the problems raised by the possibility of 'improper substitutions' (such as *picture* for *wall green* in the frame 'you paint the wall green', or *certainly* for *know John* in 'I know John was in'), and have suggested methods of avoiding such pitfalls and their consequences.[12] Others again have pointed out the objection that the test too readily presents the danger of relying upon unreasonable utterances or of depriving reasonable ones of their contextual matrix.

It is likely that Harris's criterion of 'change in response' will work when the linguist *observes* such a change in response, but he would be taking grave risks if he proceeded to equate, on this evidence alone, utterances which appeared to elicit no such change. The danger is far more apparent in the formula of C. F. Hockett who speaks of an analyst's utterance as having only to be 'capable of passing the test of casual acceptance by the native speaker'.[13] This would indeed open the floodgates and would run the linguist not only into problems of neutralization but into a total blurring of the system's outlines. It has long ago been light-heartedly claimed that many English utterances can be repeated with every vocalic nucleus replaced by schwa, and yet not only be casually accepted in London but actually rate a high social status. Even with the additional controls of Harris's formula ('change in response'), I have found that educated English speakers will not, on a substitution test, distinguish between *who* and *that* as the subject of a relative clause having as antecedent nouns of a sub-class *man*, *woman*,

---

[10] *Archivum Linguisticum* 8.35 f.
[11] See further my study of relative clauses, Paper 9 above.
[12] See M. Fowler, *Language* 28.508–9, and K. L. Pike, *op. cit.* 151. C. E. Bazell discusses this and other problems inherent in the substitution test in *Linguistic Form*, (Istanbul, 1953), 66.
[13] *IJAL* 18.98.

girl, boy: yet in a frequency survey of a considerable quantity of educated speech I found them in fact very sharply distinguished: 200 cases
of *who* as against only 19 of *that*.[14]

Use of the substitution test alone, whether with blanks for the informant to fill or with them already filled for his approval, involves the
linguist in a proliferation of forms in a misleading guise of free variation.
Such apparent free variants may be externally, that is, situationally
determined (speaking under emotional stress, or along a trans-Atlantic
telephone line, or in a state of intoxication): with these the present paper
is not concerned, and it is by no means certain that linguistics is yet
competent to handle them. Alternatively, they may be internally determined, that is by specific and identifiable formal features in the linguistic
context. The time-consuming but rewarding frequency survey would
show that at any rate many of them are what Bjarne Ulvestad has called
'structurally favored variants', and it is a vital part of the linguist's
task to analyse the 'formal conditioning factors' that determine their
occurrence – a task admirably performed by Ulvestad for the phenomenon of *dass* as against zero introducing noun clauses in German.[15]
Yet another problem is that the unsupplemented substitution test can
also involve the linguist unwittingly in a diachronic dimension, because
his frames with their simple yes/no responses throw up – along with
dominant forms and patterns – residual ones which may be very much
on the wane yet still be potentially idiomatic. Such residual forms not
infrequently clash seriously with the dominant ones which the substitution test also reveals but may not distinguish. In particular, the acceptance test, with the blanks filled, does not readily distinguish between
the merely and marginally possible and the actually normal: between
what one will accept as a hearer and what one will produce as a speaker.

It would seem, then, that the substitution test is an admirable guide
in the case of a negative response when the informant definitely rejects
the test form or the proposed equation, admirable in pinpointing a
form that is idiomatically quite impossible. But there is equal reason to
believe that an acquiescent or positive response gives an inadequate or
even a wholly misleading guide to the structural pattern. It may well be
indeed that the adequacy of the substitution test in syntactical analysis is limited, or partially limited, to simple (especially exocentric)

[14] See the Table in Paper 9, p. 104, and the accompanying discussion.
[15] 'An Approach to Describing Usage of Language Variants', Memoir 12 of
IJAL (1956), 37–59. One might profitably study in connexion with such variants
Hjelmslev's system of 'Registration of Dependencies' (*Prolegomena to a Theory
of Language*, translated by F. J. Whitfield, Baltimore, 1953).

structures: that it will expose a certain basic structure, including the very relevant bracketing of *bright, colourless, green, original* as members of a class despite the semantic absurdity of syntactic possibilities like *colourless green ideas*. On the other hand, the refinements and intricacies of linguistic structure which are involved in utterances of larger and communicationally more important scope are not (or may not be) revealed by the substitution test: they will rather appear through close examination of complex contextual variables as these occur in a corpus of natural usage. It is at this level that we distinguish collocation classes which will deny the linking of *colourless* and *green*, or *green* and *ideas*, despite the fact that such linking is permitted at the level of basic syntactical structure.[16]

But it is not only a matter of lexical collocation: the frequency survey is also a sure way of determining and ranking the features that condition variation in grammatical structure. Instead of relying only upon subjective judgment of the 'feel' involved (which is notoriously treacherous and is in any case difficult either to verify or make public), one can make formal and satisfying discriminations at a complex syntactical level by observing, comparing – as it were, 'screening' – the variant features, segmental and otherwise, in as much of the wider linguistic context as proves relevant.

[16] A call for frequency studies of collocations was made in 1952 by J. R. Firth, *Proceedings of the Seventh International Congress of Linguists* (London, 1956), 184, but little has been done in response.

Sixteen

Descriptive statement and serial relationship†

When the aims and methods of the Survey of English Usage were preliminarily drafted, analysis was envisaged as focusing upon 'the plotting of variables' (Paper 7 above, p. 78). The purpose of the present paper is to consider what types of variable need to be distinguished and what kinds of relevance the variables have for descriptive statement.

If we take the italicized pair of nominal groups in the sentence

They disapproved of *his running after Mary* and even *his liking for Mary*

the numerous characteristics in terms of which these sequences can be compared and contrasted fall into three interlocking sets of features:

$$\begin{array}{l} \text{overt} \quad a \text{ manifested} \\ \text{covert} \left\{ \begin{array}{l} b \text{ potential} \\ c \text{ transformational features} \end{array} \right. \end{array} \left. \begin{array}{l} \\ \end{array} \right\} \text{constituent features}$$

Set *a* comprises what is textually 'observable' (given the observer's knowledge of the language), the items statable at any level – or with any kind – of abstraction we choose: *deictic + head + postmodifier*, or *poss. pron. + N_{ab} + prep. + N_{con}*, or *poss. pron. + N(ing) + prep. + Name*.

Set *b* comprises the covert features which the analyst's tests reveal. They will include the fact that *him* can replace *his* in the first nominal group within certain (stylistic) limits that permit no such replacement in the second; that *running* (but not *liking*) may be preceded by an adverb such as *eagerly*; that neither N(ing) can be made plural. It should

† I am grateful to several colleagues, notably H. T. Carvell, D. Davy, J. Godfrey, S. Greenbaum, J. Mulholland, and J. Svartvik, for help and criticism in the preparation of this paper which is reprinted from *Language* 41 (1965), 205 ff.

be noted that the latter, negative comparison is only justifiable within the wider framework of knowing that number is a relevant category for the head of a nominal group and even for a N(ing) as head (*his winnings*). It is thus a 'real' covert feature, though negative, that has been attributed to *running* and *liking* here, whereas to compare similarly *after* and *for* in sharing the property of having no plural would be to set up an 'unreal' and inadmissible covert feature.[1]

Set *c* comprises the features relating to the degree of similarity with which the two sequences are related to other structures in the language by regular 'process' or 'transformation'. Thus, each nominal group has a comparably statable correspondence to a finite-verb clause, such that the possessive pronoun corresponds to the subject and the N(ing) to the verb; but in the first case the preposition remains while in the second it does not: *he runs after Mary*, but not **he likes for Mary*.

Taking account of sets *b* and *c* means, it should be noted, that the corpus-based technique of the Survey entails proceeding beyond the corpus from the very outset and that some of the objections to corpus studies (for example, that they can provide rules only for the generation of an identical corpus) are unsoundly based. On the other hand, the ability to assemble sets *b* and *c* is still too often taken for granted, and the very real problems involved[2] have only recently begun to receive serious attention and the overdue recognition that they are far from being merely scholastic pseudo-procedures of discovery. In the present paper, the convention of assuming perfected techniques is followed, but work is in progress on a series of studies in informant-reaction elicitation and assessment.[3]

It might be argued, of course, that assembly of set *a* itself made unacknowledged use of the analyst's intuition – at any rate in silently assigning 'well-formed' status to a given sequence (*his running after Mary*) and 'anacoluthal' status to another (*the most ? the the great he's daft*). Leaving aside the question of our ability to segment the latter into

---

[1] The arguments for and against taking negative correspondences into consideration are conveniently summarized in R. R. Sokal and P. H. A. Sneath, *Principles of Numerical Taxonomy* (San Francisco, 1963), 128–31, modifying Sneath's earlier views as expressed in 'Some Thoughts on Bacterial Classification', *J. of General Microbiology* 17 (1957), 194 and 'The Application of Computers to Taxonomy', *ibid.* 202; see also A. Ellegård, 'Statistical Measurement of Linguistic Relationship' *Lg.* 35 (1959), 136 ff. The question of applying taxonomic Procedures in Linguistic Analysis is examined in J. Svartvik and H. T. Carvell, 'Linguistic Classification and Numerical Taxonomy' (mimeograph, 1964).
[2] Briefly discussed in Paper 15 above (pp. 162 ff.) and Paper 7 (pp. 86 f.).
[3] See Paper 17 and the references given there.

'words' at all, it should be noted that there would be no difficulty in principle in solemnly registering such a sequence as a nominal group in terms of all its constituent features; its irregularity would automatically become clear in the course of the ordinary taxonomic process. Our practice therefore of choosing to anticipate such a classification on the basis of our knowledge of the language involves no principle of theoretical importance.

The sets of characteristics thus catalogued may be said to have three broad uses. First, and basically, they are markers of *definition*: even in a totally unordered presentation, they serve to distinguish the sequence from another.[4] Thus, if *a*, *b*, and *c* are instances of one structure, and *x*, *y*, *z* are instances of another, and they are characterized according to their having ($+$) or not having ($-$) sets of features 1–8 and I–VIII respectively, this first task of definition can be achieved by a simple display as in Table 1. The uses of such information are of course limited: we demonstrate that *a* is different from *b* and *b* from *c* (though the differences are very slight and could easily be overlooked without such a careful analysis), and that *x*, *y*, and *z* are very different from each other.

TABLE 1

	1	2	3	4	5	6	7	8			I	II	III	IV	V	VI	VII	VIII
a	+	+	−	+	+	+	+	+		*x*	−	−	+	−	+	+	−	+
b	+	+	+	+	+	+	+	+		*y*	+	+	+	+	−	−	+	−
c	+	+	−	+	+	−	+	+		*z*	−	+	+	+	+	−	−	−

But from the information we can derive analyses of much greater interest. This second use of the data is a rearrangement of the sequences and of the parameters registering characteristics to establish with precision the *degrees of identity* between the sequences – the property which M. A. K. Halliday assigns to his scale of *delicacy*.[5] Thus it is important to be able to reckon *a*, *b*, *c* as identical to a specific extent and to state in precisely which respects this identity holds; it is equally important to state that the identity which caused *x*, *y*, and *z* to be regarded as 'one' structure is manifested in only one characteristic, while *y* and *z* have a different identity in two respects, an identity which is 'lower in degree' ('further down' the delicacy scale) only of course as regards the comparison with *x*. The most striking delicacy distinctions would be shown as in Table 2.

[4] Cf. M. A. K. Halliday on 'microclasses' in 'Class in Relation to the Axes of Chain and Choice in Language', *Linguistics* 2 (1963), 11.
[5] 'Categories of the Theory of Grammar', *Word* 17 (1961), 272.

TABLE 2

$$
\begin{array}{c}
\underbrace{1\ 2\ 4\ 5\ 7\ 8}\quad 3\ 6 \qquad\qquad \text{III II } \underbrace{\text{IV I}} \ldots \\[4pt]
\left.\begin{array}{l}a\\b\\c\end{array}\right\}\quad + \qquad
\left|\begin{array}{cc}- & +\\ + & +\\ - & -\end{array}\right.
\qquad
\left.\begin{array}{l}x\\y\\z\end{array}\right\} \ +\ \Big\} \ +\
\left|\begin{array}{c}-\\+\\-\end{array}\right.
\end{array}
$$

To take a simple instance in English grammar, we may consider three important degrees of identity obtaining in the sequences *She watched the man*, *She listened to the man*, *She stood near the man*, as shown in Table 3. It is perhaps easiest to supply some of the characteristics which formed the parameters leading to the lowest degree of identity (γ) that needs to be distinguished here; γ_1 acknowledges the unique absence of a preposition; γ_2 acknowledges the inadmissibility of the shortened form **She listened to* beside the admissibility of both *She watched* and *She stood near*; γ_3 further acknowledges the difference between *to* and *near* which allows the latter to be preceded by *very*. The point on the scale of delicacy at which the identification labelled β_1 becomes relevant reflects the readiness of the passive transformation in *The man was watched* and *The man was listened to*, but not in **The man was stood near*. The basis for the maximum degree of identity, labelled α, is perhaps less obvious, but it is important to recognize in English clause structure an abstraction SVX, embracing SVC and SVA, where 'X' can be informally read as 'postverbal piece'. It is not perhaps sufficiently realized that model intransitive clauses of the type *Birds sing* are significantly rare, and that only about one in thirty of the clauses occurring in spoken or written text have this minimal SV form. We need in fact to recognize the broad but apparently basic degree of identity that is manifested not only as α in the three sentences above but also in others such as *He arrived late*, *The dress suited the girl*, *The man was seen by a porter*, and *The man was seen in the road*.[6]

The third use of the assembled characteristics is, like the investigation of delicacy, derived from the first. The complementary facet of dismissing irrelevant differences for a given descriptive purpose is the scrutiny of common features demonstrating a connexion between structures which otherwise too readily suffer the fate endemic in classificatory linguistics of being unrevealingly separated in distinct pigeonholes. Such scrutiny

---

[6] Awareness of an SV degree of identity distinct from SVX is apparently what permits special stylistic effect in such an utterance as *My father drank – so my mother ate*. An experiment in establishing degrees of identity by investigating speakers' implicit awareness of 'sames' is reported in Paper 13 above.

TABLE 3

α	β_1	γ_1	She watched the man
		γ_2	She listened to the man
	β_2	γ_3	She stood near the man

leads to the establishment of *gradience*, as this term has been used by D. L. Bolinger.[7] Thus, whereas earlier it was shown that the degree of delicacy at which *a*, *b*, and *c* were identical could be displayed as in Table 2, we now turn our attention to the two remaining parameters 3 and 6 and by a reordering show in Table 4 the gradience between *a*, *b*, and *c*.

TABLE 4

The relevance of gradience in description can be conveniently demonstrated by the structure of the English verbal group. If we consider the range of 'finites' that can operate at X in the sequence *He X (to) come every day* with seven parameters accounting for the differences as regards X in the variant sequences

1. He X_1 and X_2 (to) come every day
2. He *X* to come every day
3. Did he *X* to come every day?
4. He would *X* to come every day
5. He *X* that
6. He *X* us to come every day
7. He *X* that we should come every day

we can set up a matrix (Table 5) which will simultaneously display delicacy by means of the vertical dimension and gradience by means of the diagonal.

It is obvious that the features attributed to *used* in this matrix refer to the item [juːst] and not to [juːzd]. Less obviously, perhaps, those

[7] See especially his *Generality, Gradience, and the All-or-none* (The Hague, 1961).

TABLE 5

	1	2	3	4	5	6	7
intends	+	+	+	+	+	+	+
wants	+	+	+	+	+	+	−
seems	+	+	+	+	?	−	−
has	+	+	+	+	−	−	−
used	+	+	?	−	−	−	−
is	+	+	−	−	−	−	−
may	+	−	−	−	−	−	−

attributed to *is* and *has* would not apply to these items as head of verbal group or as aspectual auxiliaries; the distinctions are further illustrated by

> I am a soldier   :   I have been a soldier
> I am enjoying the book :   I have been enjoying the book
> I am to go   :   *I have been to go
> I have to go   :   I am having to go
> I have a pen   :   *I am having a pen
> I have enjoyed the book: *I am having enjoyed the book

Nor can the matrix be held invalidated by the existence of *He had us come* (cf. parameter 6), *He helped me (to) come*, *He need not come*, *He dare not come*, and several other examples, merely because it does not accommodate them. Rather we would claim that the usages not accommodated lead to the further important point that two-dimensional matrices are ultimately inadequate for the description of delicacy and gradience; only with a polydimensional model is a full statement conceivable.[8]

The appearance of question marks along the diagonal (indicating free variation or doubtful usage) is of course itself indicative of the gradience; it is because of the gradience, in fact, that we may expect hesitation over the use of *do* with *used to* and *ought to* and may find in speech 'mistaken' constructions of the form *He doesn't want that anyone should* ... Recognition of the gradience and of the first degree of delicacy (represented by parameter 1) alike helps us to understand the quasi-modality expressed by a wide range of finites operating at X (as in *He'd like to come*, *He's obliged to come*) and to understand too the

---

[8] Cf. K. L. Pike, 'Dimensions of Grammatical Constructions', *Lg.* 38 (1962), 221–44, and R. E. Longacre, *Grammar Discovery Procedures* (The Hague, 1964), esp. 59 and 139 f.

inevitably wide discrepancies that exist in the definition and treatment (according to descriptive standpoint and purpose) of so complex a unit as the English verbal group.[9]

One further illustration of the interrelated concepts of delicacy and gradience may be given from recent work on the prosodic features of English, especially as it provides a convenient occasion to note an alternative technique for establishing variable contrasts. By studying the degrees of accuracy with which informants repeated a tape-recorded utterance, it could be concluded[10] that, with the tone unit as that maximally identified, identities of tonicity (nucleus location), onset-location, nuclear exponent, and pitch-range followed in that order. So much for the 'vertical' distinctions, as it were, of delicacy. But the experiment also suggested that this scale maintained its neatness only when the nuclear exponent was a simple 'fall' or 'rise'. When the nucleus was 'fall-rise', 'rise-fall', or 'fall-plus-rise', two phenomena were observed. First, these nuclei could be replaced more readily by (a) other nuclei or (b) other prosodic features (stress, pitch-booster, or pitch-range) or (c) combinations of (a) and (b); this phenomenon is ascribable to the gradience between prosodic features and also indicates, within the nuclei, a distinct delicacy scale on which 'fall' and 'rise' have primacy. Second, the complex nuclei appeared to change places in relative importance with pitch-range, the latter having a higher identification (= replication) score; this seemed to indicate the operation of a subsystem, or – in terms of matrix display as expressed above – the necessity for a polydimensional model. While, however, a range of subsystems may be more readily accepted among the 'variations infinitésimales' of intonation, the point that must be stressed here is that this is not because with prosodic features 'on quitte le domaine proprement linguistique des unités discrètes';[11] rather, it is precisely the discreteness of other linguistic units that is called in question by the analogous instances of gradience.

The illustrations of gradience so far have been closely tied to illustrations of delicacy; that is, attention has been drawn to instances in which

[9] For example, cf. the recent accounts in W. F. Twaddell, *The English Verb Auxiliaries* (Providence, 1960); B. M. H. Strang, *Modern English Structure* (London, 1962), esp. Ch. 8; W. Diver, 'The Chronological System of the English Verb', *Word* 19 (1963), 141–81; M. Joos, *The English Verb: Form and Meanings* (Madison, 1964); and F. R. Palmer, *A Linguistic Study of the English Verb* (London, 1965).

[10] Paper 13 above.

[11] A. Martinet, 'Réflexions sur la phrase', *Language and Society* (Copenhagen, 1961), 117.

the starting point was gross identity. If, however, we now return to consider the properties of the sequences x, y, and z (Tables 1 and 2), we find that rearrangement to demonstrate gradience produces a different type of display (Table 6) from the others that have been presented.

TABLE 6

	6	8	5	3	2	4	1	7
x	+	+	+	+	−	−	−	−
z	−	−	+	+	+	+	−	−
y	−	−	−	+	+	+	+	+

This is probably, in fact, the commonest type of gradient phenomenon and the one whose investigation should occupy the linguist's attention most centrally. An item a_n in any set of structures whose similarity we are studying must be analysed in such a way as to demonstrate (1) all the features it shares with a_{n-1} in the set, (2) the features which make it unique, and (3) the features shared with the item a_{n+1}. The kind of overlapping gradience plotted for x, y, and z constitutes what we have come to call 'serial relationship', and z would be said to be serially related to x on the one hand and to y on the other.[12]

As an analogue to z in English grammar, we may take the structure $S + BE + said\ to\ be + C$ (as in *He was said to be foolish*), where *said* is probably the commonest member of a subclass of past participles of which *alleged* is another member. This has worried linguists because, unlike *He was considered to be foolish*, it has no corresponding active form like *(They) considered him to be foolish* of which it could be regarded as a straightforward transform.[13] If we examine the *say* subclass in relation to other subclasses of verbs taking 'factive' or parafactive complements, it seems useful to take account of at least eight parameters relating to our ability to use the verbs in the structures here

---

[12] A similar approach is outlined by H. Hiż, who speaks of sentence affiliation and of sentences entering 'a set of related sequences at the same sequence' or of being 'congrammatical' by virtue of other sets of related sequences: 'Congrammaticality, Batteries of Transformations and Grammatical Categories', *Proceedings of Symposia in Applied Mathematics* 12 (Providence, 1961), 47. Computer programmes for mechanically sorting and clumping distinctive features so as to show the kind and extent of interrelationship between grammatical structures are discussed by Svartvik and Carvell, *op. cit.*

[13] Cf. R. B. Lees, *The Grammar of English Nominalizations* (Bloomington, 1961), 63.

given in partially abstract form and in the order which appears to be serially relevant:

1. They V so.
2. They V that he is Adj.
3. It is Ved that he is Adj.
4. They V him to be Adj.
5. He is Ved to be Adj.
6. They V him Adj.
7. He is Ved Adj.
8. They V him N. (where *N* and *him* are coreferential)

It may be of interest to go well beyond the points in the series most relevant for the properties of *say* by citing thirteen subclasses of verbs, taking as their representatives the items listed in the left-hand column of Table 7.

TABLE 7

	1	2	3	4	5	6	7	8
pretend	+	+	+	?	−	−	−	−
feel	?	+	+	+	+	?	−	−
say	+	+	+	−	+	−	−	−
know	−	+	+	+	+	−	−	−
find	−	+	+	?	+	+	?	+
think	+	+	+	+	+	+	+	+
declare	−	+	+	+	+	+	+	+
regard	−	−	?	?	?	+	?	?
like	−	−	+	+	−	?	−	−
persuade	−	−	−	+	+	−	−	−
make	−	−	−	−	+	+	+	+
call	−	−	−	−	−	+	+	+
elect	−	−	−	−	−	−	−	+

In the theory of serial relationship, we go beyond noting the gradient between structures with *say, find, think,* etc., and make the claim that vertical agreement in the matrix is actually generative by reason of the total configuration of gradience. That is to say, given that it should be found convenient to set up a general rule in the language deriving passives from actives, it is reasonable of course to take horizontal agreement in respect of parameters 4 and 5 as equivalent to deriving the property of 5 from the property of 4. But while property 4 may be a usual, it is not a necessary condition for property 5. The subclass represented by *like* (other members are *want, love, need*) shows that the mere existence of the active does not entail the existence of the passive transform (**He is liked/wanted/loved/needed to be careful*). More interestingly, as we see from the description of *say* and *make* in the matrix (cf. also *find*), the existence of the passive does not entail the existence of the corresponding active (**They say/make/ ?find him to be careful*). In these instances, the configuration of gradience suggests the possibility of 'vertical' derivation; because *say* has a common distribution with *feel* and *know* in such expressions as *They feel/say/know that he is careful, It is felt/said/known that he is careful* (parameters 2 and 3), and because *feel* and *know* have a further property in such expressions as *He is felt/ known to be careful* (parameter 5, 'regularly' accountable through the postulated relation with parameter 4), there is developed directly from this the possibility of using the *say*-subclass in this structure without necessitating the prior – or indeed subsequent – acquisition of property 4. It is no doubt relevant to this postulation (and relevant also to estimating the value of observation-based description) both that we find instances of the structure type *He is Ved to be Adj* occurring considerably more frequently in the corpus than instances of the type *They V him to be Adj*, and also that there are roughly twice as many verbs for which we would register a plus in column 5 as there are verbs positive to parameter 4.

Similarly, with regard to *make*, we would claim that the matrix of Table 7 justifies our postulation that its positiveness to parameter 5 (*He is made to be quiet*) is to be explained in part by the corresponding property in *persuade*, a verb class which in turn has this property by virtue of the potentiality for the active structure represented by parameter 4. In this case, the extension to *make* of a structure possible with *persuade* is also conditioned by the grammatical identity (and of course lexicological similarity) of these verbs in respect of structures like *He was made/persuaded to do it*. This and other features not demonstrated in Table 7 would be relevant (in a polydimensional display, having an intersection as it were with this matrix somewhere below the centre) for a full account of the serial relationships involving verbs (*like, persuade, help, tempt, oblige,* etc.) whose objects can be the subjects of verbs other than *be*.

One further verb in the matrix may be briefly mentioned. The uncertain properties of *regard* (readily attested in everyday examples of speech and writing as well as in the vociferous complaints of purists) provide a good illustration of the usefulness of plotting serial relationship, not least in that it provides 'an insight into the dynamic synchrony of language' which, as has recently been insisted, 'must replace the traditional pattern of arbitrarily restricted *static* descriptions'.[14] Despite the continuing membership of *regard* in a subclass of particle-associated verbs (*regard* N *as, describe* N *as, look upon* N *as, take* N *for*, etc.), there are constantly operating tendencies to give it the properties of such verbs as *think* (cf. *OED* s.v. *regard*, v., 6); it is significant that *consider* shares more firmly than *regard* the properties of *think* and of the particle-associated verbs.[15] This 'is simply an expression of the fact that relationship is an infinitely variable quantity', that 'there are many cross-relationships between very diverse families', and that, above all, 'similarity is multi-dimensional'.[16]

Serial relationship is clearly of great importance in linguistic structure and capable of much more precise formulation than we find in the insightful but generally vague accounts of 'analogy' to which the phenomena concerned have usually been relegated. It is certainly an area of linguistics which has attracted welcome attention in recent years. One thinks of C. F. Hockett's interesting postulation of a grammatical theory that 'makes provision for the building of a grammatical form by "blending"',[17] and of his 'Grammar for the Hearer', a concept which, by its handling of sequential choices, offers an explanatory model readily associable with serial relationship.[18] Above all, perhaps, there are the closely analogous ideas on syntactic blending which are developed by Bolinger.[19] This is not to say, of course, that the concept of blending in syntax is anything new; it was advanced for explanatory purposes in Jespersen's *Modern English Grammar* (cf. 3.2.67). It is rather that such a concept has been generally unattractive in the ambience of rigid discreteness that has characterized most theoretical linguistics since Bloomfield, whether the discreteness be that of phonemic and IC segmentation or that born of the more recent interest taken by transformational-generative linguists in unidirectional transformations and unique derivations. One may in fact question the need to

[14] R. Jakobson, 'Linguistics and Communication Theory', *Proceedings of Symposia in Applied Mathematics* 12 (Providence, 1961), 248.

[15] Note that *It's too hot to eat* has been taken as demonstrating the 'existence of overlapping series with *eat* a member of more than one such series' by T. F. Mitchell, 'Some English Phrasal Types', *In Memory of J. R. Firth* (London, 1966), 340.

[16] Sneath, 'Some Thoughts on Bacterial Classification', *loc. cit.* 187, 196.

[17] 'Linguistic Elements and their Relations', *Lg.* 37 (1961), 52.

[18] *Proceedings of Symposia in Applied Mathematics* 12 (Providence, 1961), 220–36.

[19] 'Syntactic Blends and Other Matters', *Lg.* 37 (1961), 366–81.

12+

regard such divergent theories as mutually exclusive and hesitate to agree that the choice lies simply between TG's 'short list of long rules' and PS's 'long list of short rules'.[20] There is surely every reason to suppose that the production of sentences proceeds by a complex interplay involving 'transformation' and what Miller calls 'a sentence-frame manufacturing device'; we might represent the interplay as in Table 8. Though the arrow and the implied priority of the left column (*abcd* as compared with *dbca*) suggest a unidirectional process, it may turn out to be more valid to speak of a certain kind of transformational *correspondence* between the upper parts of the left and right columns. Indeed for Mitchell (*op. cit.* p. 341), 'a transformational relationship is regarded as mutual between transforms and not as unidirectional'.

TABLE 8

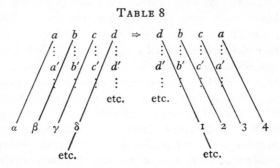

The 'diverging paths' metaphor of Table 8 may be elucidated as follows. By *abcd*, *a'b'c'd'* we understand manifestations of a given English structure; let us illustrate them with *The man gave the boy a book* and *The girl showed the inspector a ticket*. These may be regarded as having paradigmatic interdependence, being produced congruently in the structure frame. By *dbca* we understand the transformed correspondent of *abcd*: *A book was given the boy by the man*. Clearly, however, with *d'b'c'a'* (*A ticket was shown the inspector by the girl*) we have the choice of regarding it as transformationally derived from *a'b'c'd'* or as paradigmatically produced from the pattern established on the right by the transformation and manifested by *dbca*. The point has little importance until we come to consider well-attested examples like the following (one of them explicitly acknowledged as nondeviant for its user, an American linguist):

A lexicon is provided the learner by the institute.

[20] G. A. Miller, 'Some Psychological Studies of Grammar', *American Psychologist* 17 (1962), 756.

An informant was provided us by the government.
The facts were presented us by the Public Relations Officer.
The load on the left is compensated by a long extension on the right.

These clearly belong somewhere on the right-hand side of Table 8, but they cannot be ascribed to the transformational process since sentences like *The institute provided the learner a lexicon* have only a doubtful existence. In these cases, therefore, we find welcome the alternative choice of accounting for their production paradigmatically, and, to symbolize their nonderivation from the pattern on the left or from a different order of elements, they may be presented as 1234.[21]

It is unrealistic to dismiss sentences of the type 1234 as rare and minor deviations. In the first place, structures which find a place on 'diverging paths' in this way are neither few in number nor rare in frequency of occurrence. Secondly, to take a diachronic standpoint, every new development in language begins as a 'deviant' form, and our linguistic theory must face the task of providing for the essential regularity of such irregularities. Nor, of course, as we recall our allusion to Roman Jakobson's concept of 'dynamic synchrony', is this a matter of concern only from the standpoint of accommodating diachronic statement.

With reference to the left side of Table 8, we may understand by the $\alpha\beta\gamma\delta$ string one of several sentence types which can be exemplified by *The dinner cost the man a pound*. Just as 1234 has no transformational correspondence with the left, so $\alpha\beta\gamma\delta$ has no transformational correspondence on the right; but this should not oblige us to regard $\alpha\beta\gamma\delta$ as a wholly different pattern having no relation to *abcd*. Not only are the structures identical at the degree of abstraction SVC_1C_2; the identity is maintained when we state the exponents of C_1 and C_2 to be nouns (contrast *He thought the man silly* which also has a relevant abstraction SVC_1C_2), and when we proceed to describe them as animate and inanimate respectively, *The dinner cost a pound the man* being as ungrammatical as *The man gave a book the boy*. Still more delicately, C_1 is deletable but not C_2 (*He gave the boy*, *It cost the man*); there are analogous interrogative potentialities; and so on.

That the diagram's metaphor is artificially simple and that once again the need for a polydimensional concept must be stressed can be illustrated from the penultimate point. In respect of C_1-deletion, $\alpha\beta\gamma\delta$ is

[21] For a full consideration of the problems presented by the English passive, see J. Svartvik, *On Voice in the English Verb* (The Hague, 1966).

more like *abcd* than the type represented by *He taught the boy algebra*
(*He taught the boy; He taught algebra*) while nevertheless this is more
like *abcd* than *αβγδ* in respect of its voice potentiality (*The boy was
taught algebra*).

Confronted, then, with structures in which we have a range of similarity such as that between the realization of *abcd* and *αβγδ* or between
dbca and *1234*, we seek to specify the serial relationship operating through
them. Confronted by variant forms like *He is regarded as insane* and
He is regarded insane, we seek to specify the conditioning factors under-
lying the existence of such a choice. The same is true when we find a
correspondence between *The news surprised/thrilled/pleased them* and
They were surprised/thrilled/pleased by/at/with the news on the one hand,
and on the other hand between the latter and *They were sad/happy/
angry at/with the news* (manifested not least by our ability to insert *very*
after *were*).[22] The currency of *different from/to/than* is accountable with
reference to (*a*) the endorsement of the *from* selection by the existence
of *differ from*; (*b*) the conditioning of the *to* selection by the pattern
similarities of *opposite to*, *similar to*, and, more remotely, by the correlation of *from/to* in expressions like *changed/increased/converted from . . .
to . . .*; (*c*) the conditioning of the *than* selection by congruence with
the *as* Adj *as∼more* Adj *than* correlation through the *same/different*
polarity (*same as x and different than y*).

Similar considerations would apply to explaining the discreteness of
Too many cooks come from Ireland and *Having too many cooks spoils the
broth* as compared with the blend in *Too many cooks SPOIL the broth*
(compare *Are ninety-year-old men wise?* and a recent newspaper head-
line *Are ninety-m.p.h. cars wise?*). And of course they apply to the explanation of 'anacolutha'; two neighbouring examples from the Survey
material may be cited. *What I'm fascinated is to know that they are such
bad shots* (5b.16.10) obviously involves a blending of *What fascinates
me is to know . . ., I'm fascinated to know . . .*, and *What I'm fascinated
by is . . .* The other is more interestingly complex:

> . . . position to :sày [/whether it would be :chèaper [or /whether it
> would be nòt#]#]# (5b.16.51)

There are three 'well-formed' possibilities for ending this sentence
according as (*a*) the structure is to be complete with realized complement,

[22] Cf. N. Chomsky, *Third Texas Conference on Problems of Linguistic Analysis*
(Austin, 1962), 172.

(*b*) the verbal group is realized but not the complement, (*c*) only the first element of the verbal group is realized:

> (*a*) . . . or whether it would be dèarer
> (*b*) . . . or whether it wòuldn't be
> (*c*) . . . or whether it would nòt

In the event, the prosodic pattern of (*a*) is realized with the grammatical pattern of (*b*), but we should postulate the existence of (*c*) as a conditioning factor.

Finally, let us consider briefly in the light of what has been said some of the problems inherent in the adjective structures illuminatingly discussed by Lees.[23] Our first reaction may be to find it plausible to derive *He is splendid to wait* by a 'generalized grammatical transformation' from the two kernels *He is splendid* and *He waits* (219). But reflection raises doubts on three grounds:

(*a*) This postulation perhaps creates more problems than it solves, for example in the complexity of restrictions required to prevent us from deriving *He is hot to sit from *He is hot* and *He sits*, or **He is angry to walk* from *He is angry* and *He walks*.

(*b*) The postulation to some extent reverses the required direction of derivation, in that we may intuitively prefer to see the relation between *He is splendid to wait* and *He is splendid* as one in which the latter is a contracted version of the former.

(*c*) The postulation enforces too sharp a break between

> 1. He is splendid to wait
> 2. He is splendid to see
> 3. He is easy to please

(the last two of which cannot have such a derivation), and too close a relation between 1 and

> 4. He is eager to help
> 5. He must be angry to go

(for which three structures three derivations are possible and in part demanded).

Taking the primary abstraction at which 1–5 are 'sames' as SVC, we shall find that antecedent in the serial relationship toward 1, 2, and 3 there must be the propensity of S to be animate and C a congruent adjective, thus giving sequences basic to 4 and 5 such as *John is eager*,

---

[23] 'A Multiply Ambiguous Adjectival Construction in English', *Lg.* 36 (1960), 207–21.

12*

John is angry. To this is added by a subordinating process an intransitive structure (*John helps, John goes*) via

$$S_1 \ V_{be} \ Adj \ conj \ S_2 \ V_i$$

where S_1 and S_2 may be coreferential and of which a condensation for the sequence with coreferential S_1 and S_2 is

$$S_1 \ V_{be} \ Adj \ to \ V$$

(that is, 4 and 5).

A series also beginning with the primary SVC develops the propensity for having a factive S and congruent adjective as C, producing sequences like *The situation is splendid* (but not **The situation is eager*: hence objection (*c*) above). A subordinating process then allows a connexion with other structures (including those of the type *John waits, Mary sees John, Mary pleases John*) such that these can operate as S. It should be noted that what we have established here is a pattern, not a number of fully realized sentences which must be held to underlie other sentences which are indirectly related to the pattern. That is, the description so far allows us to produce *That John waits is splendid*, but it is crucial to the theory of serial relationship that we are not forced to produce **That Mary pleases John is easy.* From the 'clause as S' pattern, condensation processes (as postulated in the preceding paragraph) operate to produce patterns which may be manifested as *John's waiting is splendid, For John to wait is splendid, To wait is splendid,* and it is at this point that the series is extended by the production of *For Mary to please John is easy.*

Further stages, for which it is unnecessary to hypothesize details, include the patterns producing *It is easy for Mary to please John* and the contractions *It is easy to please John, It is easy,* the latter significantly endorsed by the factive SVC sequence determined earlier in the series. Only now need we envisage the bringing together of 1, 2, 3 with 4 and 5 by a serial interaction which neutralizes contrasts that remain in less contracted structures:

> John is eager to help + It is easy to please John
> → John is easy to please

Similar neutralizations, of course, have to be set up for the superficial but highly relevant degrees of identity in pairs like

> To consider a possible objection, it might be thought unwise that
> we . . .

To consider a possible objection, we must first understand exactly
what the objection is.

Nor is a series-influenced transfer of elements postulated ad hoc merely
to spirit away a specific problem. Analogous processes are needed to
account for *John can't seem to work* beside *John seems to be unable to work*
and *It seems that John can't work*. Similarly, there are well-known
neutralizations involving transferred aspect and modality, as in *I should
have liked to go there, I should like to have gone there*, and *I should have
liked to have gone there*; negation, as in *I wouldn't be surprised if it didn't
rain*; and number, as in *All the members present raised their arms*.

For all these phenomena, the problem is to envisage a complex
interaction between patterns and manifestations of patterns so that the
logic of our statement does not force us to specify stages that we do not
need in our description or utterances for which there can be no observa-
tional evidence. We need a descriptive apparatus that will liberally and
economically enable us to account for the 'dynamic synchrony' of the
creative linguistic process, and to this end we should recognize serial
relationship, gradience, neutralization, and blending as central.

Seventeen

Acceptability in language†

It will be widely taken for granted that a teacher of English should concern himself with 'Acceptability in Language'. Not only is it a common
experience for speakers of English to come up against problems of
acceptability from time to time, but it is an equally common experience
(for the teacher of English) to be regarded as the man to solve such
problems. Indeed, some people seem to believe that if everyone had
been taught better by the English teacher, these problems would not
arise. It may not seem unreasonable to suppose that if one knew
Fowler's *Modern English Usage* from A to Z, one's problems would be
at an end; and since an English teacher might be expected to have
learnt his complete Fowler (what else has he to do, after all?), it is a
short step for the layman to assume that an English teacher has no
acceptability problems with English.

If we say that this assumption is quite unjustified, this is no condemnation of the English teacher. One might just as well assume that a doctor
can never get ill, or that a lawyer cannot end up in the dock. Such an
analogy is imperfect as all analogies are, but the point is that doctors
do not *make* the rules of health or of cell structure: they try to determine
what these rules are and to come to terms with them. Anyone who thinks
that the English teacher lays down linguistic rules might reflect on this
example. If it were argued that a pair of scissors is a single instrument
like a knife or a chisel or a scalpel; if it were further argued that therefore scissors ought to be used just like these other words

I need a scissors and a scalpel.

A scalpel is needed.

† Delivered as a public lecture in the University of Newcastle in November
1965 and published in the *Proceedings* of the University's Philosophical Society,
vol. 1, (1966), 79 ff.

A scissors is needed.

one might well be impressed by the logic of the argument, but what chance has it of becoming a rule of language? If it were endorsed by a Congress of English Language professors or by the Minister of Education, would this make it a rule? And if we called it a rule, would we follow it in our own usage – *This scissors is blunt.* And if we did force ourselves to use it, would it seem 'right' to us or would it continue to 'feel wrong'?

But the assumption we have begun to criticize was not merely that the English teacher made rules but that he had no usage problems himself. How justified is this latter part? I have recently been reading the proofs of a book by a man who has been a professor of English for over 30 years: twice on one galley I found him using 'false concords' of the type discussed by Professor B. M. H. Strang in a paper presented to the International Association of University Professors of English at the Venice conference of August 1965 and published in the *Proceedings* of the Conference:

> . . . the language and sentence-structure of the story is completely native. Inevitably the language and style is simple and direct.

He accepted my corrections *is* to *are* without demur, but the fact remains that *is* had seemed perfectly natural to him when he had written these sentences, or rather that no clear rule dominated his choice of grammatical forms in this instance. One cannot imagine him having written

> *The little box are empty.*
> or *The cans is full.*
> or *Little the box is empty.*

In these instances there are rules of some sort operating with such dominance that the prospect of breaking them seems quite ridiculous.

It should be noticed, moreover, that rules to avoid these last sentences are not stated in Fowler's *Modern English Usage.* The knowledge that makes us reject *Little the box* and accept *The little box* has not been learnt from any book. Indeed, one can go further and say that none of the rules which are unhesitatingly observed by all speakers are ever mentioned in the dictionaries and grammars which we as native speakers use. Paradoxically, almost the only rules we seek in grammars are for points of usage which have no rules, or where a traditional rule exists in grammar books which is at variance with our natural tendencies – and hence we keep 'breaking' it.

Thus we see that rules for acceptable usage are of two sharply different kinds. First there are the so-to-say unstated rules which make us all say *The little box* and prevent us from saying *Little the box*: these have obviously not been made by a grammarian – in fact, very often, as with the rest of the users of language, his rules for these are so deeply embedded in his habits that he is unaware of their existence. Secondly, there are the man-made rules put together on one basis or another to cater for aspects of usage where opinions are divided or where for one reason or another instinct cannot be trusted. Such rules might cause *Between you and I* to be rejected and to be replaced by *Between you and me*.

There are two points in what has just been said that should be taken a little further. I mentioned aspects of usage where 'opinions are divided or where for one reason or another instinct cannot be trusted'. Let us look for a moment at the different kinds of unacceptability that we find ourselves concerned with in discussions of language. First, there are the sentences over which there can be no difference of opinion:

1. *The is empty box little.*

This is instantly rejected and requires no explicit rules for native speakers. The same can be said of my next example, though it is clearly of a different kind:

2. *Cricket paints boys.*

Unlike the first example, this one has a superficial resemblance to good usage: a singular noun as subject to a concordant singular verb, and an object *boys* where objects are expected: it is just like *War kills men*. Yet the whole sentence is a non-sentence, quite ridiculous, instantly rejected and requiring no explicit rules to prevent native speakers from saying it.

Thirdly we may consider the sentence

3. *I am come here since five years.*

This is by no means nonsense; we may have heard someone say it, though we may be confident that he would be a foreigner. It is unacceptable, bad grammar for which rules are indeed formulated – to prevent foreigners from saying it, not to prevent us natives. In fact the untrained native speaker, the person with no experience of teaching foreigners, finds it very hard to formulate the rules by which this is an unacceptable sentence, almost as hard as he would to formulate rules to reject

The is empty box little.

or *Cricket paints boys.*

The reason why a foreigner has to be taught not to say sentences of this third type but not the first or second is somewhat mysterious, but to discuss the issues involved would take us too far from the present limited objective.

Fourthly, we may consider sentences like:

4. *He don't need no help.*
   Him and her was there alone.

We have all heard people say such things: we know that here are unacceptable sentences that natives are capable of, and most of us can formulate rules showing why they are unacceptable; above all, even if we ourselves would find it difficult to state the rules, we know that such rules exist and exist for us as native speakers.

The same can be said for a fifth type of sentence:

5. *She is different than me.*
   Between you and I, she's silly.
   Who did you give it to?

Again, we have heard these things said; again we know some rules exist for them and could make a fair attempt to state them. But I think it will be agreed that these are all somehow less unacceptable than the fourth type – and some people would probably hold the opinion that one or other is not unacceptable at all.

The following may be taken as an example of a sixth type of sentence whose acceptability may be questioned:

6. *For everyone to have walked out would not have surprised me.*

Like most teachers of English, I would deplore this sentence in a piece of written work though I am aware of the difficulty of prescribing a rule which would forbid it. Finally, here is a sentence entirely without grammatical error and hence infringing no grammatical rule, but nevertheless one that would be condemned as unacceptable:

7. *The man who came to the door when the policeman who lives nearby in a tumbledown house called with his faithful dog which is lame because of a car accident on account of which the driver was prosecuted for having a vehicle which had no roadworthiness certificate although he was acquitted was drunk.*

So much, then, for some of the types of sentences that occur to one, which raise the question of acceptability. It will be understandable that, confronted by such an assortment, I should have spoken of 'man-made rules put together on one basis or another', and our next task is to look briefly at what are allegedly the bases for some of the rules. Logic is sometimes invoked: the first of the type (4) sentences transgresses the rule that two negatives make a positive: 'If you don't need *no* help, you must need some help, and if you don't mean that don't say it'. But of course this reasoning is specious since, whether we use such expressions or not, we all unambiguously and unhesitatingly understand them as strong negatives and not as positives. In any case, if logic were important, there could be no objections to sentence (7), since the sequence here is perfectly logical and complete. Sometimes a sort of universal case-law is invoked, if one can allow the feeble pun: the subject must be nominative and so it is wrong to say *Him and her was there*; *than* is a conjunction and must be followed by the nominative; *between* is a preposition so it must be followed by an accusative, so that we should therefore say *Between you and me* but *taller than I*. Here again one suspects some speciousness of argument. It leaves unexplained the fact that no one now objects to *A soldier than whom none braver has lived* while many still object to *braver than him*.

If these bases are specious, it does not make the sentences necessarily more acceptable: it simply means that we are missing the real reasons for their unacceptability. If we look at (4) and (5) again, we may have a clue: we would probably all agree that type (4) is more abhorrent to us than (5), and this corresponds to an awareness that while educated people might use (5) they would not use (4). In other words, there is a social basis to our reaction. We can extend this social basis through to sentence (7): such a sentence is hard to understand and we should have to ask the speaker to rephrase the sentence for us. Looked at from the other end, this sentence is also hard to frame: we have difficulty in remembering just where we are as we proceed and this corresponds to the social problem of communicating the sentence. What I am calling 'social basis' is of course the basis in usage, but the 'social' reference may help to prevent the misunderstanding that often occurs with the word *usage* – as though one were concerned only with a simple statistical majority.

If we now accept that usage can be the basis only in relation to social criteria – such as educational background or even a particular kind of linguistic usage ('formal', let us say) within that social background – we can begin to bring the acceptability rules for all sentences here discussed within the same framework. The rules will describe a single strain of usage: what actually occurs in (say) the formal written usage of educated native speakers of English. The only usage that can thus give rise to problems for native speakers is that which has rather sharp social or stylistic restrictions on it: examples (4), (5), (6), and (7).

What is involved, therefore, in stating the rules is no different in principle for any of the seven types of sentence that we have looked at. We may, if we wish, state the rules disallowing sentence (1) by describing the form of sentences that do occur: their nominal group structure of *article + adjective + noun head*; the sequence in clause structure of *subject + verb + complement*. We may state the rules disallowing the first sentence in type (5) by examining formal written texts and observing that *different* does not co-occur with *than* but rather with *from*, and so on. The rules that we turn round and prescribe to our students will then be in effect a statement of what acceptable usage is and a recommendation that those in doubt should adopt it (Cf. Paper 10 above).

It is of course this approach which underlies the work of Professor Strang that was mentioned earlier. Interested in the concord vacillation that we have in certain circumstances, she scrutinized dozens of examination scripts to find the linguistic conditions under which a person could have a technically singular subject with a technically plural verb, and so on. Our work in London on the Survey of English Usage proceeds similarly for the most part, but recently we have been experimenting with a direct method of eliciting usage involving doubtful points and in eliciting at the same time social reaction to such points.

Table 1 lists a set of sentences in the order in which they were presented orally to 76 student subjects in a psycholinguistic experiment. The subjects were asked to perform certain grammatical changes and to write down the resultant sentences. Test sentence 10 will illustrate one of the three objects of the test.[1] We all know that usage is uncertain with the negative preterite of *dare*, with the concord after *neither . . . nor*, and a good many other similar points. If we depend on determining majority educated usage from natural texts, we are confronted by the problem of the rarity with which these points occur – perhaps once every twenty thousand words. By requiring subjects to turn into the negative the sentence *He dared to answer me back* (which itself presents no problem), we oblige them to decide on their preferred form from among the several that they have encountered in their linguistic experience. Table 2 shows the resultant selections along with the

---

[1] The experiment and its results are described more fully in R. Quirk and J. Svartvik, *Investigating Linguistic Acceptability* (The Hague, 1966).

13

negative present of *need*. In each case there is a strong preference for the fully 'regularized' form with the *do* auxiliary, though this is stronger with *need* (61 *doesn't need to go*, 9 *needn't go*) than with *dare*, where there are additional choices available. (The results here should be compared with those from a different experiment reported in Paper 11 above).

Similarly, by confronting subjects with sentence 13, *Neither he nor I knew the answer* (which has no problem), and requiring them to change the verb from past to present, they are obliged to choose between *know* and *knows*, thus showing their natural response to the concord challenge. Number 22, *Neither I nor he felt a thing*, is another attack on the same problem but with reversed order of subjects. In the results (also in Table 2), I would draw attention especially to the preference for the unmarked or 'plural' form in each case, *Neither he nor I know* and *Neither I nor he feel*, though this preference is considerably sharper when the verb is immediately preceded by a concordant form. It is noteworthy in this connexion that hesitations are more numerous in the case of 22 where the verb is preceded by the non-concordant form.

Table 3 shows the extraordinary scatter of forms obtained as the inversion question form of *Neither he nor they know the answer*. Here, of course, several factors are involved: the incompatibility of the two subjects with respect to concord, the reluctance to keep the negative correlatives in the question form, and not least the general confusion caused by this multiple complexity. This is not the occasion to pause over the inferences one can draw from the results beyond this striking display of variation and the evidence it provides for the sensitivity of the test technique: in particular, I would stress the variation, since much has been made recently of the all-or-nothing nature of the native's sense of a 'well-formed sentence', and to this question I should like to return presently.

But finding an objective way of establishing preferred forms was only a small and subordinate part of our aim. Far more important is trying to find in what ways a listener finds a given expression unacceptable, to find what effect an unacceptable expression has upon a listener's ability to perceive what is said, and hence (though this is a remoter aim) to make inferences about the nature of linguistic rules in the human mind. As is clear from Table 1, subjects had no difficulty in carrying out the required operation on the first two sentences: 75 out of the 76 students correctly gave the required inversion question and present tense form respectively without altering anything else in the sentence. Such a result was not of course particularly surprising nor yet of any great interest in itself, but it did show (*a*) that our subjects understood how to carry out the operations and (*b*) that there were sentences where they were able or willing to do so without otherwise departing from the given form. It thus gave us a standard whereby we could judge less successful or less docile performances. For instance, although test sentence 4 has a high result like 1 and 2, it is flanked by two sentences which are treated very differently: number 3 gets a success score of 55 and number 5 a score of only 40. But this, although rather more interesting, is still not very surprising; number 3 is clumsy and there is small wonder that 20 students altered it somewhat or failed to grasp it on performing the operation, but number 5 is not merely clumsy, it is obviously unacceptable and it is only to be expected that far fewer should preserve its form when they made it into a question. All we have done is provide a measure of acceptability that corresponds to our straightforward judgment. But let us look at number 27. Here is a sentence – if it is worthy of being so called – that makes no sense at all and yet 60 of the 76 subjects dutifully and correctly performed the operation on it: more than for either number 5 or even number 3. Here is where the Operation results become interesting and make further scrutiny rewarding. While the number who do the operation correctly gives only a rough and imperfect indication of the extent to which it is acceptable or unacceptable, a better guide is provided by studying what those subjects do who get it *wrong*. We closely scrutinized the failure responses and classified the failure types, taking account even of the signs of doubt and hesitation that are provided by deletions. This produced a first classification of the unacceptable sentences as in Table 4. The seven groupings left to right are made partly on the basis of the success scores (the A horizontal row), partly on whether the errors were grammatical alterations of a peripheral kind (the G row), grammatical alterations focusing on one particular problem centre (the I line), and similar factors that both allowed objective rating and also seemed linguistically relevant. The seventh group is naturally made up of sentences that not merely achieve a very low Operation success score (line A) but which cluster the failures in line I. At the same time, it will be clear that, although the classes have characterizing clusters of result types, they shade into one another.

Now, part of our aim in this whole experiment was to investigate the rather widespread assumption that sentences fall into two sharp groups – 'well-formed' ones and non-sentences. Native speakers can, we are told, 'classify sentences as acceptable or unacceptable . . .

without reliance on extra-linguistic contexts'.[2] After the subjects had completed the Operation test we ran through the battery of sentences again, this time asking for nothing more than a snap judgment: does the sentence seem *perfectly normal, quite abnormal,* or *somewhat dubious.*

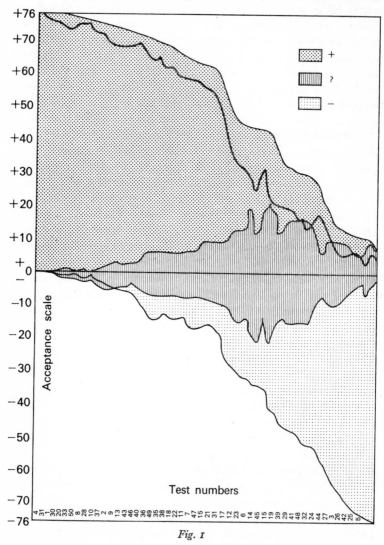

Fig. 1

[2] H. Putnam, 'Some Issues in the Theory of Grammar', *Proc. Symp. App. Math.* 12 (1961), 39.

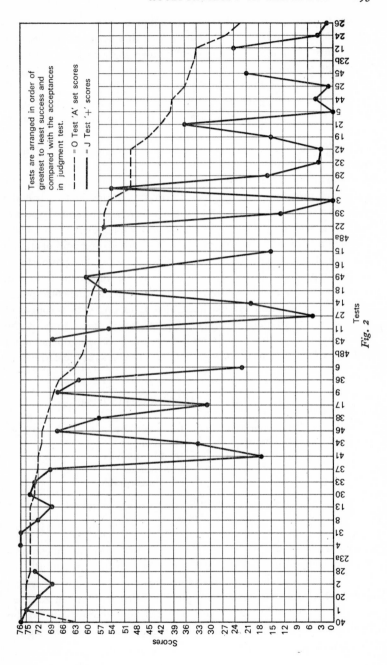

Tests are arranged in order of
greatest to least success and
compared with the acceptances
in judgment test.

------- = O Test 'A' set scores

———— = J Test '+' scores

Fig. 2

Figure 1 shows the results plotted in the left to right order of most accept-able to least acceptable, and it will be seen that very few sentences in fact struck all subjects as either wholly acceptable or wholly unaccept-able. The majority of sentences came somewhere between, and a few even had a greater query score than either approval or disapproval. Gradience is in fact much more strikingly shown in this Judgment test – despite the all-or-none assumption – than it was in the Operation results.

Clearly, the next step was to relate the Operation and Judgment results, and although space forbids any treatment here of the detailed procedure,[3] Figure 2 shows one basic aspect of the relationship. The line which broadly speaking slopes downwards to the right records the Operation test *success* scores, and although there are occasional plateaux and occasional rather steep drops, on the whole there is no sharp distinction between being acceptable enough for a successful operation and being too unacceptable for a successful operation. The more irregu-lar line represents the *acceptance* scores in the Judgment test, and, erratic as it is, it clearly shows some degree of interesting correspond-ence to the Operation success line. That is to say, with a couple of exceptions, the irregular line also registers lower scores towards the right: judgment as to acceptability is related to successful operation on sentences. On the basis of the scores in both tests and of the correlation

I: LEXICAL	II: GRAMMATICAL
(*a*) congruous	(*a*) established
(*b*) obscure	(*b*) divided
(*c*) incoherent	(*c*) ill-established
	(*d*) dubious
	(*e*) unacceptable

Fig. 3

of both sets of scores, we were able to postulate a reasonably compre-hensive categorization of acceptability. As shown schematically in Figure 3, we have first an overriding dichotomy as between lexical acceptability and grammatical acceptability: that is, between accepta-bility on the grounds of the words selected, and acceptability on the grounds of the grammatical patterns stringing these words together.

[3] See *Investigating Linguistic Acceptability*, Chapter 5.

Within the lexical category we can divide the gradient from acceptability to unacceptability into three parts: congruous, obscure, and incoherent. 'Congruous' embraces most of the sentences in the battery, irrespective of the gross success or acceptance scores in the Operation and Judgment tests. What is crucial is the absence of any trouble with lexical items in the Operation test, and this is true for sentences as different as number 2: *Jack admired sincerity* and number 24: *They painted blue their door*. The Operation test interestingly showed, in fact, that a sentence can be grammatically highly deviant while being lexically perfectly regular but that the converse does not hold.

'Obscure' is the class containing sentences scoring low acceptance in the Judgment test but reasonably high success in the Operation test. For example sentence 16: *Dusk was creeping up between the trees*. It would seem that it is to this class that metaphorical or figurative language belongs, and acceptability is sharply dependent on the degree of sentence isolation. It is not difficult to imagine, for example, that the scores would have been very different and would have removed number 16 from the 'obscure' class if it had been textually embedded as follows:

Day was over and the shadows were lengthening as I approached the forest; dusk was creeping up between the trees.

Thirdly, the 'incoherent' class embraces sentences having again a low acceptance score in the Judgment test but having also a scatter of failure types in the Operation test suggesting that subjects were unable to perceive any structure, lexical or grammatical: in other words a sentence cannot be perceived as grammatically acceptable if it is regarded as lexically deviant. An example is sentence 27: *Friendship dislikes John*.

Turning now to the second half of the dichotomy, we have first the 'established' category, which accommodates sentences that are given both a high Judgment and a high Operation score. Thus all sentences in this class will automatically be classed also as lexically congruous, since, as we have just seen, lexical congruence is primary. Examples of 'established' usage are number 1: *They always come here* or 8: *You painted your fence blue*.

Next we have 'divided' usage, by which we understand sentences for which there are competing forms of more or less equal acceptability. The experimental evidence consists of fairly high Judgment and Operation scores, plus independent substitution of the competing forms by subjects. Examples are numbers 11 and 36: *Whom did you see* and *Who did you want*, where there is switching from *whom* to *who* and *who* to *whom* in identical grammatical environments.

The next class is labelled 'ill-established', the experimental evidence being fairly high acceptance in the Judgment test and a scatter of results in the Operation or Selection tests; for example, number 47: *Neither he nor they know the answer*. Sentences are brought under this head by the fact that rules governing their form and use appear not to be well-established in the language.

We then have what we have called 'dubious' sentences, for which there is only moderate success in the Operation test and a fair number of query responses in the Judgment test, with few acceptances. For example, number 44: *Some food was provided the man*.

Finally, we have the unacceptable sentences, scoring low in the Operation test and at the same time getting almost unanimous rejection in the Judgment test: for example, number 5: *John works there either*, and other sentences which while making lexical sense, as it were, are scarcely conceivable as naturally occurring except as a slip of the tongue or some kind of joke.

We have arrived at what we hope is a rather more satisfactory spectrum of acceptability than the seven types of sentence deviation with which we started, concocted as they were apparently randomly and betraying little sign of how they might be relatable to each other. Our final classification clearly provides for such an interrelationship and also gives us the assurance that it is not groundless or entirely subjective. But classification is a rather arid aim in itself. What we are trying to do in this work is to come nearer to understanding the native speaker's problems with his own language, what makes certain language seem difficult to him, what poetic. Perhaps we even come a step nearer to understanding a person's ability to construct and comprehend sentences in the first place.

TABLE I

No.	Operation	Test Sentence	Operation Success[1]	Judgment +	Judgment ?	Judgment —
1	inversion question	They /always còme here#	75	75	1	0
2	present	/Jack admired sincèrity#	75	68	7	1
3	inv. qu. I neg. II	I was /sat opposite by a strànger#	55	0	15	61
4	past	He /wants some càke#	74	76	0	0
5	inv. qu.	/John works there èither#	40	0	1	75
6	positive	He /isn't much lòved#	63	22	41	13
7	plural	It's in the /front of the stàtion#	49	53	19	4
8	inv. qu.	You /painted your fence blùe#	74	72	3	1
9	singular	They /ăren't# but they pre/tènd to be#	68	67	9	0
10	negative	He /dared to answer me bàck#	S	70	5	1
11	present	/Whom did you sèe#	60	55	14	7
12	inv. qu.	He is /silly and crỳing#	34	24	39	13
13[2]	present	Neither /he nor I knew the ànswer#	74 S	68	5	3
14	plural	He is re/garded insàne#	60	20	32	24
15	inv. qu.	/Food was lacked by the chìldren#	57	15	29	32
16	present	/Dusk was creeping up between the trèes#	57	41	18	17
17	negative	The /old man chose his son a wìfe#	69	31	24	21
18	inv. qu.	It's the /man to whom I spòke#	58	56	14	6
19	present	We pro/vided the man a drìnk#	45	15	28	33
20	singular	They /own a large fàctory#	75	73	3	0
21	past	I /turn on the light for the room to look brìghter#	42	36	23	17
22[2]	present	Neither /I nor he felt a thìng#	56 S	56	12	8
23[2]	past	He /turns to the [misiz] Smìth#	(a)74 (b)34	31	22	23
24	inv. qu.	They /painted blue their dòor#	26	4	14	58
25[2]	negative	A /nice little car is had by mè#	36 (S)	1	2	73
26	inv. qu.	/He sits àlways there#	23	2	7	67
27	past	/Friendship dislikes Jòhn#	60	5	7	64

TABLE I—*continued*

No.	Operation	Test Sentence	Operation Success[1]	Judgment +	Judgment ?	Judgment —
28	posit. I negat. II	The /woman sat òpposite me#	74	73	1	2
29	past	They /don't want some càke#	49	16	25	35
30	inv. qu.	/Bill comes here tòo#	73	74	2	0
31	plural	It's in /front of the còllege#	74	76	0	0
32	positive	They /aren't very lòved#	49	4	20	52
33	inv. qu.	They /pushed the gate òpen#	73	73	3	0
34	singular	They /aren't but they clàim so#	71	33	29	14
35	negative	He /needs to go at tèatime#	S	59	13	4
36	present	/Who did you wànt#	67	63	6	7
37	inv. qu.	She is /clever and prètty#	72	69	6	1
38[2]	negative	Both /I and my friend saw the àccident#	70 S	57	14	5
39	plural	I re/gard him fòolish#	56	12	31	33
40	inv. qu.	/Clothing was needed by the pòor#	76	62	12	2
41	present	I/Wood II/Timber } was creeping up the hìll#	72	17	10	49
42	negative	A /wife was chosen his sòn#	48	3	5	68
43	inv. qu.	It's the /girl I spòke to#	50	68	5	3
44	present	Some /food was provided the màn#	39	4	11	61
45	singular	They are /owning hundreds of àcres#	35	20	25	31
46	past	I /stop the car for the children to get òut#	71	67	7	2
47	inv. qu.	Neither he /nor they know the ànswer#	S	53	16	7
48[2]	past	The /Miss Browns are tùrned to#	(a)57 (b)61	10	19	47
49	inv. qu.	He /pushed open the dòor#	57	60	13	3
50	negative	I have a /black Bèntley#	S	74	1	1

(1) Operation Success = 'A' set scores (Table 4).
(2) 13, 22, and 38 are scored as O tests in respect of the order of the elements operating as subject; 25 is scored as an S test where the passive is replaced by active; 23 and 48 scored as two O tests, (b) relating to 'the Misses Smith' and 'the Miss Browns' respectively.
S: Selection tests (as in Tables 2 and 3).

TABLE 2

Test Number	Range of Variants	Total Selected	Simply Selected	Selected Hesitantly	Selected then Deleted
10	didn(o)t dare to	48	44	4	1
	didn(o)t dare Ø	13	11	2	
	dared not Ø	8			4
	dare not Ø	5	5		1
	durstn't Ø				1
	wouldn(o)t dare to	1	1		
	dared not to	1		1	1
35	doesn(o)t need to	61	60	1	1
	needn(o)t Ø	9	8	1	
	doesn(o)t have to	1	1		
	needn(o)t to	1	1		
	(wrong operation)	4			
13	know	53	50	3	2
	knows	22	20	2	2
	know & know	1	1		
22	he feel	36	29	7	2
	he feels	20	18	2	6
	I feel	13	12	1	
	I feels	3	3		
	I feel nor does he	1	1		
	I, nor he, feel	1	1		
	he are feeling	1	1		
	(wrong operation)	1			

TABLE 3

Test Number	Range of Variants	Total Selected	Simply Selected	Selected Hesitantly	Selected then Deleted
47	do neither he nor they	23	15	8	
	do either he or they	26	21	5	2
	do neither he or they	2	1	1	
	do either him or they	1		1	
	do either him or them	1		1	
	do he and they	1	1		
	do either they or he	1		1	
	do they or he	3	2	1	
	do they are he	1	1		
	do they or him				1
	do either of them	3	2	1	1
	do any of them	1		1	
	do neither of you	1	1		
	does neither he nor they	1	1		1
	does neither he or they	1	1		
	does either he or they	4	4		1
	does he or they	4	3	1	1
	does either him or they				1
	does either they or he				1
	do they know or does he know	1		1	
	does either he or do they	1	1		
	do(es) . . . knows				2

Table 4

Operation Test Results Grouped by Pattern-set Totals

	Grouped Test Numbers and Respective Scores							Totals
	1	2	3	4	5	6	7	
Tests	9 17	46 34 38 36 6 48b 14 43	18 16 15 11 27	48a 39 49 22 3 32 42 29 7	19 44 21	5 25 45 12	23b 24 26	
A	41 72	68 69 71 71 70 67 63 61	59 60 58 57 57	60 60 57 56 57 56 55 49 49	49 49 45	39 42 40 36	35 34 34 26 23	1854
F	I I I (I)		4 (2)(2)	4 (I)(2)	3 (I)	I (I)(4)		16
G	3 7 I I I (I)	(3)	9 II 2 3 3 3 5 (I)(2) (4) (I)	6 2 2 I 6 7 I (2)(2)(I)(4)(I)(2)(3)(2)(5)(I)(4)(2)(2)		I 8 3 5 (I)		92
H	(I)		16 7 2 (I)	I (I)(I)	I I I (3)	I 10 I (I) (I) (2)(I)		40
I	5 3 4 6 9 13 12 16 6 3 I (I)		9 13 I 9 (4)(I)	14 17 18 16 18 17 25 27 30 35 (I)(3)	28 25 26 27 35 42 (I)(6)(2)	50 52 (I)		612
J	(I)	I 3		I (I)	I (I)	I I (2)(2)		6
K		3 I I	I	6 5	2 3 I	2 10 4	I	40
								2660